M000281373

Writers Talking

JOHN METCALF AND CLAIRE WILKSHIRE, EDS.

WRITERS TALKING

The Porcupine's Quill

National Library of Canada Cataloguing in Publication

Writers talking / John Metcalf and Claire Wilkshire, eds.

Includes bibliographical references.
ISBN 0-88984-274-4

1. Authors, Canadian (English) – 20th century – Interviews.
2. Canadian fiction (English) – 20th century – History and criticism.
3. Short stories, Canadian (English).
4. Canadian fiction (English) – 20th century.
I. Metcalf, John, 1938–   II. Wilkshire, Claire, 1964–

PS8329.W75 2003   C813'.54   C2003-906543-X

1   2   3   •   05   04   03

Published by the Porcupine's Quill
68 Main Street, Erin, Ontario NOB 1TO
www.sentex.net/~pql

Readied for the press by Jack Illingworth; copy edited by Doris Cowan.

Represented in Canada by the Literary Press Group.
Trade orders are available from University of Toronto Press.

We acknowledge the support of the Ontario Arts Council,
and the Canada Council for the Arts for our publishing program.
The financial support of the Government of Canada
through the Book Publishing Industry Development Program
is also gratefully acknowledged. Thanks, also, to the Government
of Ontario through the Ontario Media Development Corporation's
Ontario Book Initiative.

 Canada Council for the Arts   **Conseil des Arts du Canada**

 Canadä

 ONTARIO ARTS COUNCIL
CONSEIL DES ARTS DE L'ONTARIO

Table of Contents

———·≈✦≈·———

Foreword

WHEN WE STARTED working on *Writers Talking* the writers we wanted to present – or rather re-present – were curiously invisible. In 1999 they had won no prizes or awards. Reviews of their books were good but these very talented writers had not impinged on national awareness. We knew, however, that these writers, along with a dozen or so more, were at the centre of the flowering of the short story form in Canada.

Since then, Terry Griggs has been awarded the Marian Engel Award for a female writer at mid-career, Lisa Moore has been nominated for the Giller Prize, and Steven Heighton has been published by Granta and described by the *Times Literary Supplement* as 'one of Canada's most talented younger writers'.

Writers Talking is an attempt to make these writers more familiar and to move them towards the centre where they belong. The interviews let the writers introduce themselves and talk about what influences in their lives shaped them as artists. In most cases we edited out the questions to achieve a smoother flow. The interviews also suggest ways into the work; they all provide us with insights into the writers' methods and motivations.

K.D. Miller writes '... I am in fact an actor who writes ... As a writer, I still think in terms of segments of actions – acts, scenes, and "beats" like heartbeats. Sometimes when a story appears to be dying, I turn back into a director and try to revive it as I would a play. "Why isn't anything *happening?*" I bark at the hapless page. "What are you supposed to be *doing?*"'

Mary Borsky illuminates her emotional world when she writes: 'I find my slant on the world not much changed from the time I was eleven. I'm still interested in what a friend of mine calls "the good stuff", the close-up view of ourselves, which includes, of course, our rough edges and unravellings. Like, what exactly did my friend's father say when he dropped in to see her after an absence of seventeen years? And her father – who used to be a real estate agent – are his hands big or small?'

Terry Griggs, talking about fiction which influenced her, goes on to shine an interesting light on her novel *The Lusty Man* and the stories in *Quickening*.

'Which is not to say that there weren't other sources of story. You need look no further than the Catholic Church for a packed and bizarre fund of that. As well, anecdote came with the summer breezes for our camp was always full of people, many of them American (never tight-lipped), and many of whom returned year after year – so you got the ongoing saga. In town there was a whole community of interwoven narratives of which I was aware (to a degree) and a part. Hence my immediate attraction to *Under Milk Wood* when I later encountered it – I had lived the form.'

Lisa Moore writes, 'I think of words as having texture. *Lugubrious* has the texture of baked okra. *Serendipity* has the texture of rain bouncing off the surface of a lake.'

The eight stories in this volume reveal a passion for writing, a joyful intensity about language. What's special about the language of these stories is that it is striking, playful, saturated with the tactile, the visual. The words are strung taut, chosen with a scrupulousness that borders on the religious.

Lisa Moore's 'Craving' describes a dinner party which reunites old school friends; as the three women drink and smoke a little dope, the story's atmosphere becomes pleasantly floaty. The narrator's dreamlike mood is shot through with very precise observations about desire, and about the women's relationship, their understanding of one another. The story is a kind of purposeful meandering, full of the languid, languorous imagery which makes Lisa Moore's fiction so striking.

Elise Levine's writing always gives the impression that it has been whittled down by the most ruthless editor – not one word goes astray. (Her first drafts probably look like that.) The result: tough intricate fiction that makes demands on the reader, as does all the fiction in this book.

Michael Winter (like Elise Levine and, for that matter, like Norman Levine, whom he admires greatly), has a gift for ellipsis, for knowing what not to tell and elaborate.

'At the end of summer I invited Femke to my parents' cabin. Get out of the city, see some woods. We hitchhiked and it's easy. People assumed we were a couple, which, secretly, excited both of us. We played cribbage and read Edgar Allan Poe. The flax and monkshood. A fire on the beach for hotdogs and a tin of beans. I try swimming but the water cuts me at the hips. I towel off by the fire and Femke rubs my neck. We find faces in the coals. There are blankets for both beds, but I suggest sleeping together. Even with this there is mere friendship, practicality, intended.'

'A joyful intensity about language', to repeat a phrase of Claire Wilkshire's, is the core of *Writers Talking*, a joyful intensity we invite readers to embrace.

The interviews were conducted by mail. Mary Borsky, Elise Levine, Lisa Moore, and Michael Winter were interviewed by Claire Wilkshire. Terry Griggs, Steven Heighton, K.D. Miller, and Annabel Lyon were interviewed by John Metcalf.

John Metcalf, Ottawa
Claire Wilkshire, St. John's

MICHAEL WINTER
The Force of Mystery

MICHAEL WINTER'S LAST HOME in St. John's seemed not to exist at all: to pay him a visit you had to follow the wooden row houses partway down Long's Hill and look for a huge blue dumpster. Behind the dumpster: a narrow gap between two buildings, a mailbox, a white gate. Through the gate, at the end of a stone path through what appeared to be someone else's back yard, you found a pretty little house that was not on any road. To the left of the front door, a composter; inside the porch hung the bicycles of his roommates.

Although it's not the place he lived the longest, that house seems somehow emblematic of Winter's existence then and since. It offered a desirable seclusion (Winter remains at best an occasional answerer of phones) without isolation (he spends half the year in Toronto these days). It provided community in the form of assorted exotic roommates, and, when they all went off about their business, the solitude he needed to write. And there was a quirkiness about its continued existence, its defiance of convention, its refusal to line up in a row on a street like all the other houses. That was probably what he liked most.

Winter used to be a familiar figure in downtown St. John's, striding along Water or Duckworth Street, satchel swinging from his hip, a tall lean figure in a dark coat (although there was the era of the bright orange boiler suit). He was often heading for the Writers' Alliance office, or a meeting at the office of *TickleAce,* the Newfoundland literary magazine where he served as a fiction editor from 1991 to 1998. Mostly, though, what Winter has been doing since he graduated from university in 1986 is writing, and unlike many young writers, he hasn't been doing it as a sideline but as his main gig. Supporting himself through a series of grants and writing-relating jobs (workshops, competition judging, research/writing projects), he has focused determinedly on his fiction.

Michael Winter published three books in the 1990s. He co-authored a young adult novel, *Ask Me No Questions* (Prentice Hall, 1990). His first collection of short stories, *Creaking in Their Skins,* appeared with Quarry in 1994; the second, *One Last Good Look,* came out with the Porcupine's Quill in the spring of 1999. Anansi published a journal, *This All Happened,* in 2000.

Creaking in Their Skins comprises sixteen stories, many of whose settings are influenced by Winter's travels. In 1988 he spent six months in Greece, Turkey, Israel and Egypt, in 1991 five months in England, Germany and Eastern Europe. The protagonist's unfamiliarity with foreign surroundings often points to a deeper sense of unease in the context of intimate relationships. *One Last Good Look,* on the other hand, tracks the development of one character, Gabriel English; the story cycle is firmly rooted in Newfoundland and the most important relationships are familial. The images of *Creaking* are suggested by the title of the book's first story, 'Enlarged to Show Texture': they have to do with perspective and distance, the protagonist contemplating the world, zooming in every now and then to ponder its oddities. But Gabriel English, although he is a first-person narrator, appears at least as much a participant in the world he describes as a detached observer of it. *Creaking in Their Skins* exemplifies a new kind of writing which has been coming from Newfoundland in the last fifteen years or so. It does not deal in picturesque coastal communities and a vanishing way of life; it does not work with traditional and plot-driven forms such as the folktale (not that there's anything wrong with those things, but this is a different kind of book) – *Creaking,* like *One Last Good Look,* is contemporary writing with an interest in language, irony, juxtaposition, keen observation of unusual detail, the cadence of a sentence.

cw: Michael, do you see big differences between your two collections of stories, between *Creaking in Their Skins,* your first collection, and the more recent one, *One Last Good Look?*

mw: I think the difference is that in the first collection the stories sometimes come off as analytical, or cooler. But in the second I feel stronger as a writer to explore emotions in a way which is sophisticated, and before I didn't have the talent to do that. So I think the reader gets a greater sense of emotion in the stories, or of deliberation in the character.

CW: It's clear that you have greater confidence as a writer in this book [*One Last Good Look*]. It seems to me that there's an authoritative quality to the writing voice.

MW: Mmm. I don't care to try to pretend to the reader that I'm a knowledgeable person. Instead I cut through that, and I think there's something very authoritative about confessing to the reader that you're pretty ignorant about certain things, but at the same time you know that you're also giving quite a lot of knowledgeable detail and insight about people, and yet you're confessing to ignorance ... which is honest and it's not honest at the same time. I love writers who have that authority. Heinrich Böll's novel *The Clown* is like that. He says to the reader, 'I can smell the liver and onions he had for lunch: I'm like that, I can smell things over the phone,' and it's a completely bizarre thing but I believed the clown. I believe that character does that, and I can see Heinrich Böll thinking: 'OK, I'm going to keep that in, that's a pretty bizarre thing about this character.' So it's fanciful, but I think I used to be fanciful for its own sake whereas now I take those absurd moments and the reader is more convinced that I'm allowed to write about it and I haven't just written it for the sake of a laugh or the shock of it.

[There are moments of humour in *Creaking in Their Skins,* and some funny situations and characters – the roommate in 'Camera Obscura', for example. Many of the stories in *One Last Good Look,* though, manifest a kind of playfulness which is new, a willingness to pause and point out the ironies and absurdities of life at any point, wherever they present themselves. In 'Four of the World's Smallest Worlds', Gabriel spends an evening drinking and playing pool with his buddies. Winter relaxes his tight control of the form to allow Gabriel more room – to reminisce, to offer up perceptive and witty meditations on his personality and those of his friends. It's a funny, powerful story about men and intimacy.]

CW: Would you describe 'Four of the World's Smallest Worlds' as fanciful?

MW: When I was writing it I had just finished reading *Independence Day* by Richard Ford, and I loved how he spent the whole novel writing about this man on a weekend with his son, but every person he met on the street, he spoke to. The narrator would be in a parking lot and a guy would be unloading a van, and the protagonist would talk to the guy at the van, and they would get to some kind of emotional theory about what it is to be a man. Which you *know* would be impossible, it just wouldn't happen, but I was completely convinced by it, and I thought: I'm going to do that with four characters in a story and just go on at length with an analysis of the emotional state of these four men in a way that I think will be believable to the reader. So that was a conscious project of mine, which I think was quite different from the way I'd written stories before that.

[Winter completed his first two years of university in Corner Brook before moving to St. John's in 1984. By that time he had already begun to publish poetry in *TickleAce,* sometimes pseudonymously. He graduated in 1986 with a BA in economic geography and took a summer job with the city from which he was let go after he phoned to complain about the mayor's absence from the Canada Day celebrations. Winter then began work for an agency called Public Legal Information. There he met Lisa Moore (author of *Degrees of Nakedness,* Mercury, 1995); they were hired to write scripts with legal themes. Moore persuaded him to enrol in a creative writing course offered at Memorial University. He took the course in the fall of 1986 and met the people who would, he says, 'over the next decade, read and critique my work. They formed the nucleus of the Burning Rock writers' group.'

Winter describes the Burning Rock in the Introduction to *Extremities: Fiction from the Burning Rock* (Killick, 1994), a book he edited. (A second collection, also with Killick Press, is forthcoming). The core members, Winter writes, 'met in creative writing classes taught in 1985-6 by Larry Mathews at Memorial University.' 'Picture this,' Winter writes:

a group of writers living in Newfoundland who have been writing short stories for the past nine years. They meet every two weeks, lugging cases of beer across downtown St. John's, sitting in kitchens and living rooms (candlelight, tablecloths festooned with guacamole, tortillas, grapes, fruit pies, cheese scones), to read and critique their latest fiction.

(Winter is modest about most things other than the quality of his cheese scones.) He has been a central figure in the Burning Rock since the group's inception. In addition to editing *Extremities*, he organized the national tour which followed its publication. In July 1999 he toured the province for a week with five other Burning Rock writers – an expedition involving huge numbers of hours in a minivan and excessive amounts of deep-fried food. His contribution to the group has been invaluable: he's always got something new and interesting to read, and his comments on other people's writing are full of tact, humour and insight. He also takes criticism well – if you're able to point out anything truly awful in what he reads, he'll laugh a deep Ho-ho-ho and like you for it.

Winter was about twenty when the writing group started up. He valued the company of people who took fiction seriously – without it, he claims, he might not have become a writer. As for the impact of the group on the development of his work, he says that the exercise of reading stories aloud and of listening to others read has sharpened his understanding of voice. He has watched other people experiment with a variety of techniques and learned which stylistic devices interest him and which do not.]

CW: Michael, you mentioned Cormac McCarthy as someone you emulate; are there other writers who have influenced you in that way?

MW: Yes, there's a whole bunch of them. Right now I'm reading a novel by Milan Füst, he's a Hungarian writer and he wrote this book, in the fifties I think, called *The Story of My Wife*, and it's all about this sailor who talks about his wife having an affair, but really the reader suspects that the wife isn't having an affair at all, it's just his paranoid jealousy. The journal that I'm rewriting now [*This All Happened*] is a similar case where the narrator's involved in jealousy; I'm learning from Füst how to structure things so that they're funny, and how to convey that the narrator might be deluded ... I've been rereading Richard Ford, and Norman Levine a little bit. I pick up a lot of books and I look for a certain honesty in the storyline where I believe the writer is doing his utmost to convince me that what he's writing about really happened, even if it's completely made up. I have to really believe that somehow he's getting to some kind of honesty about a situation. And if I don't get that I put the book down immediately.

cw: You seem to be using the word 'honesty' in more of an aesthetic than an ethical sense. What do you mean by 'honesty'?

mw: I'm convinced that to be honest in a story is to deal with a bunch of lies about the real world, but to configure them in the best way you can to contrive some kind of truth out of it. Every sentence I write is a step down a false road that I'm constantly trying to keep out of. You read all these stories by people who believe that if they just tell a true story it's going to be interesting and publishable, and that's the furthest thing from the truth – it's boring. True stories that are earnestly told are almost without doubt going to be boring. I feel like I'm constantly lying, with each sentence, but as long as I know the effect of what I'm writing, I'll get to some kind of truth about the emotions that I want to express. I think most people, when they try to write, use words that are already around them, in the air, and those words are usually clichés, and so the reader is bored. A trained writer avoids all that, those minefields of cliché and stereotype, and says: 'I have to write a new story.' If you keep writing, you begin to learn to look at a sentence and say, 'That's a good sentence, and that's accurate to the story's centre, so I'll keep that sentence.' And then you have another sentence, or you have another situation with somebody else, and you think, 'Well, I can't have both these characters so I'll give that line to this person.' And then you have to contend with the changes: do they say it before breakfast or do they say it when they're walking to the bar? And so it's all changing. It's a complete fabrication of events to create an interesting story that somehow expresses whatever thing initially interested you about the story. I don't have a structure – it's more of a making sure that the bricks I'm making this building out of are really good bricks.

cw: It's interesting that you should enjoy a book about jealousy so much, because jealousy is an issue in your collection of stories as well –

issues of jealousy, marriage, fidelity, flirtation, those kinds of things are important.

M W: Well, I think jealousy in my personal life came late to me. I'm a late bloomer in the world of jealousy, so I'm only lately becoming an expert at it. And I love the fact that for a certain time when I was jealous, when I was a virgin to jealousy, it completely unravelled me. I was completely at a loss to deal with it intellectually. I was just a raw emotion. I couldn't think of anything else and I thought really bizarre things. And as soon as I had a word with my beloved about the situation, I was completely soothed and transformed, and looking at myself thinking: How could I possibly have thought this whole construct, how did I get in that position? So I find it to be a really delusional, powerful emotion.

[Gabriel English in *One Last Good Look* has his jealous moments as well; the similarities between the protagonist and his creator do not end there. Like Winter, Gabriel is a long-term resident of Newfoundland whose roots lie elsewhere, and he's conscious of the difference that creates. Winter was born in Jarrow, county of Durham, in the northeast of England, on 11 March 1965, the third child of Anne (Hardy) and Thomas Leo Winter. His father, a plumber and electrician, worked in the shipyards of neighbouring South Shields, and in 1968 he took a job in another shipyard, in Marystown, Newfoundland. Leo Winter had always wanted to live in Canada. In June of 1968, a three-year-old Michael and his family crossed the Atlantic for the Burin Peninsula; a year later they moved again, this time to the island's west coast, where Michael's father was to teach woodwork and metalwork in a junior high school in Corner Brook. Anne Winter worked part-time as a clerk at Sears; the family remained in Corner Brook, where Michael grew up aware of his family's Englishness. 'I learned to speak two accents,' he says. 'A Geordie, British accent for my parents and siblings, and Newfoundland accent for my friends. Neither group knew the existence of the other accent. I felt awkward if I had friends over and had to speak to my mother.'

Being from somewhere else is different in Newfoundland than in, say, Vancouver or Toronto. If you move to Vancouver, people there act as if you've finally come to your senses. Then you assimilate. Here, there's a firm divide between Newfoundlanders and CFAS (Come-from-Aways). To be a Newfoundlander means born and bred, with family dotted around the island: living here for almost your entire life does not make you a Newfoundlander. In an interview in the St. John's *Telegram* (Sun. 23 May 1999) Michael describes himself carefully as a 'permanent visitor' to the island. And geographical identity is tenuous: after spending only eight months in Toronto he was described in a *Toronto Star* review as a Torontonian.]

CW: You've been living in Toronto since September [1998]. How do you feel about that? What's it like, writing over there?

MW: It's good. I'm working on a novel now, an historical novel set in Newfoundland, so it's kind of good to be somewhere else, in a different place altogether. Newfoundland freezes in time for me and I've got a whole bunch of reference books about Newfoundland that I'm living vicariously in the past with, and I'm not confusing it at all with the Newfoundland of today, so I feel like I can get back in time. If I was living in the same landscape I'd be confusing things all the time, or I'd be writing things which were more contemporary and maybe I'd feel [the novel] was more of a chore. Whereas right now I can just spend a lot of the time writing about the past; I'm not tempted by what's out the window.

CW: Are you making a deliberate effort to represent Newfoundland in your writing? Or: is it important to you that your writing is informed by the culture that you grew up in? [It's perhaps worth noting that four of the first five stories in *Creaking in Their Skins* include references to moose.]

MW: I don't feel any responsibility to be putting Newfoundland out there as subject matter. I think it's the other way around, I feel grateful that there's a whole body of real life going on in this province that is not written about that much and it's available to me. I've lived in Toronto for a year and there's a hundred good writers in Toronto writing stories about Toronto life. Those are good stories too, but why not write about these stories here: there's only a handful of us here writing them and they're strange stories that are interesting. The other thing is I find a real distaste in how I'm seeing Newfoundland more and more being marketed as a tourist place. I remember somebody saying as soon as you start looking at your own culture, it's gone: you become static and that's the thing you recreate, you have kitchen parties that you sell tickets to mainlanders to come and be a part of, or you build a traditional Newfoundland community that tourists can go to. I'm just trying to be as accurate as I can to what's really happening rather than mimicking what I think goes on in a fishing village or what I think goes on in St. John's.

CW: Gabriel English resembles you in that he's caught between two cultures, his parents' English background and the fact that he emigrated to Newfoundland as a child, and he resembles you in quite a lot of other ways as well …I know that you're working on a journal which has implications, like the memoir, of being more truthful than fiction. What kinds of things are you doing with autobiography and truth and fiction, what ideas do you have about the different ways that you're working with those?

MW: I've constantly been accused of just writing autobiography, and it's a very hard thing to explain the difference between what I live and what I write about. When I was writing the journal [*This All Happened*], I felt a sort of a vengeance towards people who might claim that I'm just writing down my real life, because I know that that's not what I'm doing. So I wanted to write a fiction but call it non-fiction. I wanted to create this whole other world using the character of Gabriel English who's writing a journal in the stories and who's writing stories in the journal, and for one to deal more with the landscape and vignettes of everyday life, that being the journal, and the stories being more about the emotional terrain of the characters. I think that's what I was doing. But they were both getting kind of confused in my mind.

CW: So Gabriel in the stories is fiction and in the journal he's also fiction but you're calling it non-fiction.

MW: Right. Because I guess I find those separations to be strange.

I read *The Sorrows of Young Werther*, the Goethe book, and I like that conceit of a writer creating a journal of someone else. I wanted to give the journal as much of a ring of truth as I could, and to call it fiction seemed to be at the last moment pulling back and saying, 'Actually, I made it up.' I thought: just go all the way and call it non-fiction.

cw: But now you're saying you made it up?

mw: I think I want the book to be written and to be marketed as non-fiction, but if I was ever interviewed about it I would say I made it all up, sure. They always make it up.

[*One Last Good Look* is in many ways a meditation on growing up in a small town in Newfoundland, the formation of identity through the recognition of similarities and differences between self and other people. In this book the other people are mainly family: Winter's parents, his sister Kathleen (b. 1960) and brother Paul (b. 1962). *One Last Good Look* is also a testimony to the respect and affection Winter holds for his family: while the characters in the book have their foibles, they are all presented with respect, an admiration for their individuality and for the values which propel them.

Each member of his family has served as a role model for Winter. His elder sister Kathleen was always creative; she wrote stories and played guitar. Michael, several years younger, wrote a story about plants in pots; he saved money from his paper route to buy a guitar. Later he bought a manual typewriter like hers. Kathleen Winter is a writer with a popular weekly column in the St. John's *Telegram;* she has published three books, including a journal. Michael Winter has published two collections of stories and a journal. He has described his brother Paul as 'reckless and physical'. Paul, the mechanic, knows how things work, and the ability to manipulate concrete objects so that they function in a practical way appeals to Michael, who once said that you should be able to rig up an exercise bike to a fridge or a TV set. The recklessness is also attractive – the protagonist, Gabriel English, is drawn to characters whose indifference to convention places them on the fringes of society. He's torn between the conformity he recognizes as instinctive on his part and the wildness of characters such as Eric Peach and Junior. In the stories, both his father and brother educate Gabriel in getting out of trouble when the need arises. Here is a passage from 'Archibald the Arctic' – Gabriel and his friends have broken a neighbour's window; the dialogue is between Gabriel and his brother, Junior:

We ran. We ran home. Junior said, When you're in trouble, where do you run? Home.

No, Gabe, always run away from home.

The father in *One Last Good Look* emerges as a particularly striking and sympathetic figure. Like Leo Winter, he teaches shop, hunts and fishes. Gabriel English's father is a benevolent patriarch with big biceps and a compelling sense of right and wrong. At school, he teaches students how to build things; at home, he teaches Gabriel that things must be done properly, with care. 'Archibald the Arctic' closes with Junior and Gabriel wrecking an old car in the parking lot of their father's school. It's Junior's car; he has to write it off because of the insurance. The brothers look through the windows into the school:

On the board were the yellow chalk drawings our father made of the various projects: tables, lamps, chairs. There were angles and choice of wood screw and the correct use of a plane and a clamp. The work tables were cleared, the tools all hanging in their racks, the cement floor swept with sawdust and water. Everything in order.

For Gabriel, this order is profoundly reassuring; it is what makes his father trustworthy, reliable without being dully predictable: the mystery lies in the relationships between the objects – what exactly is the correct use of a plane? Which choice of wood screw is the appropriate one? These questions represent a world of knowledge the father possesses and Gabriel respects.]

MW: I would love for stories that I write to be appreciated by my parents, for instance, I would love for them to say, I really like that story. So that's a kind of thing that I'm growing into. I guess ten years ago I didn't really care what my parents thought about what I wrote, but now I really appreciate their principles and values and their wisdom, and I would love for them, not being writers or artists at all, to look at the story and go, 'That's good work.'

CW: Do you mean your parents because of their place in your life, or do you mean your parents as in people of that generation, or people who aren't writers?

MW: I guess they represent that other world, the bigger world of professional artists, but as well just them, I want to impress them, they've become more important to me, I guess I love them more now or I just appreciate them more now, and what they think of what I'm doing means something to me. But if they don't like the stories, that's not going to hurt me or stop me from writing that kind of story and I'm not changing the way I'm writing the story to fit what they want to read. But I feel like the stories are changing in a way that I think they might like them more.

CW: There's a lot of respect in *One Last Good Look* for both parent figures, especially the father.

MW: I feel more and more that I'm a product of the four people that I grew up with – my mother and father, my brother and my sister – all older than me, and I realize I spent my childhood witnessing their ways of living, and choosing what I was going to do. And the only fair thing to do is to respect their ways of living and write about them in an honourable way, in an accurate way. To write about them is to write about the love I have for them, and so that's the kind of thing the reader is getting from the stories, that feeling that I have for them. Even though they can be at times angry or villainous, I think overriding that there's a sense of goodwill between us all.

[The mother in *One Last Good Look* is quirky, religious; she meets the world with wonder and delight. She seems somehow cut off from aspects of existence most people think of as ordinary. Here is an excerpt from 'The Pallbearer's Gloves':

Junior: We were in a gas station, Gabe. Mom was looking in the coolers, she doesn't want a coffee. Orange crush, she says. Ooh, cream soda. Red cream soda. So I take her, tender like, by the shoulder and say, Mom. You don't get out much, do you.

The mother's obvious pleasure in simple things could make her seem childish but it does not; instead, it suggests an aesthetic which corresponds to Winter's own.]

MW: I get great delight out of particular small bits of my stories, and it's irrational. In Milan Füst I read last night the captain was talking about this meal he was going to create for his friends and about the cheeses and salamis he was going to buy and he said, I can hear the chuff-chuffing sound they will make in the bags as I'm carrying them home, and in brackets he said, These kinds of details delight me. In his life. And they delight me too. That's the whole thing about living, is that little sound of the rustling of the paper in the bags of the food that you're bringing home to feed your friends with. If you can appreciate that, then you're my kind of writer. And reader. And human being. I think my main delight in life is those little things, which appear trivial and maybe they are, maybe somebody who's really got a good grasp of God in the world would think that's silly and I'm small-minded but that's all I can rely on. It delights me, that's all, it makes me happy.

[It doesn't take all that much to make Winter happy. He's not a big spender. He believes in quality, a few good things, and the rest he can do without. 'My parents were children of the Second World War,' he explains. 'They survived bombings, evacuation and the post-war rationing. This formed them. They did not waste anything, and they did not purchase services (my mother cooked from scratch and my father bought raw materials). They grew vegetables, hunted moose, repaired vehicles and appliances, bartered, and cut trees. They were scrupulous with money.' It's clear that Winter admires these traits. He wants real butter in the fridge, but he might share that fridge with five or six roommates. A small room, a mattress on the floor, a desk for the computer, and a drawing by his niece. Living frugally is not exactly making a virtue of necessity: it's the way he seems to want things to be. Gabriel English says in the story 'Let's Shake Hands Like the French' that

---

he's 'never been comfortable with material comforts', that he feels 'not guilty, but responsible in a vague, collective way for the massive wrongs that are done in the world to protect my standard of living.' Money is not something Winter has had a lot of over the years, but there's always a little socked away somewhere; he'll always stand you a beer.

This sense of economy is more than a simple matter of money: it's an aesthetic principle, one which applies to fiction as much as groceries. Winter doesn't like to squander words. A recent review of *One Last Good Look* in the *Toronto Star* praises 'Winter's ruthlessly austere style – think early Hemingway or Carver, stripped to an even further minimized minimalism' ('One Lasting Good Read,' 18 July 1999). Think, too, Norman Levine, whose work Winter has been reading for years and whom Winter interviewed in *TickleAce* (*TickleAce* 26 [1993]: 16-30). One reason Winter's stories are so good has to do with the difference between leaving something unsaid and leaving it out: much is suggested by an image, an abrupt utterance, a juxtaposition. He edits fiercely, excising even conventional forms of punctuation.]

cw: Most people use quotation marks, Michael, for dialogue. Why don't you do that?

mw: When I read [Cormac McCarthy's] work I realized that you didn't need them. If I can cut anything, I'll cut it, and if it still makes sense then I'm delighted by that. I started realizing that I hated, in dialogue, putting in the 'he said' or 'I said' – I found I was writing the word 'me.' Me, colon. And then what the narrator was saying – 'Me: I went to the store.' And I didn't have to write the word 'said' any more. If the sentence became shorter, that's what I went for, as long as it remained clear.

And another thing I like doing is, in dialogue, seeing how far I can go until the reader isn't sure who's speaking, and you can also go another sentence after that point and then put in 'he said' to relieve the reader.

cw: So you don't mind making your reader go back and count, and think: he said this, she says that ...

mw: I don't think the reader has to go back, I think the reader can still have some residual memory of the line, that he can then fix in his mind.

I know that I write for readers who are like me. I really appreciate a reader who picks up on those things that I spend a lot of time working on.

CW: Is there anything that you particularly wanted to be asked that I haven't asked you, about your writing? Anything you'd like to talk about?

MW: I sometimes get slightly depressed that people think the stories are centred on the material world – they're very concrete, and objects are described – and I feel like secretly I'm injecting everything with a spiritual side, there's something larger, a larger force beyond everything that's going on, or that the love between people is a bigger force ... Maybe I fail to get that into my stories, but that never seems to come up, the idea of a bigger presence in the stories, of a force that's beyond the characters or the teapot that's on the kitchen table. It's a force of mystery that allows these absurd things to be said and done.

I have known Michael Winter since the early days of the Burning Rock writing group in the mid-to-late 1980s. I interviewed him for this piece on 4 May 1999 in St. John's, and called him a couple of times afterwards to ask another question or check a fact. Once he had been hauling clapboard off the side of a porch. Another time he wanted me to know that there's a little point of land in Antarctica called Wilksland. It is not possible to separate Michael Winter the person from Michael Winter the writer – they're inextricable – but when I think about him as a friend I am struck by his generosity, his patience, by the number of times he has hauled furniture for hours on other people's moving days. It's hard to make him say anything bad about anyone and if you tell him a secret, he won't blab. He is, most of the time, reasonable and fair-minded, and although he's meticulous and disciplined about some things – work, for instance – he also laughs easily and often. Michael is a proud and private person but the pride has to do with a certain kind of integrity which does not manifest itself as aloofness. He'll talk to anyone, he's interested in everything – how to grow a vinegar plant, replace a faucet stem, paunch a moose. He'll ask people, unintrusively, respectfully, about these things, draw out strangers on subjects they know about.

Two of Winter's comments in this interview seem to encapsulate most precisely his approach to life; they have to do with delight and mystery. He describes the rustling sound of bags of food being carried home and the pleasure of hearing that sound. It's a simple yet suggestive idea: yes, that is the kind of thing that captivates Winter, but it's worth noting that the delight has to do not only with the particularity of the sound itself but also with the fact that it's made by bags containing food, food which is to be prepared for a gathering of friends. Also, the sound is not one he's heard but one he's read about in Milan Füst's novel. So that the small sensual pleasure experienced in isolation is, in the end, connected to friendship and to literature. Winter's delight in small things goes beyond the naive, immediate and sensual, although it possesses those characteristics: it is accompanied by the sense of awe he describes in his final response, awe at 'the force of mystery that allows these things to be said and done'. Delight and awe, the force of mystery, transfuse Michael Winter's writing.

ARCHIBALD THE ARCTIC
Michael Winter

EARLY ON NEW YEAR'S DAY my mother woke me to say, calmly, that two police officers were at the door. She said this in the same way she'd say there's a fried egg sandwich in the oven. I was seventeen, home for Christmas, staying in Junior's room, in his bed in fact. I had been out with Doyle and Skizicks the night before, we ended up on Crow Hill throwing our empties down on the tracks, enjoying the wet distant crumple they made, waiting for the fireworks to sputter into the cold dark air. I remember Skizicks, who is a year older and knew we were virgins, saying he'd screwed Heidi Miller against the wall in behind Tim Horton's. Over the course of two long minutes we counted the reports of eleven shotguns, sounding small, disorganized and lonely.

I walked to the porch in my cold jeans, barefoot. I was hungry and my head hurt. I worked my mouth. The police officers were still outside. I opened the screen door. The white metal handle was frosty. Snow was drifting lightly onto their new fur hats, their epaulets, sliding off the waxed cruiser which hummed quietly in behind my father's car. There were no lights flashing. The driveway needed to be shovelled. Doyle would be up in his window, if he was up. The officers were facing each other, conversing. Snowflakes tangled in their eyelashes. Their footprints were the first to our door in the new year. They looked fit and very awake.

Are you Gabriel English?

Yes.

We have a warrant for your arrest, son.

I knew there was something you could say here. I searched for the proper wording.

Can I ask what the charge is?

We'll discuss that at the station.

Am I under arrest?

This is what my father had taught us. When the law wants you, ask if youre under arrest. I was glad I could remember it.

We'd prefer to formally charge you down at the station, son, after we've cleared a few things up.

My father, who had been in the bathroom shaving, came to the door. He was still in his undervest, mopping his neck and chin with a white towel. He wasnt wearing his glasses, which gave him a relaxed look. He said, Would it be all right, fellas, if the boy had some breakfast? I'll bring him down right after.

The way he dried himself with the towel showed off his massive, pale biceps, his thick wrists. The thickness was well-earned. There was a beat and then the older officer said that would be fine. He decided to look at my father for a moment and then they turned and made new footprints back to the cruiser.

My father turned to me and said, Well what a way to start the new year. He said this in a way that reassured me. He knew already that I hadnt done anything, that I wasnt capable of doing a bad thing. He was confident about this, all he knew about me was good things. I was the good son. His impression reinforced a faith in my own innocence. It made me realize what must have happened and suddenly I got upset.

It's Junior, isnt it, he said.

I suspect it's Junior, Dad.

And why do you suspect him.

He knew that I must be in league with Junior, had information that we'd kept from him. Over breakfast I told him what I knew. He listened as if, while the particulars of the event were new to him, they fit into the larger maze which was the interlaced lives of his sons. He said, Theyre going to begin with a presumption. That youve been driving. And you havent. Be flat out with that and the rest hold to your chin. He said, People in charge like to figure things out. They dont appreciate confessions.

We drove to the police station, which was a bunker below the Sir Richard Squires building. The building housed the first elevator in Newfoundland. There was no need for a tower – it was built so Corner Brook could lay claim to the province's first escalator.

I liked the Up and Down arrows by the elevator buttons. That was my earliest appreciation of technology's ability to appear prescient. I thought it was a considerate touch by the makers. The elevator was the avenue to Corner Brook's public library, which my father had introduced to me before I could read. I would pick up books Junior had chosen, like *Archibald the Arctic* and stare at the riddle of print. Junior loved the northern explorers, of men eating their dogs and each other.

The lobby was glass on three sides, with nine storeys of brick pressing down on it. My father took me to the sixth floor once, to a government office where he had some tax business. I could see the Bowater mill, the neck of the bay twisting around the town of Curling, the swans (the whitest things in town) drifting below in the reservoir which cooled the mill's furnaces, the secondary schools on the landscaped hill to the east. I was uneasy in the building. I was convinced the glass footing would topple. I worried for the commissionaire stationed at his desk by the fountain.

The fountain stood in the centre of the lobby behind an iron railing. It drizzled water over its scalloped and flared glass edges. A boy was carefully tossing a penny in. The fountain was a silent, enormous presence, a wordless example of grander things one could value and live for. I loved the fountain even when no one and nothing told me it was worthy of love.

My father leaned against the rail. He said if he had guts, he'd sell everything and help the poor in Calcutta. That was his base belief about what was right. His weakness drove him to self-interest, to preserving family and constantly bettering our material position. He could appreciate decorative flourishes, but never allowed himself to get carried away.

My mother would say I have these thoughts because we emigrated from England. My mother has given a lot of time to such considerations. She cultivates hindsight, and researches the repercussions of certain acts. Perhaps if I had grown up where I was born, had not felt strange in my own skin, I wouldnt be so sensitive in the world. In the house I spoke with an English accent, outside I pronounced words the way Doyle and Skizicks said them. I said brakfest, chimley, sove you a seat. I was aware of the boundary between blood bond and friends, between house and world. Junior was different. He managed to be pure Newfoundlander.

My father and I walked down to the police station and I began my brief story of never having driven a Japanese car in Alberta and the officer nodded as if he knew the truth of the matter only too well, that my arrest was a technicality, that a million brothers a month pretend to be younger brothers and he was going to add this latest infraction to the pile. I was free to go.

The station, below the library, was a place I had been to only once before, when Doyle and Skizicks and I were accused of breaking a window. We were kicking stones down Valley Road and a neighbour's window crashed in. We ran. We ran home. Junior said When youre in trouble, where do you run?

Home.

No Gabe, always run away from home.

I found the station small and casual. It didnt look hard to break out of. There were three cells in the back that I could only hear.

I never spoke to Junior about this arrest. He had left to go back to Alberta on Boxing Day. He was plugging dynamite holes in Fort McMurray.

My father has cried twice – once when a German shepherd we had ran from his knee and was crushed by a snow plough, the other when Junior left to work in the tar sands. It doesnt hurt me to think of him crying for Junior and not for my departure, or even crying for a dog we rescued from the pound, a thin, shivering creature who knew who to thank for fattening him up. He became too fierce in protecting us. Crying is an irrational act and should never be resented. I know Junior's life is a riskier thing. I know that my parents trust my good senses (I am named executor of their wills). There will be greater love attached to an incautious wild man on the brink of living.

Before Christmas I went out with Junior to a cabin belonging to one of the Brads. Junior knew three men named Brad, and my mother had begun to disbelieve him. That they had other names. She would answer the phone and say, No, he's off somewhere with one of the Brads. As if that was a joke and she wasnt to be fooled. But I believe they were all called Brad. I think perhaps naming someone Brad is not a good idea.

Brad picked us up in his black and gold Trans Am and tried his best to charm our mother who appreciated the gesture but still kept her opinion. I sat in the back and we detoured down Mountbatten Road. We stopped at a house with blue aluminum siding. Brad honked his horn and a screen door opened with two women waving and smiling and pointing a finger to indicate one moment. Brad popped the trunk from inside and waited.

Who are they.

Our wool blankets.

The girls climbed in the back and I remembered Linda from a party Junior had at the house. She had come into my bedroom, sat on the floor with a beer, and told me how she loved Junior to bits.

They nudged me with their hips to get their seat belts on. I was in the middle. Then Linda smiled: Youre gonna be our chaperon, Gabe. Danielle leaned forward and pulled on Brad's hair and kissed him on the ear and I could see the perfect contour of her breast.

Brad Pynn had a cabin up in Pynn's Brook. Junior liked to go snow-mobiling and drinking up there over the holidays. He'd flown into town, gotten his presents giftwrapped by Linda at the hardware store he used to work at, and invited her to Brad's.

Brad and Junior had a plan to rob the small bank above Co-op grocery on Main Street. I dont mind revealing this because, to my knowledge, they never pulled the heist and now, I believe, the bank is closed. It was a small bank, used by members of the Co-op. It was less formal than other banks. There were just desks, rather than counters with glass. You could walk right into the safe if you were quick. Junior was convinced you could pull off that job. The only problem was, everyone knew him. And if you did it with someone like a Brad Pynn, you could never be sure if he'd blow too much money one night, or brag, or betray you.

This bank scheme was something that always came up after a few beers, or during a vial of oil and a sewing needle, which Junior had out in the front seat, spreading the green oil over a cigarette paper on his knee. The joint was passed and I had to take it from Danielle, smoke, and hand it to Linda. Danielle kept pressing my knee saying Look at that, if she saw a cute abandoned salt box, or a crow on the melted road that refused to lift. She'd press my knee then slide her hand a little up my thigh, as though she'd forgotten it was my thigh. Linda put her arm along the back window to make more shoulder room. They were quite relaxed.

Junior had a sawed-off shotgun between his legs which I watched him load with a red number 4 shell. He asked Brad to roll down his window. Cold air pummelled into the car. He clicked the chamber closed. He lifted the barrel up to Brad's window sill, pushed off the safety, stared back at us and said, Watch this.

He saw Danielle's hand on my thigh and Linda's arm around my neck and paused.

There were three black objects ahead standing in the snow on Brad's side of the highway. Brad kept the speedometer at the limit. Junior didnt aim, just pointed at the grade and estimated the distance. He fired and the crows flew up alertly. Brad swerved.

Jesus, June.

He slipped off the road, hit bare ice, fishtailed, adjusted for the swing, pumped the brakes a little, and straightened up. The blast still echoed inside the car. June was laughing until he saw that Linda and Danielle were horrified. We all saw, through a thin veil of trees, a line of cabins.

Oh, honey. Sorry about that.

Linda clenched her jaw and stared out her window. Her arms crossed and flexed.

Brad owned a Gold Wing which he parked and chained into the cabin over winter, and this bike he straddled and drank beer from and turned on the stereo embedded in the ruby fibreglass windjammer and would have started it up if Junior hadnt, at Brad's request, drained the cylinders and cleaned his valves and left the engine to hibernate in drenched oil.

Brad and June took the purple Arctic Cat for a bomb down the lake to ice fish and to hunt with the sawed-off. They carried a small auger and they had slugs in case of a moose. The girls and I played Scrabble and drank rum mixed with Tang crystals. I missed touching their arms and hips. They were about twenty, both attending the Career Academy and slowly becoming disappointed. But that winter they were still bright, talkative Newfoundland women who wore friendship rings and small twinkling earrings and could imagine ways to have fun and succeed. They'd spent summers working in the fish plant in Curling and winters wearing white skates on ponds like Little Rapids. I could tell they enjoyed me and while each on her own may have been bored with my company, together they shared a glee in flirting, in egging me on. In their eyes I was a man in the making, and I accepted this. Women like a confidence no matter what the confidence is.

Linda said, Youre going to be something, arent you. Youre like your brother, but youre smarter and gentle.

Ah Linda he's shy, boy.

And Danielle put her arm around my neck and felt my ear. Her collarbone lifted a white bra strap. Shy? Why you got nothing to be shy about.

She slipped her hand down to my waist.

Have you ever done the dirty? she said.

I didnt have to answer and they laughed and loved the fact that now they were getting into this.

You know something me and Linda have wanted to do?

Linda felt my crotch. She put a hand in my jeans pocket.

Wow. Danielle. Guess what he's not wearing.

Go way.

Danielle slipped her hand in my other pocket. This pocket had the lining torn and her warm, probing hand clasped directly and gently.

Oh Linda we've got a fine young man on our hands.

A growing boy.

Linda unbuttoned my jeans. I shifted in my chair and prayed that the skidoo would be loud. I tried to recall the sound it made as it buzzed up the lake. But as it was, even if Brad and Junior came in the door, nothing could be seen above the table. Nothing except an astonished boy and two eager, laughing women leaning in to him.

Last fall Junior hit a moose. This was six days after the mandatory seat belt law had been established, and it was this law which had saved his life. Dad and I found him unconscious, pinned behind the wheel of his orange and chrome VW Bug. Eight hundred pounds of moose had rolled over the bonnet, crumpled the windshield, bent the doorframes and lay bleeding in his lap. The ambulance service had to wait for the jaws of life to free him. He'd loved the Bug, it had lived its previous life in salt-free Florida. Investigators measured skid marks, the animal was towed off with two canvas cables, its injuries charted, witnesses signed statements and it was declared that Junior had been driving with abandon under severe winter conditions.

He bought a Rabbit then, and two weeks later he rammed into the back of an eighteen-wheeler; the Rabbit was dragged four hundred metres before the semi braked. The trucker was furious, he hadnt even seen Junior he was that far up his ass. Up your wind tunnel, Junior said, looking for an opportunity to pass. The trucker wanted to smack him. He would have if my father hadnt stretched his big hands in an obvious way.

Junior began giving up on a Datsun, an old, whipped car. He was motoring around town, scouting for other drivers' infractions. Someone running a red light. If he saw anything, he drove into it. He was making money, he said, from other people's insurance.

When the Datsun had built up a nest egg he asked if I wanted to go for a ride. This was after supper, in early December. He'd decided, he said, to retire the vehicle. The insurance company had declared it a liability and he had to write it off before the calendar year.

We drove to the empty, carefully ploughed parking lot behind the school my father taught at. The streetlamps were just flickering on. It was terminally ill, Junior said, and we had to put it out of its misery.

He revved up the motor, spun on the slightly icy pavement, and swaggered the car towards a ploughed mound of snow at the edge of the lot.

Hold on, Gabe.

The headlights lurched, grew in concentration against the bank as we accelerated and approached. The car exploded into compact snow, driving in a few feet, snow smacking against the windshield, the hill absorbed our blow. The motor muffled, hummed, still ran happily. If it had a tail it would be wagging.

Junior shifted into reverse, hit the wipers, spun wide and galloped for the opposite end of the lot, dipsy-doodling around a streetlight pole on the way, swinging on the ice and slamming sideways into the far bank of snow.

I had to get out and push this time. The exhaust was clogged with snow. I watched as Junior aimed for a sturdier bank pressed against the school. The car whined horribly. There was no give in the snow. The seatbelt cut against his chest as he came up hard on a hidden concrete post. A crease formed in the hood of the car, the grill burst open and jets of water spouted up, dousing the windshield and melting then freezing the snow on the hood. The motor kept running as if nothing had happened. I ran to him.

Can't kill a fucking Datsun, man.

Junior got out to reconsider his approach. I reminded him that if he went through with this demolition we'd have to walk home. He popped the hood (it opened at the windshield) and cranked up the heat to transfer valuable degrees over from the engine. Then he said come look at this.

We stood on the front bumper and stared in to the dark classroom. On the board were the yellow chalk drawings our father made of various projects: tables, lamps, chairs. There were angles and choice of wood screw and the correct use of a plane and a clamp. The work tables were cleared, the tools all hanging in their racks, the cement floor swept with sawdust and water. Everything in order.

We drove home with the broken radiator, my eyes fixed to the temperature gauge which hovered past the orange bar.

It was then Junior asked me for a favour. We were parked, the lights shut off, the engine ticking to the cold. He said his insurance was sky high. What we'd do, he said, is insure his next car in my name and he'd be a second driver. It would save him a hell of a lot of cash.

At the time I wasnt driving anything and when youre not using something, it's hard to feel the importance of giving it away. There was a mature air about Junior needing my help in the adult world. But a warning hunch spread through my body. I knew there would be repercussions, though I could not articulate them. It all seemed reasonable, he just needed to borrow my driver's licence for an hour.

It wasnt just the insurance, the police told me. The car was registered in my name too. I had an overdrawn bank account. There was a bad prairie loan. A lien on a leased Ford pickup. In Alberta, his entire life had become my life. He was living under the name Gabriel English. It was as if he never expected me to live a life, so he'd better do it for me.

'Archibald the Arctic' is told in a tone different from one I usually adopt. The narrator doesn't just relate events, he often explains the actions and motives of the characters. This is the first time I've done so much editorializing. I get away with it because the story I tell is simple and strong, there is a pay-off after the last sentence. I've never been very good at plot, and so I've relied on ruthless attention to detail, an absence of judgement, and the hunch that the small moments I witness and report are interesting to a reader.

This story was one of the last I wrote for the collection *One Last Good Look*. I'd just moved to Toronto, was subletting an apartment that was filled with unfamiliar books. There was a collection of Tobias Wolff's work. Two books in particular, the memoirs *This Boy's Life* and *In Pharaoh's Army*, stood out. I loved the apparent candour Wolff's delivery exuded and the simple images and events that informed this story. His material was ordinary, infused with intelligent consideration. And I believed it all.

I felt I hadn't, in earlier stories, articulated clearly what it was about Junior and Gabriel that interested me. I hadn't been clear enough. 'Archibald' is the simplest story in the collection to read aloud because of this clarity. What makes it clear is the ease with which the images present themselves. We have the police at the door, the father's presence, the realization by Gabriel of what the truth must be. And then the ensuing digging up of that truth. There's a comfortable pattern to the telling: scene, scene, reflection. The voice is authoritative, self-deprecating, confessional but not embarrassing.

Many of the scenes are autobiographical and I enjoy turning personal experience into stories. I feel I'm making sense of the life I'm living. I was arrested on New Year's Day for something my brother did. It involved a driving infraction. I am executor of my parents' wills. There was a water fountain I loved. I'd forgotten about the fountain until I began writing the story. I'd forgotten it until I had the father and Gabriel enter the police station. Then I remembered it. Most of this story I had forgotten.

The series of incidents that occur in the story is a false conjunction of event. I haven't been true to the facts of occurrence. Rather, I've maintained an honesty to emotional truths of familial bond and duplicity. I've been true to the humour in the way Junior walks through life.

I should stress, however, that this idea of the story's meaning did not occur prior to writing down the incidents. I knew I had material, a hunch that it would be interesting. Only later did I see a form. I believe we all know what the formative moments of our lives are. Expressing what they mean is often difficult, often false, but we can muddle with those moments and after a while a larger sense emerges.

I think I've learned, within the body of the story, to speak accurately about my characters' intentions.

My favourite scene is when Gabriel and Junior, after futilely attempting to destroy the car, stand on the bumper and look into their father's dark classroom. They witness their father's order on the chalkboard, the blueprints for building things. It is directly after this witnessing that Junior asks Gabriel for the favour which is the story's hook.

This scene was not conceived beforehand. It was arrived at during the writing of the story. The leap occurred at the moment I wrote that paragraph; the contrast of the brothers' actions and the father's plans was not premeditated, and Gabriel's realization, therefore, does not feel forced or contrived. It is not even his realization, but the reader's.

I had begun to let my narrator ruminate in this story. Prior to 'Archibald' I was very stringent about what I told the reader. I am a mean writer, I strip away superfluous words, even punctuation. I give only surfaces. The reader has to glean the rest. But in 'Archibald the Arctic' I let myself tell the story. I relaxed and released segments of the apparent truth behind motivation. Stories prior to 'Archibald' lacked repercussion. They just happened, with no rumination on the causes. The scope of the story refused to allow the fruits of whatever decisions were acted upon. Their endings were snipped off.

I wanted to discuss motives or the seeds of why my characters were motivated. And so the father, not in any particular scene, but in the tone of how he addresses his sons, conveys his trust in Gabriel and his wariness of Junior. He reassures Gabriel that he is intrinsically good. Gabriel is incapable of a bad deed (unlike Junior). However, as we're told, greater love will attach itself to riskier men. Gabriel understands the love his father has for Junior, because Junior is the incautious side of the father unleashed. Junior is the man his father would not let himself be. It is this type of blatant editorializing that I have allowed to enter my story's scope.

One summation I make in the story, which I'm still not sure I've earned, is the line that the young women like a confidence (in a man) regardless of what that confidence is.

Before writing 'Archibald', I felt I must master the show-don't-tell story. In striving for this effect I have, perhaps, been too cold-hearted, leaving a barren, reporter-type examination of character and event. 'Archibald' seems to be a successful marriage of that pared-down writing style and the satisfaction that is derived from naming and examining those moments that shape or challenge our character.

There were at least six other scenes that were cut from the final story. I carved away superfluous material. When I had the right mix, when I had extracted a surplus out of the remaining images, and a resonance occurred, I stopped. I didn't care what the resonance was, just that I had one. I trust my hunches.

LISA MOORE
Kernels

POPCORN: Once, when I was seven, I was told to draw a single piece of popcorn and to change the scale: make it monolithic, make it architecture. A germ's point of view. I was doing art classes with the artist Ray Mackie at seventy-seven Bond Street, drawing on big sheets of newsprint with charcoal. Fat streaks of black, sooty shadows, foreboding and gothic. The restraint employed in leaving some of the paper white, for the highlights. I stared at a single piece of popcorn for more than an hour under a strong light, noticing the remains of blasted kernel, the curving white walls of the antechamber, swooping shadows within the busted cave of the main bulb. Ray told us to think about the kind of marks we were making. The mark was a record of the way we moved our arms, of what we were feeling while we drew. The popcorn's shape was a history of the violent action of popping. A still life should be anything but still. It should be full of gesture, action, drama. The class was a lesson in form and content. Be innovative with form, express emotion. Of course none of that was apparent until much later. But an hour with popcorn is a serious commitment for a seven-year-old (there's the overwhelming urge to just eat the thing), and the exercise stuck with me. Struggling to render its unique form, different from all the others in the bowl, I slowly became aware of its insane intricacy and beauty. I think those early classes were about being astonished unexpectedly by ordinary things.

TEXTURE: So my first forays into the world of an artist were visual. Seventy-seven Bond Street was a giant building with paint-spattered hardwood floors, a dark-room, winding staircases, easels, a pottery studio. The smell of oils, turpentine, developing chemicals. Many Newfoundland artists had a studio there. It was thrilling and strange, as a child, to see nude drawings pinned to the wall, to watch adults thoroughly engaged in what most of the people I knew considered the realm of play.

Art-making as a child is all about the physical world: the squish of mud through your fingers, a smear of paint drying on your arms so that it pulls the tiny hairs when you pick it off. It's about luxuriating in the materials. Learning the properties of each medium, its unique qualities and limitations. I think of words as having texture. *Lugubrious* has the texture of baked okra. *Serendipity* has the texture of rain bouncing off the surface of a lake. I love the feeling of having a word on the tip of my tongue, ungraspable. I feel it there, like a mothball. My daughter, when trying to figure out the spelling of a new word, writes the letters on the roof of her mouth with the tip of her tongue. I discovered this one evening while watching her write – pencil poised, eyes riveted on the opposite wall, jaw wiggling. I met a woman once who grew up in the Australian outback with Maori children. She said they learned to spell words by tracing the letters with a finger on each other's backs. When I write, my goal is to *transport* the reader. I want her to surrender her immediate surroundings for whatever I've cooked up. In order to seduce like that I have to create vivid concrete worlds with lots of texture and shadow.

During one of those early art classes each student was given a ball of wool, and told to think of it as a line. We were to draw with our line through the room. By the end of the class several balls of wool had been wrapped around chairs and table legs, tied to door handles, tossed over pipes that ran across the ceiling, flung through the curtain rods. A multi-coloured spider web, a gigantic cat's cradle, a three-dimensional linear drawing. That was my introduction to sculpture. The next class we hefted a video camera over our shoulders (it weighed more than I did) and shot the Santa Claus parade. We were told to think of the borders of the viewfinder as the frame and to consider what information we were including in the picture. Did we really want that shot of pavement? Did we really want to cut off Santa's head?

I love the parallels between visual composition and the composition of a piece of writing. What information one includes in the frame, what details one includes in a story. Recently, I have been learning to edit video on my computer at home. A shot of my daughter and me in a vaulted alleyway in France. We're holding hands and spinning in a circle, our hair flying out behind us. I try cutting the speed halfway through the spin so when our feet hit the pavement the sound is distorted, drawn out, a reverberating *thwack*. It takes more than an hour to edit less than half a minute. Around one o'clock in the morning when vibrant, frenetic pixels have implanted themselves onto my retina for good, it occurs to me that the written word is dead. That a hundred years from now the image will have taken over. The language of images will proliferate and evolve at a tremendous speed. The video blur on the screen in front of me – a splash of orange shirt, the blue shutters – all a swarming mass of tiny pixels seems to be far more *living*, more full of possibility than anything I could write. One frame of video contains so much detail. It would require several pages of writing to capture what the eye devours in a second. At one in the morning, writing seems destined to lose its privileged position as a form of communication.

BEING COOL: Marshall McLuhan talks about cubism developing at the same time as film. Cubism allows us to see an object from all angles at once: the top, the sides, the back, the front. McLuhan suggests cubism is about simultaneity rather than sequence, and the absence of sequence destroys ambiguity. Norman Levine, in an interview with Michael Winter, once said the less a writer gives the reader the better. Levine is referring to what McLuhan calls a cool medium: a medium in which the audience does most of the work. The reader is a fully engaged participant in the act of creation. It's that ambiguity, or coolness, that draws me primarily to writing rather than the visual arts in the end. Trusting that certain unsaid things are present. But I have contrary impulses as well. I want to be hot, tell all, gab, gossip, narrate. I could never really trust that it was enough to let the popcorn be a popcorn, I want it to be suffering unrequited love, or be an egomaniac.

The more skilled a short story writer is, the less action she needs to write in order to create drama. I was reading a Richard Ford story in the *New Yorker*, 'Reunion', in which almost nothing happens. A chance encounter at a train station between a man and the husband of his ex-lover. One of the characters actually says, 'Nothing happened here today.' And nothing had, but Ford managed to evoke the power of a moment, by suggesting the messy histories of each character.

THE CRAWL: Another valuable piece of advice from Norman Levine is to surround yourself with interesting people. At sixteen I went to the Newfoundland and Labrador theatre school in Stephenville, which was run by the late Maxim Mazumdar. Mazumdar was originally from Bombay. Somehow, he ended up in Stephenville, Newfoundland. Stephenville, an old army base, was small enough to have only one streetlight. It was a peculiar place for a man of Mazumdar's vision to set up shop. Every summer he orchestrated a festival of theatre that included, the summer I was there, Greek tragedy, Shakespeare, Jacques Brel, Thornton Wilder and original Newfoundland works. There were teachers, actors and directors from all over the world.

Mazumdar was a sensualist with a formidable dedication to his craft. I think that combination describes the perfect personality for any writer or artist. He had the voice a certain sort of trained actor has, not exactly a British accent, but a controlled modulation, each vowel sculpted and set down with care, and twenty years later I can still hear it. Resonance. At sixteen, I wanted more than anything in the world to go to that theatre school. I lost a contact lens on the way to the audition. I delivered a Tennessee Williams monologue with a Southern accent and one eye screwed shut. I was in.

I learned to mime invisible walls and a perfect breast stroke. The breast stroke involves standing on one leg, the body parallel to the floor, the other leg kicking behind, toes pointed at the end of each thrust. I watched the mime teacher for a long time and still had to be told the secret of the illusion. You bend the standing leg just slightly with each stroke so it looks like the body sinks a little as it pulls forward. I spent a long time cultivating the idle grace of the crawl, the muscles in my bending thigh shrieking with pain. A subtle, almost imperceptible dip of the thigh, the swimmer suddenly surrounded by water. Just like the characters in the Richard Ford story – two men who hardly know each other exchange a few words in a crowded train station, but somehow Ford manages to surround them with families, histories, spent passions.

BEING NUDE: In Montreal I'd seen an Antonin Artaud play. It was staged in a warehouse. The actors were as physically different from each other as they could possibly be. An elastic Vietnamese woman and a seven-foot man with a canary-yellow Mohawk. The man got down on his hands and knees and the Vietnamese woman picked up a giant tree stump, complete with root system and drove it through the man's spread legs again and again, in slow motion, while he tossed his head and howled. A fishing net hung from the ceiling, surrounding the performance space. Periodically, the actors rushed the net as if trying to escape. They screamed at the audience, forcing their hands through the holes, trying to grab us.

Afterward my friend the film-maker Mary Lewis and I asked to speak to the director. He was from eastern Europe. We said we wanted to join his troupe. He told us that the actors meet in the summer at a camp in Northern Ontario and rehearse nude for a month. Would we be willing to rehearse nude for a month? We both nodded vigorously. We certainly would. We both tried to give the impression that we were used to doing all kinds of things nude, cooking, bringing out the garbage, running through the trees with a crowd of actors. We took his address and I think we kept it for a very long time. I think we still have it.

TALKING TO MYSELF LOUDLY: I enjoy being jolted. Made uncomfortable. Being edged, squeezed, jammed, thrust out of some position I hold. I like being forced to give up what I believe, if only for a while. I went to the Nova Scotia College of Art and Design. NSCAD is a degree-granting institution, but students don't receive marks for studio courses, just a pass or fail. I lived in a condemned house in the North end of Halifax with six other art students. A week before the fall semester started our house filled up with all the Newfoundlanders who needed a place to stay while they looked for permanent accommodations. We put plastic on the windows but during the coldest nights of the winter there was often a skin of ice on the kitchen floor. On the weekends we had parties with over a hundred guests, and a rock and roll band took up most of the living room. The band's name, 'The Brats', was spray-painted on the wall behind them in fluorescent orange. Every other square inch of the house was covered in art. Drawings, paintings, sculpture. Jim Boyd, who lived in one of the closets, welded huge rusting car parts – a wheel rim jutting from a mass of metal like a woman's buttock – once one of Jim's sculptures sat on the sidewalk, too heavy to bring inside, and a taxi driver dropping me home said, Look at that heap of garbage, looks like modern art.

NSCAD made an international name for itself in the seventies in the field of conceptual art. Much of the fervour had died down by the time I got there in the mid-eighties but the school still had an impressive visiting artist program. I attended a lecture by Dara Burnbaum, whose 'found' video clip from the television show *Wonder Woman* is on permanent display at the Metropolitan Museum. Burnbaum looped the moment when Wonder Woman transforms by exploding from her magic belt so that she explodes continuously, without rest, for eternity. A feminist statement as elegant and ambiguous as a zen koan.

I met Kristoff Wadesco, a Polish artist who had been arrested for projecting an image of chains and padlock on the South African Embassy in Geneva during a meeting of the United Nations. He had projected the same image on tenement buildings in New York. The buildings were slated for demolition and the squatters who had taken up residence were forced onto the street. I met with Wadesco several times to discuss my work, and the political implications of art. We talked about how the meaning of a work changes according to its location, its audience. The implications of the market. The place of morality in art. Is work without a political agenda frivolous? Is it naive to imagine that art can incite social change? If a work is completed by its audience how much control over content does the artist have? I left these talks at dusk and wandered up Gottingen street, carrying on the conversation, arguing out loud with myself, stopping, starting, gesticulating when I'd made a good point.

BERGMAN: Last winter I invited a bunch of women to my house to watch the movies of certain directors and to read criticism of the work. Most of us were mothers with brand spanking new infants, or very pregnant. The snow flying, good snacks, a roomful of breast-feeding mothers watching Bergman. We started with 'The Passion of Anna.' Someone on an island was mutilating lambs. People torn apart by extravagant life-altering emotion, and the viewer is never told why; the concrete reasons for humiliation or passion barely alluded to. A horse is covered in gasoline and locked in a burning barn. Suddenly, there are the actors talking about their characters. The concerns of acting. I've been reading short French books in translation, that have a similar feel – erotic and surreal. There's something open-ended about

Jean Baudrillard, Alinas Reyes, Anne Hébert. I can't believe what those French guys get away with. It feels as though that's what they're doing, *getting away with something.* Something unexpected. Liv Ullman, as herself, in a huge red hat.

I love the illusion of simplicity that's apparent in the work of artists, writers and film-makers who have been practising their craft for a lifetime. I love the way Picasso photographed himself in a dark room drawing a bull with a flashlight. I love how that gesture, a few seconds of waving his arm around, was the consummation of so much of the work he'd done before, recurrent themes and a commitment to experimentation. Bergman has said that he writes a script by collecting 'split-second impressions that disappear as quickly as they come, forming a brightly colored thread sticking out of the dark sack of the unconscious. If I wind up this thread carefully a complete film will emerge, brought out with pulse-beats and rhythms characteristic of just this film.'

FAVOURITE BOOKS: I love the question, what are your favourite books, because the answer shifts so dramatically and frequently – like chaos theory – a whole stream of authors flood to mind all connected by a system as delicate and complicated as the flux of weather. Then a whiff of coffee hits me, or say, the smell of baby puke, and I am thoroughly devoted to and passionate about a completely different group of authors or books.

I miss the intensity of concentration and talent for suspending disbelief I had reading as a child. Books could take me over then, bodily, as if I were possessed. I remember a lunch period in grade four in the school auditorium when I was reading *Harriet the Spy.* The whole school crammed into the room, the screeching of cheap metal chairs, the roaring surf of voices, my hotdog with ketchup and mustard. Harriet, a kid from New York, who was going to be a writer. I was amazed to discover that there were actually children in New York, or that children lived in apartment buildings, or that there were Italians who ran grocery stores, or fathers who wanted to be writers and couldn't make an adequate living. When I looked up from the book, the cafeteria was empty. The bell had rung, two hundred kids had moved out, returned to their classrooms and left me behind without my noticing. It makes me want to write children's books. My list of favourite writers at this moment would include Eudora Welty, Flannery O'Connor (for the muscle behind her moral scrutiny, for being Catholic, for her humour, for owning peacocks, her collected letters, her courageous fight against lupus), Marguerite Duras (for her sensuality, the transparent clarity of her writing, for *The War* particularly, her descriptions of a certain kind of poverty, for experimenting with form and point of view, for being able to combine the autobiographical with the political without sacrificing aesthetic and formal concerns while she's doing it). Raymond Carver (for almost the same reasons as Marguerite Duras), Jane Austen for the balance of her sentences, you could put a spirit level on any one of them and the bubble would be exactly in the middle. José Saramago (the narrative voice in *Blindness*, a unique invention, like nothing I've ever read before) Susan Minot (same reason as Jane Austen). Faulkner, *As I Lay Dying*. Joan Didion, Oriana Fallaci (two interviews: one with Hugh Hefner, another with Fellini; how she lets both men bury themselves), how both women wrest journalism from its crusty formulas and allow themselves a presence in their social criticism. Simon Schamas's book *Rembrandt's Eyes*.

SKYDIVING: I had a meeting with the producers of a national sit-com to pitch an idea. I'd never written a screenplay before, and the word 'pitch' gave me butterflies. I bought a coffee on the way. I wanted one of the female characters in the series, a singer, to fall in love with a music tycoon from Toronto. We got comfortable in the office, I tore the tab off my coffee and the producer said: I'm afraid this music guy is somewhat cliché.

My hand started to tremble and the coffee slopped over the side, burning my thumb. Oh, well, originally it wasn't a record producer. It wasn't? No, originally it was something else. What was it, originally? Oh, never mind. Tell us. No, it's silly. Tell us anyway. Originally it was a naked man falling from the sky. A naked skydiver, they have them. My sister-in-law fell in love with a French adventurer, an avid skydiver. He'd come across the Atlantic in a yacht, got caught in a storm, clung to the mast while the boat capsized and was still clinging when it righted itself. He also rides a unicycle and eats flame, works for the telephone company repairing those little red phone booths all over the Alps. The next thing, my sister-in-law wants to jump out of a plane. She saw this picture of two men in the paper, naked skydivers, running across a field of grass, parachutes billowing behind. You could just see their bums. I came into the kitchen and she stood with her coffee cup held near her chest and tapped the picture with her finger. I want to do that. They gave her a two-day course, and there she is hanging onto the wing of the plane, her feet on a step, and the guy yells at her, Jump! and she says, Jump? and he says, Jump! and she says, Jump? and the guy kind of leans out and puts his boot on the step and he edges her feet off the step, just pushes her feet off the step and she was flying. So my original idea was this French guy falls from a plane naked, this flame-eating guy, and our singer has a one night stand.

The producers looked at each other. We could do that, they said. You could? We could do that.

But the editors in Toronto wanted full-blown romance. They wanted mush. The local producers kept negotiating with Toronto on my behalf for a touch of subtlety. Finally I had a call from the producer saying funding wouldn't be approved until CBC Toronto had one more romantic line. I said, 'His hands smell like orange peels.' There was a pause. He said, Okay, I'll tell them. Later in the afternoon I got a call. Apparently that line was romantic enough, and funding was approved.

The episode was shot in the middle of a snow storm. Everybody on set wore fat knee-length eiderdown jackets purchased from a special catalogue only available to Arctic explorers and film-makers. Except the leading male. He came loping through the blowing snow completely naked but for the straps of his parachute. Several crew stood waiting in the sidelines with blankets to rush at him at the end of the shot.

CRAVING
Lisa Moore

JESSICA LAUGHS VERY LOUD and the candle flames lie down stretched and flat. She moves the candelabra in front of her husband.

She says, I like aggressive men.

I say, I like aggressive women.

She dips her spoon into the mushroom soup.

But this is delicious, she says.

Vermouth, I say. On the way back from the liquor store a plastic bag of fierce yellow slapped against my shin. I peeled it away, meat juice coursing in the wrinkles like a living beast. It clung just as viciously to a telephone pole when I let it go. There was a poster on the pole just above the bag, Jessica Connolly at Fat Cat's. A band of men behind her. She looked resolute and charged, just like twenty years ago when the three of us would crush ourselves into a change room in the mall, forcing our bodies into the smallest-sized jeans we could find – she and Louise and I, twisting on the balls of our feet to see how our bums looked.

I like aggressive women too, she says.

That's because we're both aggressive.

I put my arm around Louise and squeeze her. I like you anyway, Lou, I say.

Jessica says, Oh, she's passive aggressive.

She isn't though, I say. Jessica pouts her lower lip, contemplating. We both concentrate on Louise's sweetness for a moment. Louise reaches for the bread, her brow furrowed. She's trying to think of something bad.

Lou's so wonderful, though, Jessica says, giving up. I glance at my husband. The men don't know each other. I should be drawing them into the conversation, but this is too heady. Jessica's so thoroughly herself, the genuine article.

Louise says, Do you remember when our class used to go to church? I

51

loved the feeling of the sleeve of someone's blouse touching my arm. If they were unaware of it. Just brushing against my arm. Someone else's sleeve.

Jessica says, I love my daughter.

She's holding her spoon in the air. Jessica is far away, her eyes full of her daughter. She's in the park or the delivery room – somewhere with a lot of light – and the child is vigorous, screaming or running. Jessica sent a picture at Christmas of the four of them. The boy resting his cheek on her bare shoulder. Her daughter trying to tear off a white sunhat.

I love my son too, she says, and dips the spoon. But my daughter is going to do things. She'll get into a lot of trouble too. Jessica grins at her soup, proud and grim about the trouble her daughter's going to cause.

I tell them a story about a Bulgarian woman that ends with the shout, No matter, I must have it!

I say, This should be our motto. We clink our wineglasses and shout, No matter, I must have it! But the men go on with their conversation at the other end of the table. They are talking music, the different qualities a variety of sound systems offer.

Then Jessica says, I'm going through flux right now. Her eyes flit to her husband. I slam my hand flat on the table, the wineglasses jiggle.

Stop it, I say.

Stop what? The flux?

I won't have flux at the dinner table, I say.

Okay, she says, and she laughs, but it's more of a sly chuckle. We are twelve again, in the bloating, compressed heat of the canvas camper in her parents' driveway. She and Louise are trying to convince me I have to come out now. One of her brothers noticed my new bra and made some remark. Sitting alone in the trailer, with my arms crossed so tight over my chest that the next morning my arm muscles are stiff and it hurts to pull a sweater over my head. Jessica full of worldly disgust. Louise obstinately refusing to make Jessica relent, which she could do with a single tilt of her chin. They are united in the desire to punish my vanity. They don't have bras, but they have braces on their teeth, and that makes them a club.

Jessica says, Fine, if that's the way you want it.

I start to cry, knowing it's a gamble. Louise wavers but Jessica's scorn fulminates into a full-blown denouncement. She won't let me ruin all the fun. It's sunny outside and the camper smells of her brother's sports socks.

They wander off, their voices fading, Jessica's ringing laugh the last sound, not a forced laugh, they have forgotten me. Then I listen to the wind through the maples, straining to hear my parents' car coming for me.

Jessica admired the characters of her Siamese cats, haughty and lascivious. She could suss out the swift-forming passions of the gang of boys we knew, and make them heel. She knew the circuit of their collective synaptic skittering and played it like pinball. She couldn't be trusted with secrets, and we couldn't keep them from her.

I ask her husband if he wants more soup. I won't play a part in excluding him, though I'm sure everything is his fault.

He says, I don't know what else is coming.

There's dessert, says Louise. Lou wants to save him from the flux too. Save us all, because it's a big wave that could make the panes in the French door implode and we'd be up to our necks with the soup bowls floating.

Then Louise's boyfriend says, But pollution is a by-product of industry and we all want industry, so. He shrugs.

Lou catches my eye. She's thinking, Remember the guy on the surfboard in Hawaii? I felt total abandon. An evanescing of self, my zest uncorked.

Yes, but if you had kept going, it wouldn't have been abandon. He wouldn't be a man swathed in the nimbus of an incandescent wave, muzzling the snarling lip of that bone-crushing maw of ocean with a flexed calf muscle. He would be one of these guys at the table, half drunk and full of mild love.

There's my husband, heavy-lidded, flushed. The first time I saw him my skin tingled with the nascent what-would-come. Shane Walker. Red suspenders tugging at his faded jeans. The best way to make a thing happen is to not want it. I didn't want him so bad that he strode right over to the table and dropped down his books, *Mexico in Crisis* and *The Marxist Revolution*. He rubs his hands down the front of his faded jeans.

I read your sexy poem, he says.

A sheet of water falling from a canoe paddle like a torn wing. That's the only line of the poem I remember. So much bald longing in a paddle stroke. A torn wing, big deal, yet Shane Walker is blushing. Then I decided – No matter, I must have it.

Jessica taps her spoon on the edge of her cup. She's furious – why won't I have flux at the dinner table? It's only emotion, everything blows over. What am I afraid of? Let Louise have her beach boy.

I think, What if it wasn't abandon? What if some part of Louise stays on a surfboard in Hawaii forever when this guy, who considers the politics of pollution, wants her. Would Jessica have Louise long eternally for something that never existed? It's perverted. And what about Jessica? How long can this last, this brave refusal to compromise? There's redemption in submission. If Jessica wants to strut her charisma I'll stand aside, but in the end she's wrong and I'm right.

Why does the end matter, shrieks Jessica, there is no end. She doesn't say anything, of course, she's gone to the bathroom. We're only on the soup, there are several courses, whose idea was this, the plastic bag on my shin, her poster. Wouldn't it be fun? How have we changed? I think, This may be the end.

She says, I'd rather die ignited than sated.

I realize now, totally zonked – Jessica has rolled three joints since she got here, I haven't been stoned in years, it's so pleasurable, so good, I can hardly collect the plates – that I have always believed the flaws of men are born of a stupidity for which they, men, can't be held accountable. I recognize in a flash – I have balanced the sixth soup bowl, a spoon spins across the floor – that all my relations with men have been guided by this generous and condescending premise. I see now that the theory comes from the lack of courage required to face the truth, which is that men are pricks. They're aware women like me exist, women who believe men have been shafted in terms of a moral spine, and these men welcome this low estimation of themselves, and capitalize on it.

My neighbour, Allan, in the kitchen this afternoon while I was preparing for the dinner party. He was dropping off the flyers for the parent/teachers' auction. It disturbs me that Allan has never flirted with me. He flings himself onto a kitchen chair, spoons white sugar over a piece of bread, which he folds and eats in three bites.

He says, Aren't we all hungry?

I thought, Hungry for what? But I could remember a keening, an imminence. At certain hours it was strongest, at dawn riding my bike downhill, walking home from a bar at four in the morning.

I know I am, says Allan. I'm hungry.

I used to crave something, but what was it? Approval? It was bigger than the whole world approving, bigger than anything language could hog-tie. It compelled my every action, even eating a bran muffin I could tremble with excitement, thinking something might happen now, right now.

Allan certainly looks hungry, all shoulders and elbows splayed over the table.

I say, I can't help you, Allan.

I wasn't certain I'd spoken out loud. When I said *I can't help you*, I meant, I wish you wanted me, and even, I'd like to climb on the kitchen table with you – but I didn't say that, thankfully. What I said was terrible enough, *I can't help you*. I had been unaware, until that moment, that I wished to be desired by Allan.

He says, But I don't want you to help me.

Why wouldn't he want me too? If he is so damn hungry?

Louise: Why don't we unleash a primal battle screech, our friend is in flux for fuck's sake.

I think, Oh yes, it would be great to be Jessica. Let's all be Jessica, ready to burst into flame over an unpaid parking ticket. Ready, anyway, to sleep with the window washer who lowers himself to her office window on rope and pulley, blue overalls and cap, his powerful arms cutting slices of clarity through the soapy blur.

Fabulous, says Jessica.

We are very drunk now, it seems. Or I am, not used to smoking, but Jessica has a bristling fixity. She flicks her wrist to look at her watch. I have to go downtown, she says.

But it's our dinner party. We haven't seen each other. We don't know how we've changed.

Her husband says, I'll come with you.

Jessica says, You have to relieve the babysitter.

I think, It's too late. I didn't do my part. I have forsaken the promises of our adolescence; hiding near the warm tires of parked cars while playing spotlight at dusk, holding still while curling irons burn our scalps, splashes of silver raining from the disco balls in the parish hall, mashed banana emollients, face scrubs with twigs and bits of apricot, ears pierced with an icecube and sewing needle, and the disquieting loss of a belief in God. The saturated aura, a kinetic field of blue light, that surrounded a silent phone while we willed it to ring. Our periods. Dusk, all by itself, dusk, walking home from school after a volleyball game and the light withdrawing from the pavement. I look at my husband, I try to feel dissatisfied but I can't, he's a beautiful man.

Jessica's husband wants her to give him money for the babysitter but she won't. She's angry he didn't take care of it himself. The chink of a wineglass on the marble fireplace. Louise's boyfriend rises from his chair and sways a little, he moves across the room and pats Jessica on the head.

Patronizing bitch, he says.

Jessica grins. She unfurls a peel of giggles tinny as a dropped roll of tinfoil bouncing across the kitchen tiles. She picks up her leather jacket and fires up the zipper. She grabs me by the shoulders, presses me into her big breasts. Then she holds me at arm's length.

You, she says, haven't changed a bit.

She moves to Louise, lifts her from the couch also by the shoulders, gives her a big hug.

She kisses her husband on both cheeks and hands him forty bucks.

She says, I love you, even at this moment.

She says to Louise's boyfriend, You, I'm not hugging.

She opens the French door and the window panes rattle.

Thank you so much, it was lovely.

The front door slams behind her. We each sit up a little, adjusting our posture, the draft from the front door sobering. Outside the dining-room window, we can hear her platform heels slapping the sidewalk, she has broken into a trot.

The story 'Craving' came to me almost fully formed one slightly hung-over morning after a dinner party. A fully formed story is a rare occurrence for me. I keep a daily journal, switching from the computer to a hard-cover black notebook throughout the day. The journal is full of dialogue, dreams, images, gestures and scenes. It's a journal of impressions rather than facts. My fiction almost always develops from these notes. I write the journal without looking for any cohesion or theme, though over a two-month period I usually find the material has an internal order that can become a short story. I have a kind of illogical belief that certain images are magic, super-saturated with meaning. I write fast in my journal because I want to sneak up on those moments and snag them before I know what I'm doing. Too much scrutiny at this stage can make things fusty.

I have a visceral, gut response to certain moments: a sprinkler tipping over a flashing lawn at dusk, a woman's necklace breaking, the beads clattering onto a long candlelit mahogany table, a developmentally delayed man in a fluorescent cap leaning on a shovel surveying the steaming asphalt he's uncovered, the yolk of a boiled egg dripping over the shell, the egg sitting on a wedding ring, the white of a horse's eye, her front hooves lazily pawing the clouds on the morning of my first kiss. These moments give me a tingling this-is-life-this-is-life-this-is-life feeling. They are fleeting, brief. I think the average day is jam-packed with the kind of moments I'm talking about, and any one of them could be the kernel or turning point of a short story. It's a matter of unravelling the weave of lives that has given the image or moment its aura.

When writing a story I usually start with an elusive, vague but overwhelming emotion – jealousy, loss, obsession – or a character who is in some way enigmatic to me. I discover what the story is about as I'm writing it. I like the feeling that I'm chasing after some mystery. I think most short stories are about strangers, or those we are intimate with who unexpectedly become strange to us. 'Craving' is a story about how those we love change.

'Craving' is also about intoxication. The drunken, stoned intoxication of a dinner party. The heady nostalgia for childhood friendships, the sated lull of a marriage going well, a mild love. The intoxication that rage and clarity of purpose can ignite when someone breaks out of a relationship gone sour. Desire is intoxicating; pursuing it means relinquishing control. The term 'falling in love' points to the involuntary aspect of desire. Losing control is always dangerous and exhilarating. 'Craving' is about compromises versus burning bright. Jessica is a 'patronizing bitch' because she refuses to settle for anything less than living a vivid, honest emotional life.

The narrator of this story is deliciously drunk, and therefore unreliable. She imagines Louise's longing for a boyfriend from the distant past. She constructs Jessica's arguments against acquiescence. She argues silently for compromise, and allows herself a grudging admiration for Jessica's unspoken counter-arguments. Often the narrator, and therefore the reader, aren't certain if the dialogue is real or imagined. Yet I want this imagined, drunken dialogue to be full of a truth that might be absent in what's actually said. I want to portray the particular sort of friendship that forms between Catholic girls in early adolescence. The art of communication reaches a heightened state with those friendships, an eerie clarity, thoughts are shared without visible physical effort, like pheromones or dog whistles. Though these three friends haven't seen each other in a long time they are intoxicated by the fact that nothing has changed between them, and everything has changed. They're able to share delicate intimacies as if they have lost no time. They talk in half sentences. Jessica says, 'I'm going through flux right now,' and Louise and the narrator understand Jessica is leaving her husband. Louise says, 'There's dessert' and the narrator understands that Louise wants to save Jessica's husband from the flux, although he's probably to blame for it. I wanted to create an atmosphere of inclusiveness. The reader may not know exactly what's being said at the dinner table, but I want them to recognize the truncated patter that forms in the fast bonds of adolescence.

A central image in this story is the balanced soup bowls and skittering spoon. I felt a shivery, joyful this-is-life feeling in the middle of a dinner party somewhat like the one in the story. I watched the hostess hold a pyramid of expensive soup bowls in one hand, her other hand resting on the back of a chair, supporting her through a spasm of laughter. Everybody was laughing, a spoon clattered over the hardwood floor, a dog pawed the French door. The soft puck of a cork tugged from an expensive bottle of wine. The emerald stink of marijuana, the goose's skin in a chiaroscuro of candlelight. One of the couples at the table was soon to divorce, but for the moment a delicate balance had been achieved. Whatever it was we were all hungry for, it seemed within our grasp.

ANDREW TIETZEN

STEVEN HEIGHTON
Foreigners

YOU ASK ME if I read much as a child. There were times when I hardly did anything else. It may be something of a cliché that the athletic extrovert is fulfilled enough by schoolyard successes – by the life of the body, and rowdy companionship – that books are seen as redundant, or as a burden and a nuisance. Meanwhile the bruised ectomorph retreats into fantasy and the page's private environs. The meek, in other words, inherit the library. I'm tempted to say that in my own case this tidy dichotomy holds, but then I recall whole winter Saturdays spent playing road hockey, summer evenings of neighbourhood games in the child-intoxicating dusk, bushwhacking with my one-eyed Lab cross in the hardwood ravine winding north along Etobicoke Creek. (We were trying to find the creek's source – Heart Lake, I learned years later, twenty miles to the northwest.)

Still, my childhood physique fit the stereotype well enough, from the age of seven till seventeen there would be little 'rowdy companionship', and when I did pick up a book I could forget that rough and foreign outer world for days.

The library I inherited was my father's. He taught English lit at a Toronto high school and also, two nights a week, at the Erindale campus of the University of Toronto. You ask if that affected me; you ask if our household was more bookish than the Canadian norm. In our house literature was in the air in the way hockey, say, is in the air in countless other Canadian homes. There were bookshelves in almost every room. In a couple of rooms there were no paintings or other decor because the walls were so dominated by those eclectic shelves. My parents belonged to several book clubs – historical, musical, artistic, military – and the monthly brochures lay waiting to be perused on the coffee table with issues of *Life* and *Maclean's* and *National Geographic.* For years my parents also subscribed to *Horizon*, the richly illustrated, unabashedly highbrow 'magazine' that appeared more or less monthly in a cloth format and whose many-coloured spines came to monopolize a wide shelf in the den.

This osmotic apprenticeship wasn't restricted to the page. My father, a walking jukebox of canonical quotations, brought literature to life by reciting constantly. A word or a tap on the shoulder was enough to start him up. While driving the family back and forth across Canada and the border states on summer vacations he would often break off his tour-guide patter (my younger sister and I always had to be learning something) to recite the verse of Robert Service or fragments of Frost or T. S. Eliot or passages of Chaucer, or the morose medieval ballads of Anon., or alliterative lines of Anglo-Saxon in his own impromptu translations.

But his interests weren't only literary. I think of bookish houses as being steeped in a studious quiet, yet our own house flouted the stereotype. My parents played their many LPs at volume. Saturday-night parties meant the croonings of João Gilberto and Frank Sinatra and Louis Armstrong broadcast up through the floorboards into my room along with upswellings of vibrant banter and laughter and the good smell of my mother's du Mauriers and my father's Sail pipe tobacco. My father would also bring home rock LPs like the Beatles' double White Album, and Cream albums with their sheeny psychedelic cover art and prolonged athletic drum solos. The soundtrack of our Sundays could not have been more different: sombre opera, baroque, classical, medieval monastic chanting – the melancholy leitmotifs of coming Monday and the return to school.

My first years were divided between Balmertown – a gold-mining town of about two thousand people, set in the Shield Country forests two hundred miles northeast of Winnipeg – and the suburbs of Toronto, where we moved for good in 1967, when I was six years old. In the years that followed we maintained a strong connection to the north, spending each Christmas and much of our summers at my father's parents' bungalow on Trout Lake in North Bay. Whether because I first came to consciousness up north, or because the suburbs were so unpoetic, so interchangeably nondescript (*Glendale Creek, Markland Woods*, always named for the now-absent natural features they'd replaced), the Shield became and remains my primary environment, the country whose moods and contours have conditioned my imagination, the landscape I measure all others against.

And yet I have no interest in actually living there.

You ask about public libraries in the places where I lived as a child, and did I frequent them? Actually I saw them as public branches of my first library, my parents' library; I saw them as further cantons in the exotic country of books. And I infested them. When I remember the feeling of entering a library as a child, knowing that hours of solitude, secrecy and quiet unearthings await me, the metaphor that comes is of an eager twelve-year-old arriving at a rink an hour early to find a freshly Zamboni'd sheet of ice gleaming and nobody to meddle or recite rules as he steps onto it and begins to skate, gathering speed, seized by a sort of greedy elation ... A paradoxical image – or maybe psychologically predictable – given that as a twelve-year-old I could not skate at all.

Michael Ondaatje once wrote something to the effect that if he could play the piano, he wouldn't have to write. I wouldn't have to write if I could be a gifted athlete, an artist of the body – a runner, a swimmer, a boxer. The two declarations are less different than they seem; music is much closer to the body than is writing.

So citizenship in this 'country of books' was, for me, a birthright. This fact fills me not only with gratitude but also with guilt. Some of my writer-friends grew up in more or less bookless homes; a couple were even discouraged from surplus reading by parents who seemed to see literary activity of any kind as glorified malingering. Reading could be counted on to provoke dreaminess, introspection, an unproductive idealism, anaemic pallor and other aberrancies. Art was irrelevant to the world's real work. This sad attitude is endemic among English-speaking North Americans, the culture being foundationally puritanical, practical, utilitarian, anti-intellectual; a corporate capitalist's dream.

That someone as marinated in books and culture as I was should have gone on to be a writer is no real surprise, and frankly brings me no great credit for independence of direction. That others managed to make artists of themselves despite the long odds *is* surprising – and, for me, a source of biographical envy.

Did 'anyone consciously set out to teach' me to write? Not in high school they didn't. Over the course of five years at my Etobicoke school I was given only a handful of writing assignments – an example of the systemic *Schlamperei* that so infuriated my father, with his Saxon work ethic, and confirmed him in his belief, which he put into practice at his own school, that students should be made to write often. During the two-month Toronto teachers' strike when I was in grade nine, he gave me several short-story-writing assignments, not only, I suspect, to force me to do some work, but also to give himself something to mark.

I don't need to add that at the time I had no complaints about the school system's low standards and expectations. And in my own case things may have worked out for the best; I was always drawn to the autodidact's private path, to choosing books I felt I needed to read, writing stories I wanted to write, working at my own haphazard pace. A lax system gave me the freedom to do it.

Who taught me to write, then? Writers teach themselves, by trial and failure, though they do it within certain familial, social, cultural and educational parameters that direct, shape and punctuate their learning. So much so, in fact, that I could answer the question in two very different ways: Who taught me to write? I did. Who taught me to write? Everybody else. In the one creative writing course I took at university, the poet/editor Victor Coleman simply pointed out where I was going wrong and left the rest up to me and the passage of time. Similarly you yourself, John, in editing the work in my short story collections, were clearly trying to refine me into a truer version of myself and not some satellite or imitation of you.

Books that marked me as a child. I'll list some in the order I recall encountering them, from ages five to eighteen, starting with the works of that superb comic versifier and narcotically whimsical illustrator Dr Seuss, especially his phantasmagoric road-novel *I Had Trouble in Getting to Solla Sollew*; Maurice Sendak's spooky masterpiece *Where the Wild Things Are*; Kenneth Grahame's *The Wind in the Willows*; various comic books; the Hardy Boys; J. R. R. Tolkien's epic fantasies; *The Red*

Badge of Courage; Jack London's chest-wig adventure yarns; *Horizon* magazine; Pierre Berton's *The National Dream* and *The Last Spike*; *Dune; The Left Hand of Darkness; Oliver Twist; Tom Brown's Schooldays; The Catcher in the Rye; Lord Jim; L'Étranger; On the Road.*

Do I remember when the idea of writing, of being a writer, came to me? I think it was always there. At the boys' camp in the Laurentians where I went for two summers, I was, again, a bit of a misfit – bookish, awkward, unrobust, etc. etc. To survive on the Lord of the Flies desert isle that is boyhood – especially at an isolated summer camp, where the life of the body is all – the 'sensitive' child has to make himself somehow indispensable to the tribe. I forged my belonging out of narrative. Every night in the cabin after lights out, the other boys in my group would urge me on. A story's success was signalled not by final applause – there could be none, we were supposed to be asleep – but by a wakeful silence. Failure was measured not in hisses but a ragged ovation of snores. My high moment of success and belonging – the Moment I Knew I Was a Writer, it's tempting to say, though that would make for a suspiciously apt and airtight epiphany – came when our Sunday evening movie was cut short, probably by a malfunctioning projector. In my mind's eye I see the film freezing into a still, then a hole with a fiery corona forming in the heart of the frame, like a sunspot, and eating rapidly outward till nothing remains but light. Or is that something I've seen happen since then? It seems too perfect a death for a picture called *Ring of Fire*. What I know is that the film was somehow stopped at or near the dramatic climax, and in the riot of surprise and dismay that followed I told the boys seated around me in the gym that I'd seen the film before and could tell them how it ended. Back at the cabin, improvising feverishly, I held them captive and meekly believing until the final 'frame' – although strangely I have no memory of what that was, what I told them.

The next summer one of the boys, having seen the movie on TV in the meantime, accused me of having fabricated the ending. I have no idea what I said then either. What could I have said? That since he had believed and liked my version when he heard it, it was the real ending too? What I would say now. At the time, I probably lied.

You ask if I saw myself as a poet back then, and could I have applied myself instead to painting or music? To answer both questions at once:

I saw myself as a rock musician who wrote the lyrics, composed the music, and painted cover images for the album jackets. In terms of dominant influences it was a sorry period to hold aspirations of that kind. The Druid School of hard rock, parodied perfectly in the movie *This Is Spiñal Tap*, was crowding the airwaves then, and my songs (written with a talented but equally misled friend) showed the various quasi-Nordic-medieval influences of Deep Purple, Rush, the Moody Blues, Led Zeppelin, Genesis, King Crimson, ELO, Styx, etc. Some of those bands did truly good things, but for comic awfulness even bad parodies of Donovan can't touch imitations of, say, Black Sabbath.

Eventually I sold the mock-Stratocaster, amplifier and airbrush, swore off power chords and umlauts, and began sketching in pencil and writing folk-rock songs that owed something – though not nearly enough – to Bob Dylan, Tom Waits and Bruce Springsteen. Over time I did improve, in my late teens and early twenties busking my way around Australia and Europe, but my song lyrics were changing, getting harder to set to music, standing more and more revealed as poems....

That sounds so right – the tidy evolution, the smooth and destined transition from songwriter to lyric poet. If only I could vouch for the truth of it. Maybe I just got tired of failing to find really original tunes to clothe the words in. Whatever the reason, over the course of a year or two I stopped trying to lift the words into song and let them remain on the page as poetry.

And did the act of writing those lyrics and poems 'involve a romantic urge towards self-expression?' For most sixteen-year-olds poetry has one main function – the expression of self-pity. It's a natural thing. It may even be a necessary thing. But to avoid stagnation poets have to mature out of the early phase of lyric self-involvement, poetic growth depending on the gradual reduction (if not, as T. S. Eliot said, the full abolition) of self from the work. Coming to see poems as crafted artefacts – verbal constructs into which and from which deep feeling flows – is a key step.

Taking the step is, was, difficult for younger poets like me, born into a cultural and school system where sincere self-expression was defined as the essence of art, where free verse stood unchallenged, where all 'form' was seen as reactionary – a fascist constraint on the effusions of that Noble Savage, the heart. Directly or tacitly we were taught that the form and very language of a poem were ancillary to the feelings or politics it expressed. This view of form as subordinate to content is as dimly dualistic as the old view of the body as carrier and server of a separate soul; foundational Puritanism again.

What led me to see poetry as something more than the juvenilia of self-expression was a background of hearing great poetry recited and having it available, readable, around me. Again, I get no credit for this – for being taught early on to see poetry as a kind of music made with words, not as encounter-session sharing. And because I'd always wanted to be a musician, it was natural that in the end I'd inject whatever musical instincts I had into that most musical of literary forms, the poem.

Don't get me wrong, those early poems were unpublishable. What I am saying is that young writers lucky enough to be exposed to good writing in an intense way – a way untypical of the school system and apt to become more so in the future's wired, corporate-friendly classrooms – are likely to be making the right *kinds* of early mistakes.

You ask if I was coming to see myself as being 'in opposition', or was I getting any approval and encouragement? Luckily I wasn't getting much of either. High praise for what I was writing at nineteen would have been lethal. A certain kind of nineteen-year-old – the self-involved, artsy young man, the stubbly solo brooder – is dying to believe in his own precocious mastery and importance, and will use any hints of praise as mortar for the shoddy walls of the bunker where he stores his self-image. A stronghold built in a marsh. At some point the whole bogus structure has to sink, or to crash into rubble, so the young writer can start rebuilding slowly and carefully. Premature praise and publication can defer that collapse to the point where the unwieldy structure is so large, so plausible, that its toppling is truly destructive.

When I was in my early twenties the world began tossing the odd crumb of encouragement. For a while, each crumb seemed a banquet. And I did begin to see myself as writing in opposition to something, as most young writers do and probably must. I saw myself as an isolated Romantic – at the time I was writing love lyrics derivative of Leonard Cohen – in a milieu where everyone else, or so I felt, was writing hard, aggrieved, nervy, nihilistic, postmodern poems. (This 'milieu' of my own anxious projection was Queen's University's one small creative writing class.) In part, I think, I was just envious of what I took to be the smoky hard-edged sophistication and advanced sexuality of the other students. They made me feel tame and outdated, a whimsical anachronism. Love lyrics! It riled me that they got to be both the rebels and the majority.

In the early eighties, cultural theorists were not yet talking much about capitalism's increasingly successful co-opting and merchandising of dissent – or of dissent's outward signs, styles, gestures and lingo. But it was happening. Being an outsider had become a 'lifestyle choice'. Not that there weren't (and aren't) genuine outsiders; it's just that they don't often dress the part. But I was naive enough then to believe in any façade that was enviably attractive and energetically maintained. At university, in fact, we were almost all middle-class kids playing at Rimbaud or Corso or Genet – or in my own case, at something else. Yet almost by accident my shadow boxing with phantom opponents led me into the ring with what I now see as the real enemy of artists: a culture that impersonally pressures everyone to be hip, to be cool, hyper-ironic, self-conscious, plugged in and eternally collegiate, whether in dress or in attitude, speech or range of pop-cultural reference, grasp of the latest technologies, latest buzzwords and styles. In other words: to conform, though in the guise of stylish rebellion.

At the turn of the millennium being a true rebel means being, by postmodern standards, unabashedly uncool – an aesthete, devoted to the old pursuit of truth and beauty in artistic form.

2

After high school graduation I travelled west and found work as a dishwasher in the vast hangar-like kitchen of Jasper Park Lodge, an old CP hotel in the Rocky Mountains. There I was inducted into all the small hedonisms in store for those living away from home for the first time. I was reading the Beats that summer, becoming so enrolled in Kerouac's lyric vision that I sometimes felt I was gazing out at the country – those mountains! lakes! the Athabasca river! – through his eyes. Prolonged breathless sentences, along with the feeling and smell and taste of the high country's coniferous air, are for me still deeply redolent of finding my feet in freedom, in exuberant vitality, and with no undercutting sense of limitation. With the sort of zest and energy indistinguishable (in oneself as much as in others) from confidence, I set out to write my own stories and poems. The intensity of my impressions was such that if the words would only capture a fraction of what I felt, the results, I was sure, would be stunning. They weren't, but the joy of their making was a good in itself, and part of that season's discovery: I would be a writer.

Over the course of the summer I was unaccountably promoted from dishwasher to busboy to waiter, and that fall in the 'exclusive' Moose's Nook, to the strains of a genial, jaded lounge singer named Tom Paproski, I started to make money. I formed the plan of travelling next to a place as different as possible from the Rockies. I chose the coasts, jungles and deserts of Australia. After hitch-hiking and busking my way back and forth across Australia – another story altogether – I returned to Jasper the next spring and worked to put aside money for school. Waiting on tables was a good way to do it. I was determined to avoid taking loans and going into debt. Debt now, I figured, would mean a full-time job, a real job, later.

I was at Queen's from 1981 to 1986, doing a BA in English literature (though I nearly majored in biology) and an MA, also in English. You ask if anything I studied there had a deep impact, on me or on my writing. At university – unlike in high school – the valves of my attention were wide open and set to absorb anything. All my course lists included books worth absorbing, books that sent me off in search of further books by authors I'd discovered – yes, that's the word, because although as a reader you realize thousands have been there before you, you can't help feeling, with the ones you fall for hard, that you are the first and ideal reader for whom the author wrote every line; a time-capsule letter from soul to soul.

I read fairly widely – I'm too slow a reader to read really widely – in Canadian, American, British and Irish literature, as well as philosophy. I regret never studying any languages. Sometimes I also regret (and the regrets are related) not having tried to do my BA, or at least the MA, in another country – Italy or France or Czechoslovakia, or maybe Greece, to regain my lost childhood Greek. Queen's is a solid school and more politically diverse than outsiders give it credit for (in my sophomore year we organized a symposium on apartheid, inviting the ANC and the

South African government to attend; the student campaign for 'divest-ment' that followed led to Queen's being the first Canadian school to disinvest from South Africa), but in the early eighties the place still had a strongly Upper Canadian flavour – a smell of sherry and biscuits, an aura of class entitlement and proud, provincial gentility. But luck was with me. My neighbour in the student residence was a much older guy, or so he seemed to me, a slim twenty-one-year-old Jamaican of aristo-cratic bearing and splendid arrogance, with a precise English accent acquired at the 'public school' Stowe, with unashamedly highbrow dic-tion and a tendency to use it in page-long periodic sentences, with fierce if sometimes fickle intellectual enthusiasms, with a passionate reverence for Bob Marley, whose recent death he was still mourning. Stephen – now a successful film-maker in Toronto – was fiercely sceptical and irreverent about most things and often left me feeling like a credulous rube, but about Marley he was almost religious. I loved him, looked up to him, took more from him than I can say. It was my first true intellec-tual friendship, the stuff of every *Künstlerroman*. He would force a book into my hand and command me to read it and meet him the next night at the Pilot House or the Toucan or Lino's to discuss it into the small hours. Gorgeous foreign students with names like Milagros and Arsiniée would rustle in his wake. He had no scruples about being stylish, elegant, articulate, exceptional – all those traits that most Cana-dians reflexively distrust and shun as pretentious, undemocratic. Because we are – let's admit it – a nation of levellers. Loppers of tall poppies. Connoisseurs of *Schadenfreude*. In Stephen I glimpsed for the first time the possibility of aiming high without apology.

(Here I should mention that one of the campus's few other dandies, Russell Smith, was the first editor to publish one of my stories, in an Arts and Science magazine called – can I be remembering correctly? – *The Lictor*.

As for teachers, each year I had at least one whose public enthusiasms and idiosyncrasies made for lectures almost frightening in their inti-macy. We students were being lent a glimpse of the beating heart of an authority figure. This is rarer than it sounds. For example: I managed to shirk a more or less compulsory course in crit theory by choosing the lone, seemingly token alternative, Old Norse 310, with Professor George Clarke. I and the other student – a lanky, laconic post-grad with wire-frame spectacles and Einstein hair – met the professor of Old Norse weekly in his cubicle of an office made narrower still by shelves of fat, calf-bound Eddas, Icelandic grammars, runic lexicons, obscure biographies. Ramparts of old books and papers stacked high on the sill blocked out the tiny window. The professor with his blue eyes, wind-burned face, spindrift silver locks and flowing patriarchal beard might have been standing watch back of the dragon-prow of a gale-blown Viking ship while he spent the hour reminiscing about sabbaticals in Iceland and paraphrasing Old Norse sagas. At the end of each session he would hand us a faint Xerox of a still-untranslated saga or poem and wish us luck.

I loved the course. I fell in love with the act of translation – these days I'm doing more and more of it – and I also decided that, from where I was sitting, frank, unguarded professional passion looked a lot like success. But no; 'decided' is so often a word chosen by hindsight. In fact an impression was made, certain actions ensued, and now, years later, I speak of decision when at the time there were only inspiration and possibility.

My MA thesis was called *Approaching 'That Perfect Edge': Kinetic Techniques in the Poetry and Fiction of Michael Ondaatje.* I never considered going on to a Ph.D. Over the course of my last year I found myself spending more and more time, in classes as well as outside them, writing poetry. At last some of it was starting to work. And I was fed up with thinking in therefores and demonstrablys and notwithstandings; sooner or later academic cadences and habits of thought would be colonizing my brain, housebreaking my imagination. Partly inspired by the writers I was studying, partly repelled by the studying itself, I wrote much of my first book of poems during the seminars of my MA year. In the summer of '86 the Kingston editor/publisher Bob Hilderley accepted a few of the poems for *Quarry Magazine* and offered to publish my still-untitled book with Quarry Press when it was done.

For some time I had been refining habits of deranged frugality that would eventually allow me to write full time, and in the summer of '86, having just finished my MA, I found I had almost half my scholarship left. It seemed like a lot of money. And if time is money, money, to a writer, is time. I spent that summer excitedly drafting a novel on the youth of the lyric poet latterly known as Stalin, then in the autumn flew to Hong Kong with my girlfriend Mary Huggard. From there, to a ceaseless soundtrack of Chinese opera, we travelled by train through a China as yet unaccustomed to *gwailo,* foreign ghosts. We made west for Tibet, just recently opened to tourists. (Within a year, after a Tibetan uprising, it would be closed again.) In Lhasa we stayed in a crude hostelry on Happiness Road – an affable ruin run by a team of jolly, generous Tibetans who seemed to live on barley-beer and fried Spam. Mornings around nine or ten we would push through the crowds of the public market in total darkness, the Chinese government having decreed that the whole immense country be a single time zone. In sickness I discovered the best possible view of the sublime and many-tiered Potala Palace: through the jail-barred window of the hostelry's tiny toilet cell. I spent most of a night there gripped with dysentery, bunched over a hole in the dirt, shaking with cold. When the late dawn arrived I stood hands frozen on the iron bars and gazed south to where the palace, lit by a sun edging over the Himalayas, reared like a golden precipice above the city. I'd never felt so trapped in the isolation cell of the body. In my exhaustion, weakness and fear, it seemed like a deathbed vision of the afterlife.

We travelled on through Nepal, Thailand, Malaysia, Indonesia and Singapore, before washing up road-worn and broke on the shores of Japan. We easily found jobs teaching English – like thousands of other *gaijin,* foreigners – and an eight-*tatami* flat in Ōsaka. During our ten busy, happy months there I strove to learn the language, mainly from a second-hand book published a few years before by two elderly, venerable Tokyo philologists. Page by page, chapter by chapter, the sentences the student was asked to render into English grew more disturbing and macabre. *Shitai* – corpse or cadaver – was one of the first words I was required to learn. *When I looked through the window, there was a corpse lying on the floor.* This from the exercise section of chapter 2. I referred to the book's index. My translation was perfect. Within a chapter or two I was learning to manage the oft-used passive voice in phrases like *kodomo-tachi made mo korosaremashita*: 'Even the little children were slaughtered.' At first I had no idea what to make of this. I began to wonder if the authors were playing some bizarre Nabokovian game or maybe, as survivors of the war, offering subtle, even subconscious punishment to their mostly American readers. Not to mention subtle discouragement to the foreign student of Japanese. But I pressed on, was helped by the gabby owners of local coffee houses, and wound up totally lost on a college radio talk-show with a glib, merry host who looked like a Japanese Sammy Davis Jr.

I was finding out I loved languages other than English. In learning to cross the borders between tongues, trying to sneak meanings across undamaged, I experienced an almost transgressive pleasure. And living in Japan, learning Japanese, writing stories in the breaks and spares between the classes I taught, I found out what kind of writer I was. Some writers – the chroniclers of home – find inspiration in the small yet vital details of domesticity, in mental maps of known locales; others – the explorers of elsewhere – are imaginatively cramped by the familiar and the familial. Writing of what she knows, the chronicler of home renews or reorients our view of the familiar, showing us how strange and foreign the domestic really is. ('She' because I think first of Alice Munro.) Writing of what he doesn't know, so as to discover it in the telling, the explorer of 'away' makes the foreign and exotic feel as familiar as home. ('He' because I think first of Malcolm Lowry and Paul Bowles.) Clearly I was that second kind.

We returned to Canada in '88 with fresh savings and settled in Kingston, an inexpensive harbour city with plenty of writers, bookstores, pubs, live music, and weird turreted Victorian houses, along with a volatile mix of population groups: the inbred local gentry, ex-prisoners, the profs and upper-middle-class professionals of the downtown, soldiers from the base, Royal Military College cadets, factory workers, bike gangs, the largely affluent student body, young artists, thousands of retirees. I've been here since then. I found work as a waiter in a newly opened Japanese restaurant, and as editor of the literary journal *Quarry Magazine*, where I stayed on until 1994. And I wrote steadily – poetry and Asian short stories.

Revisits to earlier work are a good gauge of progress. I found I'd developed past the point where I wanted to do anything with the novel I'd drafted two years before. From its remains, though, I harvested the poems that became the central part of my first book, *Stalin's Carnival*, published by Quarry Press in '89. Later that year Oberon published my second book, in the Japanese form of the *utaniki*, or song-diary – a kind of travelogue in poetry, prose and journal entries. I'm relieved now that the print run was so small, but at the time, of course, I was soaring: two books in the same year from established publishers, excited reviews, small but coveted prizes falling into my lap, my new position as editor of a well-known literary magazine ... So was it a good thing, all this 'early success'? It didn't make me lazy. But it probably made me too confident. It led me to believe that if I kept putting in the hours, the writing would keep getting better, the responses more positive, which of course are no sure things. The imagination can tire temporarily as surely as the body can, and as for the public's response to the work, the writer has no control. All a writer can directly control and exert is will – effort, focus, craft – and although will is clearly essential to the enterprise, it is never enough. Magic and surprise often refuse to be conjured, and all the industry, technique and intelligence in the world are useless. Part of the art of becoming a writer, I see now, is learning how to lose – learning to relinquish certain cherished hopes, to accept that a book has refused to gel.

Which brings me to my hooking up with the Porcupine's Quill. You, John, read the manuscript of Asian stories I was working on and told me the Japanese ones were alive and the others not. You also wrote to me that 'It is too easy to get published and praised in Canada.' I wanted to believe you were wrong on both counts – for one thing, a larger publisher had already expressed interest in the book – and so I continued on my hopeful course. Six months later you wrote again and repeated your offer to work with me on a book of Japanese stories. I was surprised and flattered by your persistence. It made me take a cold, close look at the non-Japanese stories, and finally, reluctantly, I had to agree with you. I'd had a larger structure in mind, involving stories from all the countries where Mary and I had travelled, and I was trying to force the material to conform. In the case of the weakest things, magic-realist tales of Bali and Malaysia, I'd been like someone doggedly performing CPR on a bog man. I decided to go with you and the Porcupine's Quill. Two years later the Japanese stories appeared as *Flight Paths of the Emperor,* and three years after that came a second collection, *On earth as it is.*

You ask for details about foreign publication. Besides individual poems and stories appearing in various languages and countries, the full short story collections were translated into French by Christine Klein-Lataud and published in Quebec by L'instant même, a quixotic small publisher in Quebec City that specializes in stories and has done other English-Canadian writers such as Douglas Glover and Isabel Huggan. The collections also appeared, both in '97, with Granta Books in Britain, Holland and Australia. Granta also took my first novel, *The Shadow Boxer*, and published it in July 2000, a month after Knopf Canada did it here. The book will appear in the USA with Houghton Mifflin in 2002, and in 2003 with Edizioni E/O in Italy. Finally, Vintage has recently published, with the paperback of *The Shadow Boxer*, revised editions of *Flight Paths of the Emperor* and *On earth as it is*. And this is a wonderful thing – two early books lent a second presence on the shelves, a new chance to find readers.

Your last question: how I see my career now, what I hope for in literary terms. In writing a 'coming of age' novel and then revising my short story books for republication, while approaching my fortieth birthday, I sensed that I was coming to the end of something, which should be a good thing, except that any end necessitates a new beginning and I haven't been able to find it yet. In the media I'm still referred to as a young writer, which is fine – this culture with its cult of youth and newness on the one hand, and ensconced elder stars on the other, can lose sight of writers in 'mid-career' – but I don't want to just repeat youthful gestures of last year or last decade. In fact I've spent much of the last year numbly watching the squirrel circus in the phone wires and Norway maple boughs out my window while fiddling with remunerative but minor freelance projects. And feeling lost, stalled, sad and disaffiliated. The encouragements of a novel's publication, here and elsewhere, have been less ratifying than you might think. A writer only feels like a writer when in the act. And the will, as I said, is never enough. I have plenty of will. Plenty of 'good ideas'. Where does inspiration, that sacred rage, originate? Maybe in the end it's just a matter of stubbornly starting something new and writing your way into the slot.

Kingston, May 2001

FIVE PAINTINGS
OF THE NEW JAPAN
Steven Heighton

A National Gallery

I. SUNFLOWERS   I was the first foreigner to wait tables in the Yume No Ato. Summer enrolment was down at the English school where I taught so I needed to earn some extra money, and since I'd been eating at the restaurant on and off for months it was the first place I thought of applying. It was a small establishment built just after the war in a bombed-out section of the city, but when I saw it the area was studded with bank towers, slick boutiques, coffee shops and flourishing bars, and the Yume No Ato was one of the oldest and most venerable places around. I was there most of the summer and I wish I could go back. I heard the other day from Nori, the dishwasher, who works part time now in a camera store, that our ex-boss Mr Onishi has just fought and lost a battle with cancer.

'We have problems here every summer,' Mr Onishi said during my interview, 'with a foreign tourist people.' He peered up at me from behind his desk, two shadowy half-moons drooping under his eyes. 'Especially the Americans. If I hire you, you can deal to them.'

'With them,' I said automatically.

'You have experienced waitering?'

'A little,' I lied.

'You understand Japanese?'

'I took a course.'

'Say something to me in Japanese.'

I froze for a moment, then was ambushed by a phrase from my primer.

'*Niwa ni wa furu-ike ga arimasu.*'

'In the garden,' translated Mr Onishi, 'there is an old pond.'

I stared abjectly at his bald patch.

'You cannot say a sentence more difficult than that?'

I told Mr Onishi it was a beginners' course. He looked up at me and ran his fingers through a greying Vandyke beard.

'How well do you know the Japanese cuisine?'

'Not so well,' I said in a light bantering tone that I hoped would disarm him, 'but I know what I like.'

He frowned and checked his watch, then darted a glance at the bank calendar on the wall.

'Morinaga speaks a little English,' he said. 'He will be your trainer. Tomorrow at 1600 hours you start.'

'You won't be sorry, sir.'

'I shall exploit you,' he said, 'until someone more qualitied applies.'

Nori Morinaga leaned against the steam table and picked his nose with the languid, luxurious gestures of an epicure enjoying an after-dinner cigar. He was the biggest Japanese I'd ever seen and the coke-bottle glasses perched above his huge nose seemed comically small.

'Ah, *gaijin-san!*' he exclaimed as he saw me, collecting himself and inflating to his full height. 'Welcome in! Hail fellow well-hung!'

I wondered if I'd heard him correctly.

'It gives me great pressure!'

I had. I had.

Nori Morinaga offered me his hand at the same moment I tried to bow. Nervously we grinned at each other, then began to laugh. He was a full head taller than I was, burly as a linebacker but prematurely hunched as if stooping in doorways and under low ceilings had already affected his spine. He couldn't have been over twenty-five. His hair was brush-cut like a Marine's and when he spoke English his voice and manner seemed earnest and irreverent at the same time.

'Onishi-san tells me I will help *throw you the ropes,*' he said, chuckling. 'Ah, I like that expression. Do you know it? I study English at the university but the *gaijin-sensei* always says Japanese students must be more idiomatic so I picked up this book' – his giant hand brandished a thick paperback – 'and I study it *like a rat out of hell.*'

He grinned enigmatically, then giggled. I couldn't tell if he was serious or making fun of me.

Nori pronounced his idiomatic gleanings with savage enthusiasm, his magnified eyes widening and big shoulders bunching for emphasis as if to ensure his scholarship did not pass unremarked. I took the book and examined it: a dog-eared, discount edition of UP-TO-DATE ENGLISH PHRASES FOR JAPANESE STUDENTS – in the 1955 edition.

'We open in an hour,' he said. 'We are *oppressed for time.* Come on, *I'm going to show you what's what.*'

Situated in a basement, under a popular *karaoke* bar, the Yume No Ato's two small rooms were dimly lit and the atmosphere under the low ceiling was damp and cool, as in an air-raid shelter or submarine. I wondered if this cramped, covert aura hadn't disturbed some of the earliest patrons, whose memories of the air raids would still have been fresh – but I didn't ask Nori about that. The place had always been popular, he said, especially in summer, when it was one of the coolest spots in Ōsaka.

A stairway descended from street level directly into the dining room so on summer days, after the heat and bright sunshine of the city, guests would sink into a cool aquatic atmosphere of dim light and swaying shadows. The stairway was flanked on one side by a small bar and on the other by the sushi counter where I'd eaten before. An adjoining room contained a larger, more formal dining space which gave onto the kitchen through a swinging door at the back. Despite the rather Western-style seating arrangements (tables and chairs instead of the traditional *zabuton* and *tatami*) the dining area was decorated in authentic Japanese fashion with hanging lanterns, calligraphic scrolls, a tokonoma containing an empty *maki-e* vase, *bonsai* and noren and several framed, original *sumi-e.* The only unindigenous ornament was a large reproduction of Van Gogh's *Sunflowers* hung conspicuously on the wall behind the sushi bar.

'Onishi-san says it's for the behoof of the American tourists,' Nori said, 'but I'd *bet my bottom* he put it there for the bankers who come *in the wee-wee hours.* It's the bankers who are really interested in that stuff.' He sniffed and gestured contemptuously toward *Sunflowers* and toward the *sumi-e* prints as well, as if wanting me to see he considered all art frivolous and dispensable, no matter where it came from.

I didn't realize until much later the gesture meant something else.

Nori showed me around the kitchen and introduced me to the cooks, who were just arriving. Kenji Komatsu was head chef. Before returning to Japan and starting a family he'd worked for a few years in Vancouver and Montréal and his memories of that time were good, so he was delighted to hear I was Canadian. He insisted I call him Mat. 'And don't listen to anything this big whale tells you,' he said affably, poking Nori in the stomach. 'So much sugar and McDonald's the young ones are eating these days. This one should be in the *sumō* ring, not my kitchen.'

'*Sumō* is for old folk,' Nori said, tightening his gut and ironically saluting a small, aproned man who had just emerged from the walk-in fridge.

'*Time is on the march,*' Nori intoned. '*Nothing can stop it now!*'

Second chef Yukio Miyoshi glared at Nori and then at me with frank disgust and muttered to himself in Japanese. He marched to the back of the kitchen and began gutting a large fish. 'Doesn't like the foreigners,' Nori said with grin. 'So it is. You can't pleasure everybody.'

The swinging door burst open and a small white form hurtled into the kitchen and disappeared behind the steam table. Nori grabbed me by the arm.

'It's Oh-san, the sushi chef – come, we must hurry.'

Mr Oh was a jittery middle-aged man who scurried through the restaurant, both hands frantically embracing a mug of fresh coffee. Like all the elder folks, Nori explained, Mr Oh worked too hard.... We finally cornered him by the walk-in fridge and Nori introduced us. Clearly he had not heard of Mr Onishi's latest hiring decision – he put down his mug and gawked as if I were a health inspector who'd just told him twenty of last night's customers were in the hospital with food poisoning.

The *yukata* which Mr Oh insisted I try on looked all right, and in the change room I finally gave in and let him Brylcreem and comb back my curly hair into the slick, shining facsimile of a typical Japanese cut. As he worked with the comb, his face close to mine, I could see the tic in his left eye and smell his breath, pungent with coffee.

'You look *marvellous,*' Nori called on my return, 'and you know who you are!' He winked and blew me a kiss.

Mr Onishi entered and snapped some brusque truculent command. When the others had fled to their stations he addressed me in English.

'I hope you are ready for your first shift. We will have many guests tonight. Come – you will have to serve the aliens.'

From the corner of my eye I could see Nori clowning behind the grille, two chopsticks pressed to his temples like antennae.

As I trailed Mr Onishi into the dining room, two men and a woman, all young, tall, clad smartly in *yukata,* issued from behind the bar and lined up for inspection. One of the men wore a pearl earring and his hair was unusually long for a Japanese, while the woman had rich brown, luminous skin and plump attractive features. Mr Onishi introduced the other man as Akiburo. He was a college student and looked the part with his regulation haircut and sly, wisecracking expression.

With patent distaste Mr Onishi billed the long-haired man as 'your bartender, who likes to be known as Johnnie Walker'. The man fingered his earring and smiled out of the side of his mouth. 'And this is Suzuki Michiko, a waitress.' She bowed awkwardly and studied her plump brown hands, the pale skin on the underside of her wrists.

My comrades, as Mr Onishi called them, had been expecting me, and now they would show me to my sector of the restaurant – three small tables in the corner of the second room. In this occidental ghetto, it seemed, Mr Onishi thought I would do the least possible damage to the restaurant's ambience and reputation. Michiko explained in simple Japanese that since my tables were right by the kitchen door I could ask Nori for help as soon as I got in trouble.

The *tokonoma,* I now saw, had been decorated with a spray of poppies.

'We open shortly,' Mr Onishi said, striding toward us. His manner was vigorous and forceful but his eyes seemed tired, their light extinguished. 'We probably will have some American guests tonight. Your job will be to service them.'

'I'll do my best, sir.'

'And coffee – you will now take over from Michiko and bring Mr Oh his coffee. He will want a fresh supply every half-hour. Do not forget!'

For the first hour the second room remained empty, as did the tables of the front room, but the sushi bar was overrun within minutes by an army of ravenous, demanding guests. 'Coffee,' cried Mr Oh, and I brought him cup after cup while the customers gaped at me and hurled at Mr Oh questions I could not understand. The coffee yellowed his tongue and reddened his eyes, which took on a weird, narcotic glaze, while steam mixed with sweat and stood out in bold clear beads on his cheeks and upper lip. Orders were called out as more guests arrived. Mr Oh's small red hands scuttled like sand crabs over the counter, making predatory forays into the display case to seize hapless chunks of smelt or salmon or eel and then wielding above them a fish-silver knife, replacing the knife deftly, swooping down on speckled quail eggs and snapping shells between thumb and forefinger and smearing the yolk onto bricks of rice the other hand had just formed. Then with fingers dangling the hands would hover above an almost completed dish, and they would waver slightly like squid or octopuses in currents over the ocean floor, then pounce, abrupt and accurate, on an errant grain of rice or any garnish or strip of ginger imperfectly arranged, and an instant later the finished work, irreproachable and beyond time like a still life or a great sculpture, would appear on the glass above the display case from which it was whisked within seconds by the grateful customers or attentive staff.

The process was dizzying. I was keenly aware of my ignorance and when I was not airlifting coffee to the sushi bar I was busy in my own sector studying the menu and straightening tables.

Around eight o'clock Mr Onishi entered the second room, carrying menus, followed by a man and woman who were both heavyset, tall and fair-haired. The man wore a tailored navy suit and carried a briefcase. The woman's hair was piled high in a steep bun that resembled the nose-cone of a rocket, and her lipstick, like her dress, was a pushy, persistent shade of red.

'Take good care with Mr and Mrs Cruikshank,' Onishi-san said in a low voice as he passed me and showed them to their seats. 'Mr Cruikshank is a very important man – a diplomat, from America. Bring two dry martinis to begin.'

Mr Cruikshank's voice was genteel and collected, his manner smooth as good brandy. 'How long have you been working in this place?' he inquired.

'Two hours,' I said, serving the martinis.

'Surprised they'd have an American working here.' With one hand he yanked a small plastic sabre from his olive, then pinched the olive and held it aloft like a tiny globe.

'I'm not American,' I said.

There was a pause while Mr and Mrs Cruikshank processed this unlooked-for information.

'Well, surely you're not Japanese?' Mrs Cruikshank asked, slurring her words a little. 'Maybe half?'

Mr Cruikshank swallowed his olive then impaled his wife's with the plastic sword. He turned back to me, inadvertently aiming the harmless tip at my throat.

'*Nihongo wakaru?*' he asked in plain, masculine speech. *You understand Japanese?* I recognized his accent as outstanding.

'Only a little,' I said.

'I'll bet he's Dutch,' Mrs Cruikshank said. 'The Dutch speak such beautiful English – hardly any accent at all.'

'You'll find it hard here without any Japanese,' Mr Cruikshank advised me, ignoring his wife, drawing the sword from his teeth so the gleaming olive stayed clenched between them.

'Coffee,' Mr Oh called from the sushi bar.

'I'll only be serving the foreign customers, sir.'

Mr Cruikshank bit into his olive. 'Some of the foreign customers,' he said, 'prefer being served in Japanese.'

'Or maybe German,' said Mrs Cruikshank.

'I can speak some German,' I said. 'Would you like it if – '

'*Coffee,*' cried Mr Oh from the sushi bar.

Mrs Cruikshank was beaming. 'I was right,' she said, lifting her martini glass in a kind of toast. '*Wie geht's?*'

'We'd like some sushi,' Mr Cruikshank interrupted his wife, who was now grimacing at her drink as if trying to recall another German phrase.

I fumbled with my pad.

'An order each of *maguro, saba, hamachi,* and – why not? – some sea urchin. Hear it's full of mercury these days, but hell, we've got to eat something.'

'Yes, sir.'

'And two more martinis.' He pointed at his glass with the plastic sword.

'Got it.'

83

'*Danke schön,*' roared Mrs Cruikshank as I hurried from the room.

While waiting for Johnnie Walker to finish the martinis I noticed an older guest rise from the sushi bar and stumble toward the washrooms. As he saw me, his red eyes widened and he lost his footing and crashed into the bar, slamming a frail elbow against the cash register. He righted himself with quick slapstick dignity and stood blushing. When I moved to help him he waved me off.

Johnnie Walker smirked and muttered as he shook the martinis and for a moment the words and the rattling ice took on a primitive, mocking rhythm, like a chant. The older man began to swear at him and reached out as if to grab his earring, his long hair. *Shin jin rui,* the old man muttered – Strange inscrutable creature! I'd heard it was a new phrase coined by the old to describe the young.

'Wake up, old man,' Johnnie snapped in plain Japanese as he poured the martinis. 'Watch out where you're going.'

The man lurched off.

'Always drunk, or fast asleep in their chairs.'

'*Coffee,*' cried Mr Oh from the sushi bar.

II. THE DREAM   'Tell me something about the restaurant,' I said to Nori, sweeping my hand in a half circle and nodding at the closed bar. 'How old is the place?'

Nori finished his Budweiser and balanced the empty tin on a growing tower of empties. 'It was built after the war ends,' he said, belching – and I couldn't help noticing how casually he used the word war. His expression was unchanged, his voice was still firm, his eyes had not recoiled as if shamed by some unspeakable profanity. That was how my older students reacted when the war came up in a lesson. No doubt Mr Onishi would react the same way. But not Nori. For him the war was history, fiction – as unreal and insubstantial as a dimly remembered dream, a dream of jungles, the faded memory of a picture in a storybook. He wasn't much younger than me.

'What about the name,' I said, 'Yume No Ato? I mean, I can figure out the individual words, but I can't make sense of the whole thing.' *Yume,* I knew, meant 'dream', *no* signified possession, like an apostrophe and an 's', and *ato,* I thought, meant 'after'.

Nori lit a cigarette and trained a mischievous gaze on my hairline.

His capacity for drink was larger than average for a Japanese but now after four tins of beer he was flushed, theatrical and giddy. He wrinkled his broad nose, as if at a whiff of something rotten, and spat out, 'It's a line from a poem we had to study in the high school. Ah, Steve-san, university is so much better, we have fun in the sun, we make whoopee, we live for the present tense and forget all our yesterdays and tomorrows.... I hated high school, so much work. We had to study this famous poem.'

He stood and recited the lines with mock gravity:

'*Natsu kusa ya!*
    Tsuwamono domo ga
        Yume no ato.'

'It's a *haiku*,' I said.

'Aye, aye, captain.' He slumped down and the tower of beer cans wobbled. 'Do you watch *Star Trek?*'

'I'm not sure,' I said, 'that I understand it.'

'Oh, well, it's just a TV show – about the future and the stars.'

'I mean the poem, Nori, the *haiku*.'

'Ah, the poem – naturally you don't understand. It's old Japanese – old Japanese language, old Japanese mind – not so easy for us to understand either. It's Matsuo Bashō, dead like Shakespeare over three hundred years. Tomorrow and tomorrow and tomorrow. We had to study them both in school. Full fathom five and all that.'

'But about that last line ...'

'*Yume no ato?*'

I nodded.

'That's the name of the restaurant. You see, when Mr Onishi's uncle built the place after the war he gave it that name. It's a very strange name for a restaurant! Mr Onishi was just a boy then.'

'What does it mean?'

'I don't think Mr Onishi would have called it that, but when his uncle went over the bucket he didn't want to change the name. Out of respect.'

I finished my own beer and contributed to the tower of cans. The other staff had gone upstairs to the *karaoke* place but they'd drunk a lot of Bud and Kirin beforehand and the tower was growing high.

'I wonder,' I said, 'if the words mean "when the dream is over?"'

Nori took a long drag on his cigarette. 'I don't think they do,' he finally said. 'And besides, the dream had only just begun. The uncle was smart and he built Yume No Ato to attract foreigners as well as Japanese and it's done really well, as you can see.' His eyes brightened. *'We're going great guns.'*

Mr Onishi's telephone began to ring from the back of the restaurant, where he was still working. We heard him answer.

'The first line,' I said, 'is "Ah! Summer grasses", right?'

Nori seemed to be weighing this, then blurted out, 'Yume no ato means … it means what's left over after a dream.'

Mr Onishi's voice could be heard faintly. I surveyed the shaky tower, the ashtrays, the skeletons of fish beached on the sides of our empty plates.

'Leftovers,' I said, ironically.

'There's another word.'

'What about vestige? No? Remnant?'

Nori stubbed out his cigarette like a game-show panellist pressing a buzzer. *'Remnant!'* he cried. *'Your choice is absolutely correct, for five thousand dollars and a dream home!'* Suddenly he grew calm, thoughtful. 'So many foreign words sound alike,' he said. 'There's a famous Dutch painter with that name.'

'You mean Rembrandt?'

'That's him. A bank here in Umeda just bought a Remnant for nine hundred million yen.'

'Yume no ato,' I said, 'must mean "the remnant of dreams".'

Nori furrowed his brow, then nodded.

'Funny name for a restaurant,' I said. 'You like game shows?'

As if in a fresh wind the paper *noren* in the doorway behind the sushi bar blew open and a haggard phantom came in. Mr Onishi. He seemed to look right through us. Nori suggested we clean up and leave. We began to pile the chopsticks and empty plates onto a tray. I glanced up and saw Mr Onishi beckoning Nori.

'Please go examine the guest toilet,' Nori told me.

The washroom was immaculate – I'd cleaned it myself two hours before – but I spent a few minutes checking it again so that Nori and Mr Onishi would know I was thorough. For the second time that night I was intrigued by a notice in the stall, pencilled on the back of an old menu and taped to the door –

TO ALL FOREIGNERS:
OUR TUBES ARE IN ILL REPAIR, PLEASE
DO NOT THROW YOUR PEEPERS
IN THE TOILET.

When I came out of the washroom Mr Onishi was gone. 'The boss looks awful', I whispered to Nori, my smile forced. 'When he was on the phone before – maybe a guest was calling to complain about the new waiter, eh?'

'Possibly,' Nori said, 'but more likely it was a banker.'

'What, at this time of night?'

Nori shrugged. 'The elder folks, I told you, they're working late. And early, too – there was a banker here first thing this morning to talk at Mr Onishi.'

'Bankers,' I said, shaking my head. 'Not trouble, I hope.'

Nori laughed abruptly. Arm tensed karate-style he approached the tower of cans.

III. THE KERMESS
KAMPAI!

A month has gone past and the whole staff, gaijin-san included, are relaxing after a manic Saturday night in the Yume No Ato. August in Ōsaka: with other waiters and students and salarymen we sit in a beer garden under the full moon above twenty-two storeys of department-store merchandise, imported clothing and cologne and books and records, Japanese-made electronics, wedding supplies, Persian carpets and French cigarettes and aquariums full of swordfish and coral and casino-pink sand from the Arabian Sea, appliances and appliqué, blue-china chopstick-holders computers patio-furniture coffee-shops chefs and friendly clerks and full-colour reproductions of well-known Western portraits, etchings, sketches, sculptures, landscapes that Japanese banks are buying like real estate and bringing back to Ōsaka, anything, anything at all, SPEND AND IT SHALL BE GIVEN, endless armies of customers and ah, summer tourists billowing like grain through the grounds of Ōsaka's most famous department-store. SURELY, quoth the televangelist from the multitudinous screens, SURELY THE PEOPLE IS GRASS.

(For a moment the tables shudder as a tremor ripples through toxic earth under the Bargain Basement, and passes.)

KAMPAI! Western rock and roll music blasts from hidden speakers. In a few minutes the *O-bon* fireworks are due to start and we've got the best seats in the house. The plastic table sags and may soon buckle as another round of draft materializes and is swiftly distributed. A toast to this, a toast to that, *kampai*, KAMPAI, every time we lift our steins to take a drink, someone is proposing another toast: in a rare gesture Komatsu toasts the wait-staff (Akiburo and Johnnie and Michiko and me) because (this in English) we were really on the balls tonight and made no errors at all. *Kampai!* Akiburo toasts Komatsu and Mr Oh and second chef Miyoshi in return, presumably for turning out so much food on such a busy night and making it all look easy. *Kampai!* Mr Oh raises his glass of ice-coffee in thanks while second chef Miyoshi, drunk and expansive, in a rare good mood, toasts Nori for not smacking his head in the storeroom when he went back for extra soy sauce, *kampai*, (this translated by the delighted Nori, who immediately hefts his stein and decrees a toast to Michiko, the waitress, simply because he's mad about her and isn't it lucky she doesn't speak English?).

The blushing Michiko lifts her heavy stein with soft plump hands and meekly suggests, in Japanese, that it might be possible, perhaps, to maybe if it isn't too much trouble drink a toast to our skilful bartender, Johnnie Walker, without whom we would hardly have survived the night, it seems to me, after all, or maybe we might have? *Kampai! Kampai!* The flesh of Johnnie's ear lobe reddens around his pearl stud. He smirks and belts back another slug of whisky.

'To Onishi-san,' he says in English. 'To Yume No Ato.' And he quickly adds some other remark in harsh, staccato Japanese.

'KAMPAI!' I holler, hoisting my stein triumphantly so that beer froths up and sloshes over the lip of the glass. But no one has followed suit. They are all gazing without expression at the table or into their drinks. Johnnie Walker's head hangs lowest, his features hidden.

Komatsu glances at his watch and predicts that the fireworks will start in thirty seconds.

I turn to Nori. 'Did I do something wrong?'

Miyoshi and Mr Oh both snap something at him. I can't make out a word.

'Well, not at all,' says Nori, softly, 'I guess people just don't feel like talking about work after a busy night.'

I purse my lips. 'I have the feeling you're not being completely honest with me.'

'Of course I'm not!' he says loudly – and I wonder if we've understood each other.

At that moment the fireworks start. Everyone at our table looks up, relieved. '*O-bon*,' Nori says to me, relaxed again. 'Tonight the ancestors return.' Flippantly he rolls his eyes, or only seems to – I can't be sure because his coke-bottle lenses reflect the moonlight and the fiery red glare of the first rockets. One after another they arc up out of the dark expanse of Nagai Park, miles to the north, then slow down and pause at their zenith and explode in corollas of violet, emerald, coral, cream, apricot and indigo. *Hanabi,* they call them in Japanese: fire-flowers. The steins are raised again, glasses rammed together, toasts made and spirits drawn skyward by the aerial barrage.

My flat is somewhere down there on the far side of Nagai Park and now I picture a defective missile veering off course and buzzing my neighbourhood, terrifying the old folks, plunging with a shriek like an air-raid siren through the ceiling of my flat....

Nori grabs my arm with steely fingers. 'Steve-san, listen – do you hear what I hear?' I'm still concentrating on the look and sound of the exploding flowers, but suddenly I pick it out: the bouncy unmistakable opening bars of 'Like a Virgin'.

'It's the Madonna!'

'I hear it, Nori.'

He lumbers to his feet. 'You want to dance? Hey, get up! Come off it!'

Michiko and Johnnie Walker are already up beside the table, strobelit by the fireworks, shaking themselves to the beat, Michiko with a timid, tentative air and Johnnie with self-conscious abandon. The older staff sit motionless and watch the exploding rockets. Nori glances at them, at Michiko, at me, and I can tell he doesn't want to lose her. As she dances her small hands seem to catch and juggle the light.

'Life is so curt,' he pleads. 'You only lived once!' He gives me a half-smile, a sly wink, and I'm no longer sure he doesn't know exactly what he's saying.

KAMPAI! Nori hauls me to my feet and heaves me from the table in a blind teetering polka, out towards Johnnie and Michiko, his big boorish feet beating a mad tattoo on my toes. Komatsu and Mr Oh, the elders in the crowd, link arms and start keening some old Japanese song. Steins raised they sway together to a stately rhythm much slower than Madonna's, their voices rolling mournfully over the antique minors and archaic words. The rockets keep exploding. Their sound takes on a rhythm which seems to fall between the beats of the opposing songs – then as I watch, one of the rockets fails to burst. Like a falling star it streaks earthward in silence and disappears over the city.

IV. GUERNICA   I woke early the next morning with a headache and a burning stomach. I'd been dreaming. I dreamed Michiko had come home with me to my flat and we stood together hand in hand on the threshold, staring in at a gutted interior. The guilty rocket, however, had not actually exploded – it was resting in perfect condition, very comfortably, on an unburnt, freshly made futon in the centre of the room.

Michiko took me by the hand and led me into the ruin. When the smoke began to drown me she covered my mouth with her own. Her breath was clean and renewing as wind off an early-morning sea and when she pulled away the smell of burning was gone. She removed her flowered kimono and stood naked before me. The nipples of her firm small breasts were now the accusing eyes of a seduced and betrayed woman – then I was naked too, and utterly absolved, and we were lying side by side amid the acrid wreckage by the futon. She climbed atop me and took me inside her, slowly, making small articulate sighs and rolling her head back and forth so her dark bangs rippled like a midnight waterfall across my nipples, and the blue-black hair was curved as space-time and full of sparks like the Milky Way, which in the Japanese tongue is called *ama no gawa,* the river of heaven.

I wanted to come, to fill the gathering space inside her, and I wanted to run my tongue down the soft pale line of hair from her breasts to her belly and on up the wooded mound of Venus and lick the nectar from her tender orchid, as the Japanese poets say, but then it came to me that Nori had meant to tell me something important – about Michiko? About a poem? Or was there something I'd asked him that he hadn't answered?

Summer grasses ... Something left over after dreams ...

What a stupid time to be thinking about poetry.

I woke embarrassed but with a feeling of desperate tenderness for Michiko, to whom I'd hardly ever spoken and who had inspired, I thought, no more than a generic interest on my part. It was like missing a lover who'd slept beside me all night and had just left and gone home before I woke.

Well, I reflected, a dream like that was better than the constant wait-ering nightmares I'd been having until recently, and still woke from now and then. Usually I'd enter the restaurant and be told I was two hours late and none of the other wait-staff had shown up and the restaurant was full and we were booked solid until midnight. Other times I would realize I'd forgotten a couple or threesome who'd been seated two hours ago in the back corner of the second room and would they believe now it was just an honest mistake and I'd really been busy and meaning to get to them all along? Sometimes they were the Cruikshanks, and some-times Mr Sato, who (Nori had told me) had been a professor at the uni-versity in Kyōto but was demoted and now taught primary kids in Nagai, and that was why he drank so much and was so cold and pedantic when he spoke to you. In fact the unrequited dream-diners could be just about anyone, because the summer had been busy and now I was serving both foreigners and Japanese alike.

It had been the busiest summer in years, Komatsu said, and we were attracting more tourists than ever before – so why the visible anxiety whenever talk after hours came round to the restaurant? Mr Onishi did not look like a man with a flourishing business. Perhaps he was ill and everyone was worried? I'd been reading articles lately about the soaring incidence of cancer in Japan, the spread of big business and factories into the countryside, toxins in the soil, polluted water, poisonous seafood....

'I think you'd better level with me,' I told Nori the night of my dream. Miyoshi was standing by the walk-in fridge, reading the *Sangyo*

Keizai, and Komatsu was behind the steam table chopping onion. But I had the feeling they were listening to us, and so did Nori.

'Not here,' he whispered.

'Ah, such good news,' Miyoshi growled, lowering his paper with an unpleasant smile. Since he hardly ever spoke English I knew the remark was aimed at me. 'Such good news about the yen!'

Nori shook his head. 'For some the war has never ended.'

'Nihon ichiban!' Miyoshi cried. 'Japan is number one!'

'And he wasn't even born till after,' Nori said. 'I don't understand.'

'Maybe we should talk somewhere else,' I said.

Nori nodded but Komatsu set down his knife and said quickly, 'No. It's all right. Steve-san is part of the restaurant now – we should tell him the truth.' Eyes pink and glistening, he walked out from behind the steam table and pulled the newspaper from Miyoshi's hands.

Miyoshi scowled, did an about-face and marched into the fridge.

'Look at this,' Komatsu said, handing me the paper.

'You know I can't read Japanese.'

'Of course. Don't read, just look – the pictures.'

In the lower right-hand corner of the front page several well-known pieces of European art were reproduced in hazy black and white. One was a Rousseau, the second a Gauguin, the third a Brueghel. I couldn't read the caption beneath but I could make out the name of a prominent Ōsaka bank, written in *romaji.*

'And Van Gogh,' Komatsu said, sniffling. 'I hear they have just bought another costly painting by Van Gogh – so many paintings they are buying and bringing to Japan.'

We could hear Miyoshi in the fridge, muttering to himself, furiously shifting things around.

'They're buying everything in their sights,' Nori said, his usual gusto tangibly absent.

I told them I knew a bit about these purchases, but didn't see what they had to do with us.

'Well,' Komatsu started, 'they need some place to put these paintings …' His voice tapered off on the last words; I sensed I was being counted on, in customary Japanese fashion, to finish the sentence mentally so that everyone would be spared embarrassment.

'Chagall, too,' Komatsu resumed, 'and Rembrandt and Picasso.'

Bigasshole, it sounded like, but I knew who he meant. 'Costly things ... they need to find a place to put them all ...'

'Like an art gallery,' I said.

Komatsu rubbed his eyes with a corner of his apron. 'I'm afraid so.'

It had been just like *Dallas,* Nori told me, describing how the bank had first made polite offers to the dozen businesses operating in the block where they meant to build, and most were politely accepted. But several proprietors (including Mr Onishi and the owner of the Idaho Caffeine Palace, a large coffee shop dating from the late forties) had refused to consider them. Secretly the bank made more attractive offers, then a final offer which the firm's representative begged Mr Onishi to accept, because if a negotiated settlement proved necessary then payment would revert to the level of the initial sum – or, conceivably, somewhat less.

Mr Onishi had ignored the bank's covert threats and a negotiated settlement proved necessary. Unfortunately it did not involve negotiation. The bank produced lawyers who showed that actual title to the land had belonged to the bank until the end of the war, and they argued that the transfer of deeds had been improperly handled by the over-worked civil authorities of the time.

The young lawyers (I could just hear them) moved further that since the art gallery would be a public facility of great benefit to all citizens of the prefecture and would attract hundreds of thousands of foreigners to Ōsaka, it was in effect a civic institution, albeit privately owned, and the city should urge Mr Onishi to come to terms.

'The court is asking Mr Onishi to accept,' Nori said, 'but he just says no.'

'*Nihon ichiban,*' we heard faintly from the fridge.

Komatsu took the newspaper from me and walked back around the steam table. He began to giggle, like a bad comedian setting up a punchline. 'They're going to tear us down,' he said, laughing openly. 'Soon!'

Nori was chuckling, too, as the Japanese often will when speaking of their own misfortunes. Komatsu was laughing harder than I'd ever seen him, so I knew he really must be upset.

I paused respectfully. 'Listen, I'm really sorry to hear this.'

Komatsu roared with laughter. Nori continued to cackle. I asked them if they knew when these things were going to happen.

'There's no time like presently,' Nori said, slapping me on the shoulder a bit harder than he needed to. 'Come on, it's a busy night tonight, we'd better get happening.'

'Please take coffee now to Mr Oh-san,' Komatsu said weakly.

Miyoshi was still marching around in the fridge.

v. the starry night   September in Ōsaka is just as hot as July or August, and this year it was worse. Though many of the tourists were gone, the Yume No Ato was busier than ever: Mr Onishi's struggle with the bank was now common knowledge, so old customers came often to show their support and the sushi bar was crowded with curious locals. Meanwhile enrolment was picking up at the school and I had to cut back on my hours as a waiter.

Mr Onishi was upset when I told him, but since I knew now of the epic struggle he was waging each day in the courts (Nori got the details from Komatsu and passed them on to me) I found it hard to feel angry in return. The boss, after all, was showing tremendous pluck. Sure, he was of another generation, a hardy breed of industrious survivors, and as a child he would have absorbed with his mother's milk the bracing formula of bushidō, but this was valour way beyond the call of duty. He was giving Japan's second biggest bank the fight of its life. Already the original date for demolition was three weeks in arrears...

I heard that after receiving the court's final decision, Mr Onishi sighed and said, '*Yappari, nah*. It is as I expected. They will build a museum and a new country and fill both with foreign things.'

The demolition was set for the end of September and the Yume No Ato was to close a week before.

On the last night, a Saturday, the dining room was booked solid from five until closing with regular customers, both Japanese and foreign. We assembled by the bar a few minutes before five to wait for Mr Onishi and at five sharp he emerged from his office. He marched up to us, a menu tucked under one arm like a swagger stick, then briefed us in a formal and highly nuanced Japanese that I could not follow, though the general tenor of his speech was easy enough to guess. Or was it? Sometimes I wondered if I'd ever done more than misimagine what these people felt and believed.

A current of laughter rippled through the staff and Nori nudged me appreciatively, forgetting for a moment that I did not understand.

Mr Onishi dismissed us and we hurried off to complete our preparations as he climbed the stairs and opened the door. A long dusty shaft of sunlight pierced the cool gloom, and a few seconds later our guests began to descend, bringing with them the hot muggy air of the street.

'Meet me in the back,' I told Nori.

We stood in the kitchen on either side of the open rice machine, slowly filling it with the contents of two clay cooking pots. Thick billows of steam rose between us and Nori's face was intermittently clouded, his eyes nacreous, indistinct, like a man under a foot of water.

'So what did Onishi-san just say,' I asked, scooping the soft, sweet-smelling grains into the machine.

'He was apologizing.'

'Apologizing,' I said.

'Sure. He was apologizing for letting the bank close the Yume No Ato. He says it's all on his shoulders. He feels responsible for the jobs we will lose. He says he is sorry because he has felled us.'

The steam was thinning and I could see Nori clearly. His big face was pink and sweating.

'He says his uncle was a soldier in the old navy and after the war he built this restaurant with his own two hands. So he says that by losing the restaurant he has felled his uncle, too.'

'But isn't his uncle dead?'

Nori put down his pot and gave me a faintly disappointed look. 'For many years. But so the old people believe – they can fell the dead as well as the breathing. Like being caught *between the devil and the deep blue sea, neh?*'

I nodded and stared into the rice cooker, its churning steam spectral and hypnotic.

'I feel sorry for him,' I said.

'So it is, all the while. The big fish eat the little.'

There was a sharp grating sound as he scraped rice from the bottom of his pot.

It was the busiest night of the summer but the customers were gentle and undemanding and the atmosphere, as at a funeral reception, was chastened and sadly festive and thick with solidarity. The foreigners left huge tips and Mr Oh grunted graciously whenever I freshened his coffee. It fell to Michiko to serve the disagreeable Mr Sato for the last time and though he usually deplored the grammar and fashions of her generation, tonight he was tolerant and even remarked at one point on her resemblance to his own daughter. The Cruikshanks were among the last to arrive. When they left, just before closing, Mrs Cruikshank said she trusted I wouldn't have to go home to Germany just yet and surely with my good English I could land another job.

The last guests, our oldest customers, intoxicated and teary-eyed, staggered up the stairs around midnight and we dragged together a few tables and sank down for a last meal. Mat and Nori and second chef Miyoshi filed from the kitchen bearing platters of steaming rice and salmon teriyaki; at Mr Onishi's behest Johnnie Walker opened the bar to all staff. And now, though I'd felt more and more a part of things over the last few months, I sensed my saddened colleagues closing ranks, retreating into dialect, resorting to nuance, idiom and silence, a semaphore of glances and tics and nods. Nori loomed on the far side of the table with Michiko beside him. They were talking quietly. In the shadows by their chair-legs I could see two hands linked, like sinuous sea-creatures, twined and mating in the deep.

Johnnie had finished the last of the Johnnie Walker Red and was now working on a bottle of Old Granddad. Mr Oh was not drinking. He sat mutely, his agile hands wrapped around one beer tin after another, crushing them and laying them to rest among the plates and ashtrays. Komatsu and second chef Miyoshi were smoking side by side, eyes half-closed, meditating on the fumes that rose and spread outward over their heads.

Mr Onishi, I suppose, was in his office. At one-thirty he came out and told everyone it was time to leave. There were some last half-hearted toasts and deep bowing and then we all stumbled upstairs and outside. The night air was cool and fresh. We looked, I thought, like a beaten rabble. As if wounded, Nori tottered over and proffered a scrap of paper the size of a cheque or a phone bill. 'Here,' he said, his speech slurred, 'I almost forgot. That poem they called the restaurant for.... Remember?'

He and Michiko swayed before me, their features painted a smooth ageless amber by the gentle light of the doorway. Behind them the brooding profiles of bank and office towers and beyond those in long swirling ranks the constellations of early autumn.

I took the slip of paper and held it to the light:

Ah! summer grass/this group of warriors'/remnant of dream
(this poem by Matsuo Bashō, lived same time as Shakespeare)

So long and take care of yourself. Nori.

He shrugged when I thanked him. 'We had to study it back then. A real pin in the ass.'

'Drop by the school sometime,' I said. 'Please, both of you ...'

I knew they wouldn't come.

Gradually the rest straggled off alone or in pairs and I headed for the station. Waves of heat rising out of sewers and off smokestacks and the vacant pavement set the stars quivering, like the scales of small fish in dark water. In the late-summer heat of 1945, after the surrender, Japanese armies had trudged back through the remains of Ōsaka and there was little where these buildings now stood but rubble, refuse, dust and blowing ash. A stubble of fireweed and wildflowers bloomed on the ruins, rippled in the hot wind. There was nothing for the children to eat. I heard these things from a neighbour, a toothless old man who had been a soldier at that time, and I heard other things as well: how faceless Japan had been, how for a while it had been a different place – beaten, levelled and overrun, unable to rise – waiting for the first touch of a foreign hand. For a sea change, into something rich, and strange.

On the train to Nagai I had a half-hour to experiment with the words on Nori's farewell card. By the time I got home I had the translation done, though the line 'Yume no ato' was still troublesome and I found it hard to focus on the page.

Ah, summer grass!
    All that survives
        Of the warrior's dream ...

I keep thinking I should send a copy to Nori.

The slow process of forgetting a story's origins and intended aboutness eventually allows the writer to experience the work the way the reader does, in its full freshness and mystery – if it has them. And if it doesn't, the writer as re-reader will find out. I have just reread 'Five Paintings of the New Japan.' I feel uncomfortable writing about my own work, not because I have so little to say but because if I broached things I could probably go on talking all night, like that drunk at the bar trying to catch your eye with angling glances and half-grins, watching for his in. Writers are alone with a story for so long and become so intimate with its characters, landscapes, interiors, its very furniture and draperies, not to mention motifs and language, that they long to speak of that hidden world. If the story gets published, readers may say they enjoyed it, or found it interesting, or didn't understand it, but it's rare for anybody to bring up the specificities – the actual physical details, scraps of skewed dialogue, hard-won phrases – that a story is constructed of, piece by piece.

What I will say in general is that my fiction is meant to move, and (to the extent that this is possible with words) to sound, like a musical composition, whether a brief moody nocturne or a folk ballad or a blues tune or a piece of jazz improv or a symphony. I write my first drafts very fast: one convulsive sitting. The aim with this approach is not only to satisfy my need for a sort of tentative closure – that first draft done and in my hands – but also to ensure that the piece has emotional coherence and sustained vitality. As David Manicom (who tackles first drafts in a similar spirit) once wrote to me, 'You can edit order into a text, but not energy...' Energy has to be there from the start. And in the course of a manic first draft, writing your way into a kind of trance, you trick your subconscious into participating. You jump-start the machinery of dreams, though fully awake. You open the story up to happy accidents – to the possibility of astonishing yourself – while accepting that much of the writing will be rushed, clumsy, sketchy. But there will be time to fix that.

It will seem to take forever.

Finally, I try to locate the form in the central themes and images, the main metaphors of the story, rather than pre-imposing an existing form – say, the form of the traditional 'epiphany' story – on the material. I try to find the form that's radically appropriate. So that 'Five Paintings of the New Japan' is set up in five parts, or chapters, each drawing on a famous painting for its imagery, its colours, its tone, its rhythm and pace. Here's one example. Part V, called 'The Starry Night' after Van Gogh's painting, moves toward its close with an image of the night sky over Ōsaka – and then, at greater length, the ruins of Ōsaka at war's end – written in sentences meant to swirl like Van Gogh's brush strokes: 'He and Michiko swayed before me, their features painted a smooth ageless amber by the gentle light of the doorway. Behind them the brooding profiles of bank and office towers and beyond those in long swirling ranks the constellations of early autumn.' The flow of that 'long swirling' second sentence, unbroken by any of the four or five commas that could have gone in; the internal rhyme and alliteration which, I hope, pull you through along a chain of sound, sprocket by sprocket; the spatial and temporal movement from youthful faces up to older buildings and on into starry, timeless skies – all are meant to give a sense of soaring, looping motion.

My aim is to play strong music, to please your ear, while rendering everything richly present to your eye. Somehow, synaesthetically, the right word-music, like a well-chosen soundtrack, makes a scene or detail more vivid and memorable.

Sound is the way I try to make you see.

MARY BORSKY
The Last Bullring

WHEN I WAS ELEVEN, my aunt from the city sent us a set of the *Encyclopedia Americana*. My mother told me that in the encyclopedias, you could look up anything in the world.

The first thing I did after we unpacked the twelve promisingly heavy wine-coloured volumes was to look up Mrs Hill.

Mrs Hill had a boarding house across the street, where she kept six boarders, including old Mr Clock who'd been stapled by his clothes to the chair in the chemistry lab by the grade eleven boys, Fredrick Fenstock, who was known to eat anything that was placed before him (he was Mrs Hill's favourite), also Venus Scott, who used too much water, and who, with her tiny eyes and blond sausage curls, resembled a very beautiful pig.

I didn't find Mrs Hill in the *Encyclopedia Americana*, nor any of the boarders, nor myself for that matter. I was startled by the way we were viewed by the world, which is to say, we were not viewed at all. I was also somewhat embarrassed by my mistake. Clearly, I'd been foolish to think we would be included right along with the Sahara Desert, World War II and the Beaufort Sea!

I find my slant on the world not much changed from the time I was eleven. I'm still interested in what a friend of mine calls 'the good stuff', the close-up view of ourselves, which includes, of course, our rough edges and unravellings. Like, what exactly did my friend's father say when he dropped in to see her after an absence of seventeen years? And her father – who used to be a real estate agent – are his hands big or small?

Only fiction – the reading or the writing of it – (or sometimes, good conversation) gives us the luxury to consider these kinds of things. (The candy that man brought for the grandchildren he'd never seen, what kind was it, and was it in a box or a cellophane bag?)

A sticky note on my wall has a verse from William Stafford's poem, 'The Discovery of Daily Experience'.

> You see the people around you – the honors
> they bear – a crutch, a cane, eye patch,
> or the subtler ones, that fixed look, a turn
> aside, or even the brave bearing: all declare
> our kind, who serve on the human front and earn
> whatever disguise will take them home.

Brian Moore said that he was more interested in failure than in success. 'Success alters people, while failure reveals them as they truly are.'

Success shows us the finished side of the garment, the side we show to the world. But in fiction we – like good dressmakers – want to see both sides of the garment, to feel the quality of the fabric, to check the seams, to learn the exact price of the materials used.

I grew up in High Prairie in northern Alberta, the first child of Ukrainian immigrant parents. The sign on the outskirts of High Prairie said:

WELCOME TO HIGH PRAIRIE

POPULATION 2,500

'WHERE CULTURE AND AGRICULTURE MEET'

High Prairie had (and, mostly, still has) six grain elevators, two farm implements dealerships, a hardware store, several garages, three grocery stores, two movie theatres, a pool room (this was my father's), a hospital, an RCMP detachment, a school, a liquor store, a bus station, a train station, an undertaker's, churches of every hue and colour.

Stories were important in my family and in town – for what else is gossip than a form of storytelling? People were known by things they'd done and things they'd said. *The High Prairie Progress*, the town newspaper, carried accounts of various social and club events, weddings, showers, the comings and goings of the more prominent citizenry.

There was, of course, formal story-telling too. One of my early memories is of my grandfather telling my brother and me a story about two children who climb a tree to escape a witch. They are carried off – just in time! – on the backs of rescuing geese. I clearly remember the rhythmic movement of the flying goose as it carried me off, the feel of its feathers against my legs (I had my own goose and did not have to share my brother's), the cool air rushing over my skin. I remember also the fear of being so high, and of being so precariously seated on the flying goose – all this naturally mitigated by the joy and rightness of having escaped the horrible witch. (Move over, Shirley Maclaine!)

The Ukrainian community wrote and put on its own plays in the Red Hall (so named for the political persuasion of its members). One memorable play was about a farm husband and wife who, on a wager, trade jobs for the day. The hard-working husband expects that doing his wife's chores will be basically a day of relaxation, but he is comically overwhelmed by the demands of laundry, cleaning, mending (which involves his hilarious attempts to thread a needle), also the problem of getting the perogies to stick together. In desperation, and to our great delight, he even tries spitting on the perogy dough. The wife, meanwhile, finishes haying, comes in singing, puts her feet up and slams her fist on the table to demand supper.

(Oddly enough, I later married a man who never told stories. What is that person like, I might ask, how does he act? 'He looks ordinary. He acts ordinary,' my husband would answer. Once, however, he surprised me. What is so-and-so like, I asked. 'He looks,' my husband said, 'like a veterinarian.')

High Prairie had a public library from which I read basically whatever was available. I loved the *Anne* books, the *Little Women* books, the usual animal stories and mysteries.

I remember my father being pleased to see me reading *The Cherry Orchard* by Chekhov (which I was reading strictly for the story line). In that very tense Cold War era, I think my father was pleased to see me reading a Russian writer. (Chekhov for some reason remained on the public library shelves, though I do remember hearing complaints about 'that Russky', Boris Pasternak, being allowed there. I don't remember if Boris Pasternak survived or not.)

In general, however, my home did not encourage reading, other than the reading that was required for school. Reading was what you did in the evening when your work was done, not what you lay about doing during the day, so a lot of my reading had to be done in secret, jumping up and trying to look busy whenever I heard my mother coming. (This is harder to do than it sounds.) To this day, I marvel at pictures of people reading in drawing rooms or deck chairs. My own best reading is still done in bed or in front of an uncleared breakfast table.

My absolute favourite childhood book was *Girl of the Limberlost* by Gene Stratton Porter. It is a story about a girl who lives with her cruel and embittered mother on the edge of a hauntingly beautiful swamp. The girl collects and eventually sells moths in order to go to school. (I've looked at the novel recently and still find it an excellent story, though it is marred by a sentimental ending.)

One of my finest moments as a writer occurred when I was in grade four. Miss Bennett, our teacher, was reading aloud the stories we'd written. When she announced she was going to read my story, the class turned to me, then back to her, saying, 'Oh, good.' It seemed to my ears not just any sort of 'oh, good', but a quiet, hunkering down kind of 'oh, good' you say, almost to yourself, as you're setting down to a story. I was thrilled beyond words.

I was lucky enough to have an exceptional English teacher, Marjorie Daniels, when I was in grade eleven. The high school English curriculum at that time was wonderful but other teachers had us simply read the stories, then complete the questions at the end of each story. In Marjorie Daniels' class, we discussed the stories, a simple enough idea, but radical in that time and place. I remember her knowing the words to a Shakespearean song, and teaching us to sing it.

Once she told me the exact thing it seemed to me I'd always wanted to hear – that she thought I could make my living as a writer. I ran home and told my mother, who slammed down the newspaper she was reading, and said, angrily, 'And what good's that going to do me?'

Of course, my mother was very young, for she'd married young and had children young, and she had her own disappointments, her own burdens. But I was even younger, and not able to reason out her response. And somehow, in whatever ways these decisions are made, I think I picked up that little package of a dream, and put it on a shelf. Some people wouldn't have done that, of course. Some people would have thought, well, I don't care what you think, and would have gone ahead doing whatever it was they were wanting to do. But I think that given that time and place, given who I was, given the fragility of that particular hope, this was somehow a signal that I couldn't just go off and do what I wanted, and it took a while for my own dreams to resurface.

In grade twelve, a story of mine was used in the yearbook. As I recall, it involves a woman criticizing her husband for having forgotten the shrimp for a party. My only experience with shrimp would have been canned shrimp, but I think shrimp seemed awfully sophisticated to me.

I went to the University of Alberta in Edmonton in 1963 and several years later got a B.Ed. University split the world open for me, and I infused it with the same hopes and high expectations that I had the encyclopedias, years earlier.

In one of my English classes I was taught by Henry Kreisel, an outstanding professor. He had an obvious love of literature (I remember the dreamy look he got on his face when he talked about how to enter a particular poem) and his classroom was always crowded on the day each term he read T. S. Eliot. Henry Kreisel was a short story writer and novelist, and in one of his novels, *The Betrayal,* the main character stands on the banks of the North Saskatchewan and watches the ice break up. This amazed me, for though I too had stood on the banks of the North Saskatchewan and watched the ice break up, I didn't know this simple thing was worthy enough for a novel. I knew that a character in a novel could watch a sunset in San Francisco, and I knew that a character in a book could watch a parade in New York City. For that matter, I must have known that Anne of Green Gables could stare into the apple blossoms in PEI. But I did not know a character in a novel could watch the ice break up in Edmonton. (Even my beloved *Girl of the Limberlost* was set in Indiana.)

The ground I walked on was more real then, more significant, more holy – as were those of us who walked upon it – now that I had entered this place and time through this other means, through this novel.

Mel Hurtig had a wonderful bookstore on Jasper Avenue in those days, a bookstore with a sign that simply said, *HURTIG* BOOKSELLER. (Down the street his father had another store, with a sign that said, HURTIG, FURRIER.)

This bookstore was a beacon of light in Social Credit–dominated Alberta. It had a fine collection of books, large black-and-white photographs of writers on the walls, free coffee, chairs where customers were welcome to read, play chess, talk.

In that period, the Social Credit government banned several literary books. (They also banned the film *Tom Jones*, though the MLAS saw fit to hold a private viewing for themselves.) Mel Hurtig's store window had a display of books that had been banned in other times and places: *Catcher in the Rye, Ulysses, Canterbury Tales, Black Beauty, Leaves of Grass, Call of the Wild.*

Recently, I was wondering aloud to a friend why I did not do more writing in that period. She said, you know, you were always writing something. And I remembered that was true. I was always carrying a scribbler or sheaf of papers in my oversized purse, and writing in coffee shops.

What did I write? Thoughts, personal essays, letters, a few very bad poems, usually a journal of some sort. The first time I actually wrote a short story, however, stands out in my mind.

This was years later, and I was at home with my husband and a friend who was staying with us. I went to my bedroom, shut the door and wrote a story based on a childhood visit of my aunt from the city. The story, which later became 'The Blue Dress', seemed true, it seemed to have formed a small but real world of its own. My husband and my friend liked the story. I thought, well, that's that. I don't think I can think of another one.

Finally, one spring, when the second of my three children started kindergarten, I enrolled in a creative writing course at the University of Ottawa with Frances Itani.

One of Frances's greatest strengths as a teacher was her own absolute, unswerving dedication to writing. ('A story needs no defence,' she often repeated, a statement by Rudy Wiebe.) Frances let nothing come between her and her own writing, she never questioned the value of it, and she was willing to share whatever she could of what she'd learned.

She wore what appeared to be the same pair of black stretch pants each day of class (a further source of inspiration to me) and led us into that world where the only things that mattered were the answers to questions like, does this work on the page? are all the lines going in the same direction? is this character alive? do we care about this?

My notes from that class read,

Precise detail, precise gesture.

Cut down – slash! – and leave the spirit whole.

Write for the most intelligent reader.

Don't tell what the reader should feel / think.

Describe in concrete detail, leave interpretation to the reader.

Read 'The Lost Salt Gift of Blood', Alistair Macleod – a perfect story.

Read Frank O'Connor – characters are not heroes but lonely individuals.

Describe a building as seen by a man whose son has just been killed in the war.

Don't mention the son, the war, the death, or the old man doing the seeing.

Frances suggested I publish 'Blessing' and introduced us to some of the literary magazines. We had an in-class reading where I read 'Blessing' and another participant did a marvellous and generous thing: she reached for her Kleenex and wiped away a few tears.

My memory is that we sat like disciples at Frances's feet, though this could only have been figuratively true, for we were in a university classroom with the chairs bolted to the floor. One young woman wrote a wonderful piece about working in a chocolate factory, and Frances told her, 'Don't ever stop writing.' Instantly, I plunged into a black quicksand pit of envy. How I would have loved to receive such a benediction!

However, one evening Frances did say to the class at large, 'Just hang in. You'll get there.'

I was stunned. *Just hang in?* Is *that* what was required? *Just hang in?*

Well! I could certainly hang in!

I didn't know if I could write about any place that was not a kitchen, I didn't know if I could write about anyone who was not my mother, I didn't know if I could create the vivid and continuous dream that Frances urged on us, but I could certainly hang in!

Some time later I entered a story, 'World Fair', into the *Ottawa Citizen* Short Story Contest and won first prize. John Metcalf, who was one of the judges, called and later wrote me to say the Porcupine's Quill would be interested in publishing a collection of my stories.

John's encouragement was generous and invaluable, both then and later along the road. Steve Heighton once said to me, 'John doesn't care if you're a man or a woman. He doesn't care about age. He doesn't care about background. The only thing he cares about is what's on the page.' This was my experience as well.

A simple sentence of John's became very important to me, 'You must *carve out* the necessary time,' he said, in that emphatic way of his. And *carving out time*, with its forceful, almost violent connotations, was not an inappropriate metaphor for finding time for one's self in a family of five.

I confess I wasn't the world's easiest beginning writer to help along. I was busy with my children, with part-time teaching, with a marriage that was in trouble, and I had very little confidence in anything, let alone my ability to actually write the required stories. Sometimes I questioned John's judgement for asking me to write a collection in the first place (maybe John Metcalf's had a nervous breakdown! I thought at one point); other times – when it became obvious I wasn't going to dash off the stories in a hurry – I despaired that John had forgotten about me anyway. (This may not be a bad thing. In *Writing Past Dark*, Bonnie Friedman says of such difficulties: 'One must be sure one's editor has forgotten one's name.' Before one can settle down and begin to write, she means.)

A group of participants from Frances Itani's class continued meeting in each other's homes, forming a writers' group that became indispensable to most of us. We drank a lot of ,wine, talked about stories, about our marriages, our mothers, our children. We workshopped each other's stories too, though sometimes workshopping got the short end of the stick.

Gradually, I began to publish short stories in various magazines, *Queen's Quarterly, Quarry, The New Quarterly, Geist, Grain, Prairie Fire, NeWest*. At some point I realized that the characters in different stories seemed very alike. I decided to set about writing them as a set of linked short stories.

I attended the May Writers' Studio in Banff, and also did a workshop in Sage Hill with Edna Alford. These workshops were important in helping me with my stories, but even more important in creating a network of friendship and mutual support. Until I had this, I didn't realize how vital it was.

Still, I sometimes worried about writing such *domestic* stories. I'd sent a story to a particular magazine and got it back, along with a list of rules. 'No he-said, she-said stories,' one rule read. 'No domestic dramas,' read another.

But my stories were *all* he-said, she-said stories! My stories were *all* domestic dramas!

At one point I discussed this with another writer, Brian Moon. 'My stories all have a kitchen in them,' I complained. 'Hemingway had bull-rings in his!' I blamed this on my childhood where my brother had had interesting summer jobs, like one where he worked on a road crew with a man who tried to shoot down airplanes with a rifle. I'd, meanwhile, been stuck working in a restaurant or a hospital, having only totally humdrum experiences.

'But the kitchen *is* the bullring!' Brian passionately and memorably argued. 'The kitchen is the *last* bullring!'

John Metcalf and I also had a similar conversation where he encouraged me not to write for the market, but to write what I wanted.

Write what I wanted! What a radical idea!

(Later, incidentally, I used the detail about the man shooting at air-planes in 'Eclipse', so I was able, at least, to appropriate my brother's experience.)

In 1995 my collection of stories, *Influence of the Moon*, came out with the Porcupine's Quill.

In the time I'd been working, quietly, almost secretively, on the sto-ries for *Influence of the Moon*, I often thought of my father on the trapline. (Before he had the poolroom, he'd had a trapline.) I felt I was doing something similar to what he'd done, in quietly exploring my own terrain, making my own paths, building my own cabins, inventing any other devices I needed from what was at hand or learning how to do without.

But when the book came out, predictably, I had to go to town. In town, good and bad things (again, predictably) happened. I admired the bright lights, I sold my pelts, I bought new boots, I went into a restau-rant and ate a hamburger – something new. But, before long, I found I'd also spent my money, lost my boots in a poker game, forgotten the exact way back into the bush and, having tasted the ease and comfort of life in town, was no longer sure I even wanted to go back.

Recently I read Liz Hay's novel, *A Student of Weather*, and was later telling Liz how much I enjoyed the parts about the painter simply working each day, without fanfare or external reward of any kind. We talked about how the real centre to writing – the golden core – is exactly that – the hours spent in solitary quiet work, the hours spent sitting with one's story, not engaging with the world, or seeing one's self reflected in the eyes of others.

'So laziness is the only thing that can keep you from your work?' I asked, trying to figure this out as we spoke (forgetting, for a moment, flood, fire, illness, bank foreclosures, and other disasters).

'Laziness,' Liz said, 'or rejection. Real or perceived rejection.'

Later, I mentally added a third deadly sin, ego. Wanting or needing to look a certain way can also keep you from your work.

THE UKRAINIAN SHIRT
Mary Borsky

THE FIRST MORNING Norman and I were at my mother's, her eavestroughs had to be put up and everyone was mobilizing for it.

My sister-in-law, Bonnie, was flipping pancakes, and my brother, Amel, was eating them, swearing meanwhile on a stack of invisible Bibles that he would never vote again now that Trudeau had given the finger to the people of the West.

'The prime minister of Canada!' Amel shouted, thumping his hand to his heart. 'The man we-the-people put into office! The *prime minister!*' He looked around the table to see whether we were following him.

Uncle Walter, who farmed nearby, rubbed his sunburned neck and laughed along in a melancholy way.

Mother was somewhere, likely checking on her potatoes or sweeping glass from the road.

'Have another pancake, Amel-my-man,' Bonnie said in her sparky little way. 'It'll make you feel better.'

Norman and I were wedged in at one end of the table, both of us wearing green jade wedding bands. We hadn't slept well that first night in my childhood bed.

'I thought Ukrainians would be so different,' Norman had complained, turning away from me in bed. 'You made them sound so different.' He held the bedcovers under his chin and stared up at the cracks in the green ceiling.

'What are you talking about?' I said. I couldn't believe he was saying this. Especially considering how understanding I'd been about his less than perfect manners when we arrived. I hadn't said a word about the way he'd ignored all my relatives and started reading a two-year-old newspaper that was lying an my mother's coffee table.

'You made them sound so extreme,' Norman insisted, still holding himself away from me. 'So rough and ready. I thought they'd be hanging off the rafters. But they're really quite ordinary.'

I decided to switch off the light, which meant I had to get out of bed, thereby banging my ankle on one of the numerous pieces of furniture that were crowded into the room.

Before long, drunks, wandering outside on the street, began yelling in a belligerent but forlorn way, '*Parrr-ty! Parrr-ty!*' I had to get out of bed yet again, clamber through dusty curtains and clattering venetian blinds to wrestle with the window.

The bed was a double, extremely soft, and Norman and I each hung onto our own side, as if stranded in the middle of the Atlantic on an inadequately inflated life raft.

Toward morning, huge delivery trucks began their incremental, interminable backing up into the gigantic twenty-four-hour supermarket that had sprung up across the street from my mother's. At some point, Norman and I got dressed, went to the Super-A across the street where we pushed a cart down the long, chilly aisles, and came home with cornflakes and milk.

'Our duly elected prime minister!' Amel continued. 'He looks out his first-class train window – paid for by *our* taxes! – and gives *us* the finger! Am I the guy who's got it wrong? Am I the guy who's missing something?' He cast a dark and aggrieved look up and down the breakfast table.

'Sure, it's insulting,' I said. 'Sure it is.' I turned to Norman who usually had plenty to say on topics like this, but this time, Norman was silent as the soggy cornflakes before him.

Norman had never met my family all at once and on their own territory before. He was from New Zealand, and had only recently arrived in Canada to study anthropology at UBC and to embark on his life as world adventurer. His hope was to study different peoples in far-away places, to immerse himself in their ways of life, to learn their languages and study their cultures. Norman's moving into my apartment in Vancouver, where I had a job teaching school, had been mostly his idea, our subsequent marriage, mostly mine.

'So, Norman,' Uncle Walter said, in his polite self-effacing way. 'You're a few miles from home.' His faded blue eyes registered mild surprise, as if something about Norman presented a puzzle, but one he expected would resolve itself in due course.

Norman sat up straight, as if called upon in school, and inclined his head quickly toward Uncle Walter.

'I beg your pardon?' he said, in his South Seas twang.

'You're a long way from New Zealand,' I translated, smiling at Norman to encourage him. I wanted this visit to go well. I wanted my family to like Norman, to think I'd done not too badly. 'You're pretty much as far away from New Zealand as you can get,' I continued, with yet another smile, 'mile-wise, anyway.'

'Mile-wise!' Norman echoed, brightening. He turned to me with a show of scholarly interest. '*Mile-wise.* That's fascinating. Tell me, is *mile-wise* a regional expression?' He waited for my reply, holding one finely tapered finger contemplatively in the air.

Everyone stopped chewing and turned to study Norman, taking in his peach-coloured hair and beard, his sharply scissored nose, his hands – now somewhat primly folded on his lap – pinkish, finely formed, barely bigger than my own. They looked at his green jade wedding band, at his tan plaid shirt, at his khaki shorts.

There was a lengthy silence.

Finally, they returned to their pancakes.

'Now, some guys would throw the eavestroughs up with tin snips and a hammer,' Amel announced, washing down his pancakes with coffee. 'But I came prepared to do the job right. I brought my acetylene torch, I brought my steel pipes, I brought my crimper, my threader, my cutter. When I do a job, I do it right!'

'Isn't that a fact!' Bonnie said proudly, holding up Amel's well-polished plate for general admiration.

'And don't forget,' Mother said, emerging from somewhere with a pail in her hands and what appeared to be a rag around her hair. 'Don't forget the pipes for the rain barrels and the cistern.' Her face had the pale, caught-off-guard look of a mushroom suddenly held up to the light of day.

Amel remained motionless for a moment. 'Let's get one thing straight here,' he said slowly, taking time to sift her words for some nugget of offence.

Bonnie refilled Amel's coffee cup, scooped in two spoonfuls of sugar, a dribble of condensed milk, then clinked the spoon in his cup.

Amel pulled his hand across his chin, rasping his whiskers. He shifted his bulky shoulders and raised his eyes to Mother's. 'Who's in charge of this job here?' he said. 'Me? Or you?'

'I didn't say you'd go and do nothing wrong,' Mother said, hunching stubbornly over her pail, but looking back at him.

'Irene,' Amel demanded, turning to me. 'You're the schoolteacher. You choose, Irene. Mum can't make up her mind. Good workmanship or shoddy workmanship?'

'Good sounds good,' I said, finding myself springing up to refill my coffee cup at the stove. 'Good sounds just fine.' I looked over to catch Norman's eye, but Norman was reading the list of ingredients on the back of the pancake syrup. 'Don't worry, Mum. They'll do a good job,' I added.

'Don't waste my time if you want to settle for something less,' Amel rumbled ominously.

'No one's not asking you to do nothing that wastes your precious time,' my mother answered, still facing Amel, pale and puffy, from over the top of her bucket.

It was so shadowy in the room, I could barely make out the dirt-covered tubers in the bottom of my mother's pail. The Super-A across the street seemed to block the light from the front and had sent cracks laddering up my mother's kitchen wall.

'Was it always this dark in here?' I asked, looking around the kitchen. 'Didn't there use to be more light than this?'

'A cistern!' Amel shouted, laughing to deflect the conversation back to a more friendly footing. 'A cistern to hold rainwater! Who else has a cistern these days?' His even white teeth shone in his face. He pushed himself back from the table in a lordly way.

'Look at it, Mum!' he continued. 'You got your own self-contained system here! You got your own wood stove! You got your own cistern! You got your own sauerkraut and canned beets and whatnot! Do you all realize if we're hit by an atomic bomb you're going to live a few days longer than the rest of us?'

Amel's laugh boomed out again. Uncle Walter shook his head and grinned along in an unhappy way.

I poured my cup of coffee into the sink, and began to stack the dirty plates while Amel, Uncle Walter, Mother and Bonnie trampled noisily outside to survey the eavestrough project. Already, Norman had a paperback from his back pocket, and was reading, his bare legs crossed, his book angled toward the net-curtained window.

I looked at him. The book was called *Head-hunters of Central Borneo*.

I looked outside the kitchen windows. The breeze through the screen had a slightly metallic smell. Amel, Bonnie, Uncle Walter and Mother were standing in a row facing the kitchen window and looking up. I saw Uncle Walter point, heard him say something, heard everyone laugh.

I turned to Norman, hugging my elbows, rocking lightly on my feet. 'Norman, are you going to go out and give them a hand?' I asked.

Norman stopped reading and looked up with a start.

'Me?' he said.

Through my mother's orange net kitchen curtains, I was aware of men's voices, of pipes passing through the air, of the positioning of a plank horizontally outside the kitchen window.

I washed the dishes quickly, leaving them to air-dry. My mother, who did not trust any avoidance of work, even unnecessary work, had never air-dried a dish in her life, or even soaked a pot to make the scrubbing of it easier. Nothing was done right unless it was done the hard way.

I wiped off the stove, taking more time with it than I ordinarily would, pushed a broom across the linoleum, examined the cracks in the front-room ceiling. I was doing anything I could to avoid looking out the kitchen window.

When at last I could take the suspense no longer and pushed the kitchen curtains aside, I saw Amel's yellow work boots on the right end of the plank, Uncle Walter's darker shoes close beside. After a tense lapse, I spotted Norman's scuffed runners on the opposite end of the plank.

Something like a stone lifted off my chest, releasing me, releasing the sun, in fact, for at that moment a shaft of sunlight pierced the room, making the kitchen more roomy and cheerful, making the world a more benign and habitable place after all.

Husband, I found myself thinking as I polished the knobs and faucet of the stainless steel sinks to a shine. *Husband*. I liked the word, which suggested to me a certain safely harnessed male energy, something dark, polished, valuable: a mahogany dining table, for example, or a shiny-rumped Clydesdale. *Wife*, on the other hand, I reflected, I did not like nearly so well, sounding as it did, so, well, … *wifey*.

As I folded the dishrag and draped it over the faucet, I thought that from the corner of my eye, I caught a glimpse of the Ukrainian shirt I'd made for Norman.

But when I pushed the curtains aside and looked more closely, I saw Norman was wearing the same ordinary tan plaid shirt he'd worn at breakfast. It made sense that Norman hadn't run in to change his shirt in the middle of putting up the eavestroughs. Besides, I didn't know if Norman had even brought the shirt I'd made for him.

Then, moments later – from the edge of my field of vision – I once more saw the flash of unbleached linen, blue and tan embroidered flowers – Norman's Ukrainian shirt. So he *was* wearing it, I thought.

But when I peered out a second time, I found that, for the second time, I was mistaken.

I'd made Norman the Ukrainian shirt for his birthday. Sewing had never been a particular strength of mine, but I had taken three years of high school home ec, and in my final year, made the two-piece, fully lined, brown wool suit that I wore the first day of teachers' training. Since that time, though, I hadn't done much sewing, apart from very infrequently machine-stitching a cushion.

Still, I passed a fabrics store everyday on my way home from school, and the notion of making a shirt for Norman tugged at me until at last I gave in to it.

After studying the patterns for men's shirts, the one that most appealed to me was a Cossack-style shirt, a basic straight-cut man's shirt with a front slit at the neck, and a mandarin collar. I chose a good grade of unbleached linen to cut it from, and machine-embroidered strips of tan and blue flowers to sew around the neckline and the cuffs.

I worked on the shirt in the evenings while Norman was at the library, no light in the room except for the small yellow pool cast by the light of the sewing machine itself, no sound but the crinkle of tissue paper and the quick metallic clatter of the machine. I joined small dots to small dots, big dots to big dots, and sewed French seams throughout, happy in my own little world of cutting, pinning, sewing and ripping.

'You made this?' Norman asked, when I presented the shirt to him at his birthday dinner. 'You made this yourself?'

He examined the shirt under the reading lamp, then pulled it on when I urged him to. He looked down at it, smiling uncertainly, stretching his arms to see the strip of embroidery around the cuffs.

'My father was wearing a shirt like that in his immigration photo,' I said. 'Only his would have been hand-done. Even the linen. Can you imagine the work?'

Candlelight shone steadily from the table and again, but more erratically, from the ceiling which I'd covered with aluminum foil to offset the gloom of the west coast climate. Until I'd met Norman I'd been plotting my escape back to the prairies, but now the rain, the damp, the porridge skies didn't seem to have anything much to do with me. Those things seemed like something happening outside the window. They seemed like weather.

'I'll have to save this for a special occasion,' Norman said carefully. He looked down at the shirt again. He was still holding his arms straight out.

I cut myself another sliver from the birthday cake which I'd also made from scratch, carrot with cream cheese icing.

'It's a casual style,' I explained happily. 'It's a peasant shirt. It's the kind of shirt you can wear anywhere.'

Chuloveek, I remembered, was the Ukrainian word for husband. It had, to my ear, a more forceful, less tameable sound than the more smoothly rounded *husband*. This was the kind of thing Norman would find interesting, and I made a mental note to mention this to him later.

Husband, chuloveek, I said to myself, *chuloveek, husband.* I was balancing the words like balls of bread dough in my hands when Mother and Bonnie came back into the kitchen, each of them carrying a pail of pin cherries. Mother looked around, surveying the damage I'd done to her kitchen, then brushed past to pull her colander from the cupboard.

'Well, Norman looks about as happy as a drowned cat!' Bonnie announced, pretending to laugh, but her eyes sparking darkly.

Mother and Bonnie turned together and thundered their pin cherries into the sink, their feet side by side, Bonnie's ample blue-jeaned hips lined up beside my mother's more scrawny ones, their shoulders and heads tilted at the exact same working angle over the berries.

I'd always told myself that the reason I couldn't work with Mother was that she was impossible to work with, that she had no clear system of doing things, that she expected you to read her mind. But Bonnie, who was born in Lebanon, knew instinctively how to work with her.

I made my way out through the oven-hot porch which smelled faintly of pesticides.

Outside, the blinding midday sun made something behind my eyes clench into a fist. I walked to the side of the house, shielded my eyes with both hands against the brilliant sky, and looked up at the men at work on the plank.

Amel and Uncle Walter still stood on one end, talking in their easy working way as they raised the eavestrough to the edge of the roof. At the other end, Norman, bare-legged, stood alone, his figure slight, his shoulders sagging. He was holding the dangling end of the eavestrough in his hands.

Whatever it was that Norman should be doing, it was clear he wasn't doing it. Shouldn't he be, for instance, holding the eavestrough *up*? It didn't seem to serve any purpose to hold it while it was dangling down like that. Why didn't Amel or Uncle Walter tell him what to do? Why didn't Norman, for that matter, *ask*?

My vision darkened, and my skin felt tight and hot. Norman looked as dejected as a prisoner of war, but I found it impossible to pity him, the way he submitted to the weight of the pipe, and did not in any way exert himself against it.

I walked quickly around the house to the grove of pin cherries, but I'd stood there only a moment when a man I'd noticed hanging around the dumpster outside the Super-A ambled amicably in my direction. By his bowling-pin shape, his sedate low-slung belly, I recognized him as one of the drunks who'd kept us awake the night before. The man started to touch the peak of his baseball cap, as if he was about to say something, but I was already turning to go back inside the house.

In the darkened front room where Norman and I left our suitcases, I spilled out my hairbrush, shampoo, toothpaste, then suddenly – sensing someone in the shadows behind me – spun around, my heart slamming hard in my chest.

It was Norman. Norman was sitting in an armchair in the shadows, a book almost to his face. He couldn't have been in the house longer than a minute or two.

'This is fascinating,' he said, raising an eyebrow. 'The system of marriage among the Australian Aborigines is considerably more complicated than ours.' He looked at me as if inviting a response. 'Everything is based upon what clan or section or subsection you belong to, and you can or cannot marry into other clans or sections or subsections according to a complicated set of rules, including agreements that may have been made before you were born. The system is so complicated even a mathematician can have trouble with it.'

I stared at Norman for a moment. 'Did we bring aspirin?' I asked, dumping my underwear onto the floor.

In my chest and arms I could still feel the shock of sensing the presence of a still dark figure in the shadows behind me. Sometimes drunks came into my mother's house. Mother'd found one sitting in the porch, another time she'd found one asleep on the couch. She called the RCMP who drove down to pick them up and to sympathize with her. 'You shouldn't have to put up with that,' the RCMP officer said, and Mother liked to tell about it, about what had happened, the kindness of the young RCMP officer, and what exactly he'd said to her.

In the kitchen, Bonnie, who was standing at the stove in front of a steaming pot of pin cherries, had a snappy smile for me.

'I see Norman's reading again,' she said.

'He has a paper due,' I said, passing between her and my mother who was pouring boiling water into glass jars on the table.

'Does he always read in the dark like that?' Mother asked, the large aluminum kettle still in her hands. Through the cloud of steam she looked toward the darkened doorway to the front room. 'Tell him he can turn on the light if he wants.'

The Super-A across the street had part of a brightly lit aisle devoted to headache remedies. I selected the most potent-looking, and took two tablets even before I went through the cash with them.

I bypassed the in-house coffee counter and walked down the block to a coffee shop where I seated myself at a small table along the wall.

I watched the waitress fill my cup from a prepared pot and admired the geometric order of the tables and chairs, each place set with a paper place mat, a chrome serviette holder; salt, pepper and ketchup at the side. Behind the counter, a coffee-machine shone and hummed. Lemon meringue pies, butter tarts, and jewel-coloured bowls of Jell-O were brilliantly illuminated inside a glass case.

Three men at a window table were talking about fencing, the cost of different wires, the advantage of page-lock versus hinge-lock.

'You drill your posts two feet deep, run hinge-lock along the top, a strand of electric wire, and you got yourself a fence,' one of the men said.

'It's going to run you anywhere from four dollars a foot up,' another of the men added.

I felt something inside my brain unfold and take its proper shape. What a relief not to be hearing about marriage systems of the Australian Aborigines, or kinship lines of the Kwakiutl, or taboos of the Trobriand Islanders!

Give me real things any day, I thought.

But I knew, deep down, that I was mostly fooling myself. I knew things weren't really that simple. I knew the Trobriand Islanders were likely real enough, once you got to the Trobriand Islands.

There was, I decided, only one fact in this entire array of events that held its shape no matter which way I looked at it. This was the fact: It wouldn't have killed Norman to help with the eavestroughs.

I could feel my banished headache open one bleary eye, like an improperly anaesthetized patient. I turned my attention to the menu, which had been neatly typed out and slipped into a tidy plastic sleeve. When the waitress came by, I let her refill my coffee, then ordered a club sandwich.

As I approached my mother's house again, I saw the blue flame of Amel's welder, saw my mother pouring water from her aluminum kettle into the cup of a man who was standing on the other side of the fence. When I got closer, I saw it was the party-man who'd tried to talk to me earlier.

'I thought you didn't want them to come around,' I said to my mother. 'You shouldn't encourage them.'

'They get teabags from the dumpster. Why not give them hot water?' she said.

'Get a shot of this top corner, Bonnie,' Amel called out to his wife who was snapping pictures. 'Look at this! Isn't this a beauty? Pass me the camera! I got to get a picture of the bonnet!'

'Feel it,' Amel invited Mother. 'It's solid as a rock! You could do chin-ups on these eavestroughs!' He was, again, standing on the plank.

I saw that he'd made a complicated system, anchoring the eaves-troughs to steel posts on each corner of the house. The eavestroughs themselves were galvanized tin, but reinforced underneath with long thin steel pipes, while wider steel pipes went down into the rainbarrels.

'These eavestroughs are going to be here after the rest of us are dust!' Amel yelled happily.

'Why did you put something over the top like that?' Mother asked, squinting up at the eavestroughs. She was still holding the aluminum kettle. 'How's the rain supposed to get in?'

'The rain can still get in,' Amel said.

'I want it the way it used to be,' Mother said, pushing against the steel drainpipe. 'And why are those ugly posts at the corners? They're not going to stay there, are they? I thought they were just here to get the other part up!'

'What's the matter?' Amel said, his face tumbling down into a pud-ding. He held his hands toward her, palms upward. 'You like cleaning eavestroughs? I made it so you will never need to clean an eavestrough again!'

Mother pushed against the drainpipe a second time, looked up to see the entire structure.

'I did something *good* for you,' Amel said, looking down at her from the plank.

Uncle Walter, who was standing beside me now, rubbed his cheek mournfully.

Mother put the kettle on the ground, pulled the rag from her head. Her hair was orange, with grey roots. I was surprised, even shocked, to think my mother would dye her hair.

'Look!' Amel said, his voice hearty again. 'It's one self-referential sys-tem! It's a masterpiece!'

'How can I get it apart?' Mother asked, still pushing at the pipe that went into the rainbarrel.

'You can't! That's the beauty of it! It's cast in steel now!'

I was still thinking of my mother's hair. I knew she wouldn't pay money for hair-dye. Had someone given it to her?

'What if a stick gets in?' Mother was crying now, her pumpkin-coloured hair streaming down around her face. 'How am I supposed to get a stick out? I didn't ask you to do it this way!'

'A stick's not going to get in,' Amel explained, 'That's the whole beauty of the bonnet. Rainwater gets in, but sticks and leaves and dead birds stay out.' He jumped to the ground with surprising lightness for a man his size. 'I guarantee it, Mum,' he said, his arm around her shoulder.

She wouldn't answer.

'Anyway, it was Irene's idea,' he said at last, half-winking at me.

'Mine?'

'Sure.' Amel grinned. 'You said do a good job.'

I could see last night's reveller, sitting on the curb across the street, drinking his tea from his Styrofoam cup and thoughtfully considering the newly installed eavestrough system. Norman was out now too, smiling to himself as he looked at the same completed project.

He put his arm around me and smiled down in a complicit way. But I was not in the mood for complicity. I was not in the mood for anything I could name.

'I'll paint them green to match your trim,' Amel offered.

'I don't want them green,' Mother answered.

'A nice bright yellow,' Amel countered. 'Irene. You're the school-teacher. What do you think of a nice bright yellow?'

'I don't want them yellow,' Mother said. 'I want them how they are.'

'See?' Amel said, with a show of joviality. 'She likes them.'

'You planning on moving back to Australia?' Uncle Walter asked Norman. His manner was as quiet and as courteous as ever, but I thought I detected a thin shadow of judgement in his blue eyes.

We were in the kitchen eating supper, which had turned out to be a bucket of Kentucky Fried Chicken from the outlet on the highway.

'We haven't discussed going to Australia, have we, Norman?' I said. 'Anyway, Norman's not from Australia. He's from New Zealand.'

Amel leaned back on his chair, a pleasant expression on his face. 'Norman comes from Australia,' Amel said. He was speaking directly to me. Amel had a bottle of beer in his hand, several under his belt, was pleased with the eavestroughs, and was settling into the mood for an argument.

'Norman doesn't come from Australia,' I said.

'Norman comes from Australia,' Amel insisted.

'Norman doesn't come from Australia. Norman comes from New Zealand.'

'Australia. Norman comes from Australia.'

'*New Zealand!*' I said, laughing now. 'I must know where my own husband comes from!'

'Australia!'

'New Zealand!' I shook my head. I couldn't tell if he was joking.

'But you said Norman came from Australia,' Amel said, knitting his brow as if deeply perplexed.

'No, I didn't. I said Norman comes from New Zealand!'

Laughing again, I turned to Norman, but Norman wasn't laughing.

Headlights from a truck outside flashed once, like a warning, across the kitchen.

'New Zealand, Australia,' Amel said magnanimously. 'Why didn't you say so? New Zealand, Australia, big difference.'

'Maybe he likes it better in Austrillia,' my mother said darkly.

I unscrewed the top of another beer, reached over to refill Norman's glass.

'I would love to revisit New Zealand,' Norman said, his features tightening, 'but there are also a number of other countries I should hope to experience first-hand.'

It was silent in the room, and I realized I was afraid Norman would go on to talk about his dreams of seeing the world, of living with different peoples, learning their ways and going on to write about his observations and experiences.

I wasn't worried that my family would think less of him for those dreams, no less than they did now. Likely, they would see such notions as peculiar and far-fetched, but unsurprising in a man who was unwilling to pitch in to put up an eavestrough.

For my own sake though, I didn't want to hear Norman talk about those dreams right now. His dreams suddenly seemed to be insubstantial, cobwebby things. They seemed better talked about far away, by candlelight, under an aluminum foil ceiling. I didn't think I could bear to examine Norman's dreams just then, not by the unforgiving fluorescent light of my mother's kitchen.

I could feel Norman looking at me. I placed the ketchup, vinegar, evaporated milk, sugar bowl, the salt and pepper in a careful line, largest to smallest, in the middle of the table.

'Listen!' Amel said softly. He held up his hand. 'Listen. Do you hear that?'

We all stopped and listened.

Outside, there was the soft blast of rain on the roof, then as we listened, we heard the first slow trickle of rainwater run down into the cistern.

Norman wore the Ukrainian shirt a few times, once to an Anthropology Department party where another graduate student, when she learned I was teaching school, said in a show-offy voice, 'How very brave of you!'

The shirt was really too big for Norman, too long in the arms and so baggy in the neck it made his throat look thin. But with the embroidered strips already sewn on, it would have been a lot of work to take it in.

After one particularly bad fight, I pulled the shirt out of a drawer and tried to tear it into pieces. But the shirt proved so durable with the high quality fabric I'd used, the French seams I'd sewn throughout, that it wouldn't give anywhere. Finally, in my fury, I stood on part of it, yanked, and heard the fabric rip.

Shocked by the sound, I immediately checked to see what damage I'd done. The fabric had given along one of the side seams, though it still hung together with the horizontal threads. I remembered that the vertical and horizontal threads were called the woof and the warp, but I could no longer remember which was which.

I stared at the shirt, then refolded it and put it back into Norman's drawer.

Sometime later, Norman noticed the tear, and guessed how it had happened, even before I had a chance to blame the washing machine.

Holding the shirt in one hand, he leaned toward me, slightly embarrassed, and kissed me. I was embarrassed too, being caught out in this way. I regretted my anger and realized I could not have recalled even the main components of that particular argument if anyone had asked me.

I said I might be able to mend the shirt. The tear was not that visible, and the fit might even be improved by being taken in a little. Norman agreed that the shirt looked mendable and I put it into the

African basket where I stored the undone mending.

I never did get around to repairing the shirt though, and one of the times I left, while I was waiting for the cab, I dumped the unappreciated Ukrainian shirt with its tan and blue flowers into the chute of the incinerator.

The gift that had not been a true gift after all.

I had thought to take the basket for myself, but there was a pain in the exact centre of my chest, the taxi was honking, and it was all I could manage to pull on my raincoat, pick up the suitcase I'd packed, then step out into the thick, wet Vancouver fog.

I am presently working on a second collection of fiction in which the stories are not linked. In 'The Ukrainian Shirt', however, I return to the same cast of characters that appear in *Influence of the Moon*. In this story a grown-up Irene brings her husband, Norman, home for a visit.

My way of writing a story is to sit down and write it and see what happens. Then I put it aside, sometimes in despair, though I'm not sure how much despair I felt this particular time. However, when I went back to the story some time later, I thought, yes, there is a story here, it pulls me in. And I remember making a few encouraging notes to myself, so that through the difficulties of revision, I would not lose faith in it.

I place a lot of weight on what tugs on me, what pulls me in, both in my own work and the work of others. If a piece I've been working on feels alive or compelling in some way, however muddled and scrambled it might be, I hold out hope for it. (The only thing that matters about a story is whether it's alive or dead, Mavis Gallant once said.)

I began this story only with the idea that the family would be putting up eavestroughs and that Norman would, in some way, shirk his part. The section about the Ukrainian shirt evolved during the story and became crucial to it. The presence of the drunk was also unplanned, but fortuitous. The bristliness and competitiveness of the sister-in-law took me by surprise, as did Amel's desire to please his mother. I was especially interested in Norman's predicament as an outsider in this complicated and demanding family, something that hadn't particularly occurred to me before I began the piece.

Often in a story I come to a point where I have to choose between a simpler, more manageable story, and a bigger, messier, possibly unworkable one. From experience I've learned that the higher stakes are the more interesting. I no longer remember what simpler forms of 'The Ukrainian Shirt' tempted me, but I remember struggling with the cracks in Irene and Norman's relationship, for at first I resisted heaping new tensions onto the tensions that already existed. I was also unsure about whether it was too complicated to have Irene a bit of an outsider as well (with her mother brushing her aside in the kitchen, Bonnie bristling at her, and Amel cutting her off half the time). At one point I was also unsure what the drunk was doing in all of this.

I try to listen to the story as I work with it, to pay attention to what the story wants to do. In 'Ice', for example, I had at one point written, I thought, a publishable story. But an image of the little girl pedalling very hard just to keep up, kept tugging at me. When I allowed that into the story (how Amel is accepted simply on his own terms, while Irene must be – or feels she must be – an audience for her father) the story became much richer and deeper.

Sometimes, when I am feeling my way with a story, I am not so much working on it, as I am visiting it, spending time with it. When I run into trouble, I tend to go back to a piece of advice by Alice Munro. Get closer to the story. What this means to me, is to get physically closer to the characters, to try to see the details of the rooms they live in, the colours of their shirts, the drinks in their hands.

Sometimes, I go back to something Liz Hay once said in a telephone conversation. (I was so excited by what she said that I wrote it down on the back of an old envelope and taped it to my wall.)

Accept the value of a simple sentence. Nothing fancy is required.

K.D. MILLER
Standing Up Naked and Turning Around Very Slowly

MY IMAGINATION was fostered in the basement of 282 East 15th Street, Hamilton. It was an unfinished basement, with cinder-block walls and a cement floor. By the time my brother and I were teenagers, we could entertain friends in a typical sixties rec-room, complete with fake wood panelling and snooker table. But during my childhood, the basement was a cold, damp, dark place that I associated with dungeons and torture chambers.

Certainly, there were complicated instruments down there that could do a lot of damage, and sometimes did. The wringer washer, for instance, that my mother got her hand stuck in twice. Even when it wasn't crushing hands, the wringer was a fearsome thing, taking billowing, sudsy clothes in on one side and extruding them flat and defeated on the other.

Then there was my father's table saw. It had a circular blade whose jagged teeth spun into smoothness that was horribly tempting to touch. When wood was fed to those teeth, it actually screamed – a high, keening shriek that tightened every muscle in my body. It didn't help that my father was an amputee, having lost his leg to blood poisoning as a boy. Or that his father had fainted while running his own table saw, and lost a finger. By the time I was five or so, I had seen enough stumps and was sufficiently familiar with the concept of loss of limb that I could never hear the sound of wood screaming in the basement without imagining somebody being cut up.

Finally, there was the burning fiery furnace. We burned coal well into the fifties, necessitating a coal bin – a wooden shed-like structure filled from a basement window. The furnace itself had twisting metal arms like a squid, and a grilled door in front that my mother opened with a

129

pot holder before shovelling in the coal. Years later, when studying theatre history, I would come across that ubiquitous prop of medieval religious drama – the hell-mouth. No matter how ghastly these things were, with dripping teeth and mechanical jaws that chomped the howling actors, they had nothing on the writhing flames I glimpsed whenever my mother opened our coal furnace door.

I was in fact never punished by being locked in the coal bin. Nor were the fiery furnace, the table saw or the wringer washer so much as invoked as means of keeping my brother and me in line. But they were *there*. When I heard about Shadrach, Meshach and Abednego in Sunday school, I saw them being marched down the steep, open-backed stairs of our basement and squeezed through the door of our furnace that somebody in biblical garb held open with a pot holder. And when I read in school about Fathers Brébeuf and Lalemant being tortured by the Iroquois, I couldn't help reflecting that at least they had been spared the table saw and the wringer washer.

It would be fair to say that I was a rather morbid child. But I came by it honestly.

My mother, Isabel Milne Barclay, was a talented artist and a frustrated actress. She was born into a nouveau-riche family that measured all things in terms of dollars and cents. Though her parents could easily have sent her to the Ontario College of Art (the way they sent her three brothers to Ryerson) they saw no purpose in educating a girl, and ridiculed her dream of becoming a commercial artist. Obediently, she quit school, got a factory job earning 'good money' (a phrase I grew up hearing) and in a matter of weeks suffered a complete nervous breakdown.

She came out of it (God knows how, in that punishing, Presbyterian atmosphere) determined to do something with her art. Those were the days of hand-tinted photographs. She apprenticed for six months in a photography studio, learning to colour and retouch. While she was there, she met a framer named Robert Edgar Miller.

At the age of fourteen, my father got blood poisoning in his right foot. It spread, necessitating several operations that finally left him with his leg off above the knee. His mother died of a stroke shortly before or after this – I'm not sure which, because my father hardly ever talked about himself, and never indulged in self-pity. In fact, though I grew up seeing his artificial leg leaning in a corner of my parents' bedroom and his stump poking out the leg of his swim trunks at the beach, I was fully ten years old before I became consciously aware of him as a man with a handicap.

The father who appears in the stories 'The Lure' and 'Egypt Land' is a very accurate portrait of my own father, so much so that the 'Bill' stories could be called creative non-fiction. I have always found him relatively easy to write about, perhaps because he was my 'easy' parent – the one who was kind, rational and even-tempered. Also, his major hurts were external – the loss of his leg, the early death of his mother, the extreme poverty his family suffered during the Depression and the major stroke that left him wheelchair-bound in his sixties.

My mother, on the other hand, was inwardly wounded, and remains the most unhappy human being I have ever known. June Chandler, who appears throughout my second book, *Give Me Your Answer*, is a pastel-tinted, overly retouched portrait of Isabel Miller. In only one story, 'To Hell and Back', do I come close to biography – so much so that I seriously considered pulling it from the collection.

My mother was as close to being a recluse as a woman with a husband and two children can be. She had no friends, and could hardly bear to attend family gatherings. She was plagued by headaches, and very likely addicted to the 222's I was constantly being sent to the drugstore to buy for her. Judging from the cycle of her depressions and rages, she might also have suffered from seasonal affective disorder. Her life was dominated by worries and fears that, however groundless, shrivelled her talents and sapped her joy.

Yet she managed to give my artistic attempts all the praise and encouragement her own had been denied. Using her story as a negative example, I determined early on to escape the attitudes and influences that had blighted her. The distance between Hamilton and Guelph, where I got my BA, is nothing in terms of miles, just a forty-five-minute drive. In terms of the psychological energy I needed to get out of Steel Town, however, it might as well have been the distance to the moon.

But I'm getting ahead of myself.

I was lucky to grow up at a time when Ontario public schools still offered an excellent education, and in a household where reading was tantamount to breathing. Even my brother, who hated school until he got to university, was always reading something – comic books at least, or Hardy Boys or Zane Grey. I was read to both before and after I could read for myself, most often by my mother, whose voice and delivery were those of a born actress. I remember her serializing *Heidi* for me into half-hour bedtime chunks. Sometimes she would pause and study the text before going on, mentally paraphrasing sentences like 'Heidi was not to be hindered in her kind intentions' for my six-year-old ears. Later, when I was able to handle the language, I read *Heidi* for myself. I read other books in stages too – starting with the Classic comic book versions of *Oliver Twist, Jane Eyre* and *Frankenstein* (whose nightmarish illustrations fascinated me) before moving on to the real thing.

At the library, I was allowed to borrow adult books on my parents' cards, as well as children's books on my own. No reading matter was ever forbidden me – another piece of luck. I had a friend who was not allowed to read comic books, Nancy Drew or anything else her mother considered trash. One day when I was visiting her, I picked up a book her parents had borrowed from the library. 'Put that down!' my friend said. 'I'm not allowed to look at it, so neither can you!' The book was *How to Encourage Your Child to Read.*

What did I read? Well, starting with *Black Beauty,* just about every horse book ever written. (I was as horse-crazy as Arley is in 'The Ice Horse'.) Gods fascinated me too – Zeus and Glooscap, Odin and Loki and Manitou. Their stories were as familiar to me as the Jesus stories I heard in Sunday school. In between horses and gods, I read everything by Louisa May Alcott, all of Laura Ingalls Wilder's *Little House* books and all the *Anne* books, plus the obligatory Nancy Drews and Trixie Beldens. I was very taken with Susan Coolidge's *Katy* books, especially *What Katy Did at School.* I had a *thing* about boarding schools, and was convinced that if I could attend one, I would be a completely different person. Someone like Rose Red, the girl in the *Katy* books who is loved in spite of, or perhaps because of, the 'scrapes' she keeps getting into. Rose Red was likely the first of a character type I've always admired in fiction and in life – someone who not only sticks out like a sore thumb but takes pride in doing so.

I had the first part down pat. In school I used to look at other little girls – docile, feminine, interested only in their dolls, their hair and the contents of their plastic purses – and envy what I took to be their easy, uncomplicated lives. For all I might admire Rose Red, I still yearned to fit in with the crowd. My high marks and my artistic talent tended to put me in the spotlight, as did my 'compositions', which teachers liked to read aloud to the class. Though I was not friendless, I lacked a social role model. When it came to dealing with my peers, I more or less had to make it up as I went along.

So I became a watcher and a listener. I would observe ordinary exchanges between people, then run them over and over in my mind like films. Anything spontaneous or natural was strange to me. Maybe that's what made me an artist. I've always felt a strong impulse to depict my own life. To enact it somehow. Record it.

Drawing was my first writing. The pictures I made with crayons and finger paint told stories, and were increasingly bedecked with wobbly, misspelled words.

As I graduated to charcoal, watercolour and oil paints, my subject was almost exclusively the horse. Horses still obsessed me – their beauty, their speed, the universal love they seemed to attract. I lived for my weekly rides at the local stables my father drove me to, though 'ride' is a bit of a misnomer. Usually, the horse just stood there and grazed, ignoring the heel and rein commands I had taught myself from diagrams in library books. Once, my mount lay down and fell asleep, leaving me standing on the ground with a large, snoring animal between my stirruped feet. But I never gave up hope. It was the *drama* of the ride I was forever seeking and never finding. The danger, the freedom, the strangeness of communing with a creature of a different species.

By junior high school, I was taking English riding lessons and starting to jump, after a fashion. But riding is an expensive hobby. There's only so far you can go in the equestrian world before you simply have to own your own horse. Other things were coming to an end too as I approached my teens. Drawing and painting were suddenly not enough. I was feeling restless – wanting to express myself in some bigger, grander way.

I don't remember being suddenly stage-struck. The attraction developed gradually. Though I had always enjoyed acting in school plays, I assumed my teachers gave me the larger speaking parts because I had a good memory. I couldn't help noticing, however, that whenever I was on stage, people actually laughed or were quiet in the right spots.

My first published story, 'Now, Voyager', is narrated by an unnamed 'I' who idolizes an eccentric, slightly glamorous elocution teacher living up the street. Well, an eccentric, slightly glamorous elocution teacher *did* live up the street. Marie Jean, or Miss Jean, as I called her in fiction and in life, was like a little dot of colour in the greyness that was Hamilton in the fifties. Her French name and her being Catholic were enough to make her exotic in my eyes. But there was also the way she spoke – as if words were more than conveyors of information. As if they had colour and shape. As if speech could be music, or painting, or even dance.

Besides the influence of Miss Jean, there was my mother's girlhood infatuation with movie stars, which she managed to pass on to me. I still have the book of charcoal sketches she did from photographs in movie magazines of the thirties and forties – Bette Davis, Clark Gable, Joan Crawford, etc. She and I would check the *TV Guide* each week to see what was going to be playing on *Saturday Night at the Movies*. All that week, she would act out bits for me of *Now, Voyager, Dark Victory* or whatever melodramatic weepy we were going to see. By the time Saturday night rolled around, I was so pumped that the real thing could not possibly live up to my expectations. But for days afterwards, I would be Greer Garson in *Random Harvest* or Barbara Stanwyck in *Stella Dallas*. 'You like *old* people!' a classmate accused me one day when we were listing our favourite movie stars. It was true. I was living in the wrong decade.

But at least I had discovered what I wanted to do. From junior high on, the energy I had reserved for riding and art was poured into acting. I still have the dog-eared copy of the book that became my Bible in those days – Bette Davis's *The Lonely Life*. Over and over, I would read her account of the turning point in her career – the night she got her first standing ovation, hours after being dumped by her fiancé because she wouldn't quit acting: 'It is impossible to describe the sweetness of such a moment. You are at once the indulged beloved and the humble lover. Alone! All those marvelous people. My heart almost burst. This was the true beginning of the one, great, durable romance of my life.'

I rode around on that emotional bubble for five years. My first 'grown-up' part, which I played at the age of twelve, was Anne Sullivan in *The Miracle Worker*. In high school, I was Portia in a scaled-down *Merchant of Venice*, and, though I neither sing nor dance, managed to steal a few scenes of the musical *Bye Bye Birdie* as the protagonist's possessive, manipulative mother. I won Best Actress in the 1967 Hamilton District Collegiate Drama Festival as Winifred in *Impromptu*, an expressionistic, all-the-world's-a-stage one-act whose playwright's name I've forgotten. Winifred is a cynical, abrasive actress who knows she's third-rate and takes it out on everybody around her. Playing her was something of a breakthrough for me. I had a reserve of anger that found an outlet in Winifred and brought her to life. In turn, she left me with a taste for the unsympathetic characters I still have the greatest sympathy for, on the stage and on the page. I'm particularly fond of unreliable narrators. The ageless, genderless speaker in 'Rocks' and the three stories narrated by Raymond Mayhugh in *A Litany in Time of Plague* all gave me a chance to act with my pen – great fun.

But back to high school. For all the experience and confidence I was gaining, I was also picking up every bad stage habit going. I had a good voice and a strong presence. Unfortunately, I also had an eye and ear for theatrical cliché. My acting was essentially mimicry – all slick, hollow surface.

I was riding for a fall, and I took it, in first year university. At Guelph, I began to learn the hard way what Rosalind Russell meant when she said, 'Good acting is standing up naked and turning around very slowly.'

'I suspect that line was so beautifully delivered that I shall always wish I could have *heard* it.' Well, *I* shall always wish I could bring Robert Shafto back to life, grant him immortality and let him teach every young person on earth. It wouldn't matter what he taught – acting, geometry, flower arranging – because his students would learn lessons in diligence, integrity and respect for the task at hand that would last them the rest of their lives.

In my second semester at Guelph, I was disappointed to learn that I would be taking Acting 100 from Mr Shafto. I had wanted to be in Dr Murphy's class, because Dr Murphy was young, good-looking and peppered his speech with sixties buzzwords like relevant. Mr Shafto, on the other hand, was rumoured to be almost sixty, and talked like a Dickens character. I had a more personal reason to want to avoid him, however. In first semester, I had been cast in the leading role of Sophie in Peter Shaffer's *The White Liars,* a one-act directed by a fourth-year student whose staff adviser was none other than Mr Shafto. He would drop in to rehearsals and speak quietly to her in the shadows beyond the stage. Out of the corner of my eye, I would see the glint of his glasses or the shine of his white hair, and feel vaguely uneasy until he left. Though nothing was ever said, I had the impression that he disapproved of me.

But what did it matter? On opening night, it was obvious that I was making a brilliant debut. The compliments I was getting from both students and faculty all but drowned out Robert Shafto's pointed silence.

After a couple of weeks of Acting 100, I began to relax with him. He was a gentle, courteous teacher who managed to find something positive to say about what each of us was doing. An early assignment was a dramatic reading of the poem 'Richard Corey'. He used my delivery of the phrase, 'he glittered when he walked' as an example of taking a line and making it one's own. So one day I asked him what he had thought of my performance last semester.

Thirty-two years later, I still remember every word of his reply. 'You were acting from the chin up,' he said. 'Nothing was felt. There was no heart. No gut. Furthermore, you were monitoring your every word and gesture in such a self-complimentary manner that I was nauseated. As late as three days before opening, I was begging your director to replace you. Any other actress in the department, script in hand, would have been an improvement.'

Those words look so cruel in black and white. In fact, they constitute one of the greatest kindnesses I have ever received. Shafto was saying what I had been suspecting for some time. My first reaction was relief, followed by a growing exhilaration. The false apprenticeship was over. At last I was going to start to learn to act.

It was like returning to the womb. Being remade, cell by cell. 'You took a step forward,' Shafto would say after calling *Cut.* 'I did not understand that forward step. And *my* not understanding it was a direct result of your not understanding it. Please take that step back. And if you do step forward again, do it for a *reason.* Do it because you *want* something, and taking that step is the *means* of getting it.' And so it would go, with every step, every gesture, every word, every tear. Nothing superfluous was allowed – nothing affected or easy or just thrown in for show. ('It should *cost* you something to act!') Cliché, he impressed upon me, was the hallmark of dishonesty. Worse, of cowardice. And the way to reach an audience was not to play directly to them but to make them cease to exist through total immersion in the character and the world of the play.

Needless to say, what I was learning during those thirteen weeks in Robert Shafto's class was not just how to act but how to live. And how to write. To this day, whenever I get bogged down in pedestrian prose, I hear Shafto's crisp diction in my ear: 'It's too easy. It's not costing you anything. Take that step back and start again.'

I had another marvellous teacher at Guelph, Rex Buckle, with whom I am still sometimes in touch. Rex came to theatre via dance, and taught me much about movement, the stage picture and the essential *theatricality* of theatre. In fact, if Shafto served to turn my gaze inward, Rex helped me turn it back out. Time and again, he paid me the compliment of stretching me – casting me against type. So it was that a studious, vaguely religious virgin ended up flogging the Marquis de Sade with her hair as Charlotte Corday in Peter Weiss's *Marat/Sade*. Rex's directorial notes to me during that show were educational in more ways than one: 'With everything leading up to the assassination of Marat, you're being diddled. And when you stab him in his bathtub? That's when you *come*.'

My performance caught the eye of a poet who was finishing his master's degree in English. We became lovers, and in my fourth year I directed his one-act verse play *The Pawns*, which was based on Euripides' *The Bacchae*. This was my first contact with a published author. I remember thinking of his writing, the writing side of him, as something mysterious and strange – a holy of holies into which I could not venture.

My production of *The Pawns* was set up like a chess game, the actors wearing masks and making stylized moves, and the set painted in black and white squares. In hindsight, it was pretty awful. At the time, however, I was convinced I was the next Peter Brook.

I sometimes wonder now what would have happened if, instead of going on to graduate school at UBC, I had done what many of my classmates did – strike out for Toronto and wait on tables while doing the rounds of auditions. This is without doubt my own 'road not taken'. I was a good actor by the time I was through at Guelph. I had played an average of two roles per semester, including the Mother in Luigi

Pirandello's *Six Characters in Search of an Author,* Second Voice in Dylan Thomas's *Under Milk Wood,* the monologuist in Jean Cocteau's *The Human Voice* and Winnie in Samuel Beckett's *Happy Days.* As for directing, though my ambition outweighed my talent, I was energetic and organized, which counts for much when the audience is coming at eight. In addition to *The Pawns,* I directed *Shelter* by Alun Owen, Eugene Ionesco's *The Bald Soprano* and Edgar Lee Masters' *The Spoon River Anthology.*

One morning in 1973, weeks before I was to leave to start my master's in directing, I was working on a costume for one of the shows our summer theatre company was mounting. That afternoon, I would conduct a rehearsal of another show I was directing, and that evening act in a third that was already up and running. At twenty-two, I had applied for and gotten an Opportunities for Youth grant to employ myself and nine of my student colleagues for the summer. We toured parks with a children's show, visited libraries with two puppet shows, gave acting workshops for teenagers and produced three adult plays in between. As the company's artistic director, I was working twelve hours a day, seven days a week, earning $440 a month, and as happy as a clam. The eclectic, labour-intensive jumble of live theatre had me in its thrall. In a few years, I told myself while working on that costume, I would graduate as a journeyman director. Then I would recruit a company and run it on government grants until such time as it could survive on box office alone.

In 1973, this was not an unreasonable expectation for a young person to have. Pierre Trudeau was prime minister and Canadian culture a sacred cow. A future embracing theatre in all its aspects – acting, directing, setting props, hanging lights, balancing budgets – was one I could believe in as unquestioningly as I could believe in the fabric I was stitching.

It occurs to me that this is supposed to be an essay about how I became a writer. Well, one thing I've concluded as a result of rehashing my past is that I am in fact an actor who writes. The exercises I did in acting classes to train my powers of concentration, observation and emotive memory still serve me well as a writer. Knowing how to handle stage fright enables me to relax and enjoy a public reading or an interview.

What I learned as a director comes in handy too. I was taught to 'parse' a script, then go over and over a single line or bit of business until it worked. The recommended formula was one hour of rehearsal per minute of performance. As a writer, I still think in terms of segments of action – acts, scenes, and 'beats', like heartbeats. Sometimes when a story appears to be dying, I turn back into a director and try to revive it as I would a play. 'Why isn't anything *happening?*' I bark at the hapless page. 'What are you supposed to be *doing?*'

But that's the extent of my directing now. At UBC, I bumped my nose on a few hard realities. Academic politics was one of them, plus a degree of sexism (the department head's stated opinion that women couldn't cut it as directors) that simply would not be tolerated now. But in all fairness, I came up most painfully against my own limitations.

Directing, like painting or choreography, requires an 'eye' which I simply don't have. The idea of directing plays appealed to the organizing, controlling side of my nature. That side gets put to good use now in my day job, and sometimes leads me into church committee work. It plays a role in my writing, too. In the *Holy Writ* essay 'Travels with Harold', it appears as the apoplectic King dealing with a group of monks who have washed up on his shore in a boat without a rudder. The monks, of course, are the creative impulse – blind, trusting and, in their childlike way, courageous. The King is the internal editor – potentially as damaging as he can be helpful.

But back to 1978. I did finish my master's degree, more out of spite than anything else, and have not had the slightest inclination to direct a play since. In my years at UBC, I produced several one-acts and two full-length plays, Steve Gooch's *Female Transport* and Tennessee Williams' *The Glass Menagerie*. I also played a number of roles on stage, including Miss Y in Strindberg's *The Stronger* – the part Arley is playing in the story 'Giants in the Earth'.

In my second term, I was given an exercise that would have serious ramifications for me, both artistically and personally. The graduate-level directors were teamed with graduate-level playwrights in hopes that we would all learn something about the process of lifting a play up off the page and onto the stage. Linda Svendsen and Dennis Foon, both now accomplished writers, were among the playwrights. Linda, student then, is now director of the UBC creative writing department. My first choice of script was Linda's *Bags,* a one-act about four young girls camping out in their sleeping bags. But I didn't jump fast enough, so I got to do Dennis Foon's *Peach,* a fantasy about a young man who is socially marginalized by his inability to lie.

Once all the plays had been produced, Dennis and I were the only playwright/director team still speaking to each other. This was pure generosity of spirit on his part, given that I had locked him out of rehearsals at one point and rewritten the final scene of *Peach* myself. (So much for the 'holy of holies' when the audience is coming at eight!)

Workshopping a script taught me much about a play's need to be playable. It left me with a lifelong aversion for self-consciously pretty prose that sits there like a flower arrangement and doesn't *do* anything. It also left me with an ex-husband. In 1974, I became engaged to an actor I had cast as one of the characters in *Peach.* We lived together in Vancouver for five years, then moved east to Toronto, where we married in 1979 and divorced in 1986.

My marriage was essentially the stuff of fiction, and became literally so in the stories 'The Real Halloween', 'Giants in the Earth', 'Requièm', 'Beastie' and 'Sparrow Colours'. As for my divorce, I suppose I can credit it with shifting my focus once and for all from stage to page.

Shortly after we moved to Toronto, my ex and I were signed on by some theatrical agents. The agency regarded us very much as a team, which made things awkward when we split up. It was time to be practical. Though I had been getting some TV and voice-over gigs, I still didn't have my Equity or ACTRA cards. Being suddenly single made my full-time job that much more necessary, leaving me unavailable for stage work.

So I wrote a letter of notice to my agents, thereby effectively closing the door on an acting career. At the same time, however, another door was starting to open.

I'm told that musicians are encouraged to hum or sing a difficult passage of music they are trying to master. The act of taking the notes in, of becoming their instrument, can break down technical and psychological barriers between player and score.

For four years when I was in Vancouver, I was employed by the BC Library Services Branch to tape-record books for the blind. I narrated works by Alice Munro, Margaret Laurence, Margaret Atwood, Marian Engel, Audrey Thomas, Mavis Gallant and many other authors who were coming into their own in the mid-seventies. Though I didn't realize it then, that job was in large part my training as a writer. Not only was I being exposed to significant new works, but I was acting as their 'instrument'. I'm still convinced that the best way to appreciate a piece of writing is to read it aloud. In those four years, I probably learned more about the technique of writing – the rhythm and melody of expertly arranged words – than any number of creative writing classes could have taught me.

Not surprisingly, it was during those four years that I began to write. I had always kept a journal, had produced the obligatory tortured poems as a teenager, and, while at Guelph, had written one very bad play. But now I started to write short stories. At work, I had enjoyed recording Margaret Laurence's collection, *A Bird in the House*. That book in effect gave me permission to write about the ordinary stuff of my own life. My first finished story, 'My Grandmother' (parts of which are recycled in the story 'Give Me Your Answer') got honourable mention in the *Flare Magazine* fiction contest of 1979. The next year, I got another honourable mention for 'Miss Jean', which was a prototype of 'Now, Voyager', the story that won first prize in the *Flare* contest in 1981.

I started submitting stories to small literary magazines, and was greatly encouraged by Bob Sherrin, then fiction editor of the *Capilano Review*, and Roger Greenwald, editor of *Writ*. They each published several of my stories in the eighties and nineties, three of which appeared in issues of the *Journey Prize Anthology*. During those same years, I was short-listed half a dozen or so times in the CBC Literary Competition, winning third in 1990 for 'Inchworm', which was subsequently broadcast.

I have always found the literary community to be a welcoming one. Though there is competition, it isn't nearly as harsh or as personal as in the theatre. For eleven years, starting in the mid-eighties, I was part of a writers' group that met monthly to read aloud written critiques of each other's work. Some of my closest friends are people I met in that group, and we still read and comment on each other's manuscripts.

I kept all the critiques I received over the years from the group for 'The Ice Horse', 'Giants in the Earth', 'Author Of', 'Stigmata', 'The Real

Halloween' and 'A Litany in Time of Plague'. In 1993, when I took two months off work in order to put together my first collection of stories, I made good use of those written commentaries. I then submitted an early version of my first book to the group, who encouraged me to send it out.

So I did. And on July 8, 1993, I picked up the phone at work to hear an English-accented male voice saying, 'May I please speak with K' (pause) 'D' (pause) 'Miller.'

I have sometimes been asked why I write as K.D. instead of Kathleen Daisy. Years ago, when I was working on 'Rocks', I decided the ageless, genderless 'I' was one of the story's strengths. If I published 'Rocks' under 'Kathleen Miller' however, the 'I' would be assumed to be female. So for the first time I signed myself K.D., then decided I liked the ring of the initials.

Anyway, in 1992 John Metcalf had read the story 'A Litany in Time of Plague' in *Writ*, and thought he would like to read more by this K.D. Miller person. 'Litany' is narrated by the homosexual Raymond Mayhugh. There was a lot of nonsense in the air then about voice appropriation, so the bio I composed for that issue of *Writ* contains no pronouns. No one reading it would have had a clue what K.D. Miller was.

John phoned me in 1993 in response to the sample story and query letter I had sent to the Porcupine's Quill regarding my first collection, whose title story is 'A Litany in Time of Plague'. I've never asked him if he was surprised when a female voice answered 'Speaking' to his request to talk to K.D. Miller. I know it wouldn't have made any difference to him, one way or another. Issues of gender, race, ethnicity, sexual orientation, right or left-handedness, never distract John from the task of editing a writer's work. Neither does subject matter. You can write about any-thing from tea cosies to haemorrhoids as far as he's concerned, provided you do it honestly and well. In this, he reminds me of Robert Shafto. I consider myself blessed to have come under the influence of not one but two such masters.

John's editorial notes to me, though few, have always had a theatrical ring. 'The effect of that final page should be one of a slowly closing fist,' he wrote in regard to 'Author Of'. And when I almost abandoned my second collection, *Give Me Your Answer*, because it was getting too autobiographical for comfort, he issued a call to arms: '... you are a writer. That's what you do. That's what you are. ... What's really important is for your work to sparkle and to last. You won't connect with other people unless you connect with the primal material of your life and wrestle it to the ground with elegant and powerful language. ... the unpalatable truth is that if you wish to be important as a writer your allegiance must not be to people but to the perfected arrangement of words on paper.'

Well. I don't think I'm 'important as a writer' yet, and have no idea if I ever will be. I do know that I am happy as a writer. My three books, beautifully produced and fiercely marketed by the Porcupine's Quill, have received favourable attention overall. When *Give Me Your Answer* was nominated for the inaugural Upper Canada Brewery Company Writer's Craft Award (a.k.a. – 'The Guzzler') I reacted much as I have to other short-listings and nominations – first with excitement, then with a kind of agitation, and finally, with relief at being able to get on with my life once the winner (not me) was announced.

Whatever it's all about, it's not about prizes or best-seller lists. (Though I wouldn't turn my nose up at either.) As I confess in my third book, *Holy Writ*, I have a relationship with writing – one that is akin to my relationship with God, and is at the very centre of my life. That makes writing both dangerous and dear. To do it badly – to play safe, take it easy and not let it cost me anything – is to betray what is best in me. But to do it well? That is to stand up naked and turn around very slowly.

A LITANY
IN TIME OF PLAGUE
K.D. Miller

MY PROBLEM is that I'm so bloody conscious of everything. I keep track. God, do I keep track. If I go to a movie, I clip the ad from the paper and glue it into a scrapbook, along with my ticket stub. I keep stories and poems from magazines. Playbills. Christmas cards. I'm obsessed with keepsakes. I must make a mark, leave a dropping. I can't let a moment pass without cataloguing it. Even when I'm drunk I make a mental note of precisely how drunk I am, and the next day remember everything in Technicolor 3-D. No 'Lost Weekend' for this boy.

That's why, when I got home from having lunch with Robbie yesterday, I was able to put a finger on my condition and give it a name. A buzzword, no less. Trauma. I was traumatized. It always surprises me when I commit cliché. Yet here I was, *the* Raymond Mayhugh, fashionably traumatized.

How did I know? Well, the signs were subtle. My heart was trying to thump its way out through my ears. There was a big hole just under my breastbone, as if someone had taken an apple corer to me. But what really tipped me off was the fact that I was sitting in my bedroom closet, in the dark, knees to chin.

Now, I'm not built for foetal position. I'm too long, and too sharp. But I managed to get into it and stay in it for quite some time. It's hard to say how long. Time does funny things in a closet.

And so does the mind. I mean, you're there to avoid, right? So you concentrate on the damnedest things. The way your shoes smell, for instance. You begin analysing the smell: So many parts leather, so many parts sweat, so many parts good old-fashioned stink. And then you begin to wonder why your feet should smell worse than, say, your elbow or forehead. It isn't fair. And once you've established the unfairness of *that,* it's just a teensy mental hop to the Basic Unfairness of Life. And from there –

Oops. I was back to Robbie. I didn't want to be, but I was.

We had met for lunch yesterday afternoon at the Outré. I hadn't seen him for several weeks, and I wondered if he had been pulling himself out of yet another disastrous affair. He did look peaky and preoccupied. So I started right in talking about my book. You have to do that with Robbie, otherwise he casts a damper on everything by being sweetly brave.

So. My book. It's to be a fragmented, cinematic autobiography-cum-novel, sort of like Hellman's *Pentimento.* Dotted with observations, anecdotes and opinions, the way Ephron's *Heartburn* is dotted with recipes. It's been cooking for years, and Sam has finally ordered it dished up. Ordered is right. Jesus, I've never seen her so aggressive. 'It's time,' she keeps saying. 'You're pulling ahead of everybody you've ever been compared with. Stephen King's writing books like clotheslines that sag in the middle. Anne Rice is overexposed. Capote and Poe are both dead. It's time for the focus to be on you.'

Sam gets all fluffed up when she's in heat. She looks like a cross between Emily Carr and Gertrude Stein. She's got that hair and those eyes. Not to mention that figure. But she's a damned good agent. She's had her wet finger in the wind for me for decades now, and she's never been wrong. I may even give in to her on the title. She wants *Just Looking, Thank You* and I want *I Came, I Saw, I Left.*

Anyway. I bitched on cheerfully to Robbie about that, and about editors and advances, blah-blahing away. Oh, I love myself when I'm with book. I'm a blur. I never slow down. Everything but the book just melts into distance behind me.

Everything, that is, except too, too solid Robbie. He stayed right in front of me, and the minute I paused for breath stopped me dead by talking about his soul. His soul. He actually used the word.

'You know, Raymond,' he began in that self-deprecating way that used to get to me, 'I've been looking at my life a bit too, lately. I've been thinking again about the state of my soul.'

Now, Robbie does this kind of thing. I was at a barbecue with him once, where everybody was riding along happily on a bubble of beer. All of a sudden Robbie looked up and said, 'When the Indians were here, the sky was black with birds.' Pop.

Well, I refused to be popped. The calamari had arrived, thank God, so I speared one and held it up. 'Does anyone else know about this?' I asked him conspiratorially. It's what I used to say to him in bed.

'About what? My soul?'

'No. Calamari in lemon-garlic butter. Does anyone else – Oh, never mind.' God, I hate it when someone won't carry the ball.

'I'm sorry,' Raymond,' he said, and I had to smile. When Robbie says he's sorry, he not only looks and sounds sorry, he really is. He has one of those faces that don't change. Even at forty-two, he still looks like an English choirboy. Longish hair, collar up, ears straight out. Eyes.

'I'm sorry,' he repeated. 'It's just something that's been on my mind lately. More and more I find myself thinking back to the way I was when we first met. You remember, don't you, how I couldn't look at three telephone poles without seeing Calvary? Well, I'm starting to think that maybe I really was on a pilgrimage that ...' He shrugged and gave that deprecating smile again. '... that underwent a little detour.'

Oh God. I was bored with this kind of talk when I was an undergraduate. I got bored with it again when Robbie and I had our little affairette twenty-two years ago, and he dumped one religious crisis on me after another. I mean, my phone would ring at some ghastly hour of the morning (on top of everything else, Robbie's an early riser) and I would hear, 'Raymond? Are you awake?'

'I am now.'

'I had to tell you. I had to tell *someone*.'

'What?'

'I kept a vigil last night. I dozed off once or twice, but I meditated most of the time. And Raymond, it *came* to me.'

'What did? The ghost of Christmas yet to come? I hope you helped him.'

'Oh, Raymond. I mean I realized something. About myself.'

'Well what, Robbie? I'm on tenterhooks.'

'I realized that I'm an accidental Christian!'

The trouble with a statement like that is you can't tell someone to fuck off for making it. 'Robbie, what the hell are you talking about?'

'I'm talking about me, Raymond. I just realized that I am a product of western Christendom. My ethos, my world view, my frame of reference, everything is essentially Christian. So there's no more need to struggle with my faith. It's a given, like my hands, or my eyes, or …'

'Robbie, take two altar boys and call me in the morning.'

Well, over lunch, I felt the old familiar boredom setting in again. So I decided to head it off. 'Robbie,' I said, 'about your alleged soul. Two things. First, nobody's come back to tell us what's on the other side of the big D. We're not even sure there's anything to worry about, one way or another. Second, supposing somebody does come back and says, here's the scoop. If you're good, you spend eternity sitting on a stream of Jacuzzi bubbles, sipping Chablis. But if you're bad, you stand forever in a cashier's lineup listening to "Attention, Kmart shoppers" over and over again. So what? What do you do? Change the past? Change what you are? Start taking the homeless out for dim sum?' I speared another tiny perfect squid and gestured at him with it. 'There's no piece of paper inside the box this board game came in, telling you the rules in seven languages.' I twiddled the squid in the lemon-garlic butter and put it in my mouth. 'Where's all this soul crap coming from just now anyway?' I asked when I had swallowed. 'You're not dying, are you?'

'Well,' he said. 'Yes. I suppose I am.' Then he reached out, put his hand on my wrist and said, 'I'm sorry, Raymond.'

The thing about hiding in a closet in foetal position is that it's not the hysterical action it appears to be. Traumatized, yes. Hysterical, no. I was quite calm about hiding in the closet in foetal position, once I had figured out that that was what I wanted to do.

The first thing I did when I came home was go into the kitchen and putter. I cleaned a clean counter, then opened the fridge and stared at the milk, the juice, the coffee. Milk, juice, coffee. Milk, juice …

Well, when the excitement of that finally palled, I closed the fridge door and went up into the living room. I sat on the couch and flipped through a magazine, just long enough to ascertain that it was upside down.

Then up into the study, where I opened and closed my desk drawers a few times, then on to my bedroom, where I sat on the bed and at last eyed the closet door.

Don't think for a minute that the irony of what I was doing escaped me. Back in the closet again. Back where a friend's just a friend.

While I was in there, I tried concentrating on something else, anything else but what Robbie had told me over lunch. The strip of light under the closet door. I stared at that strip of light for a long time. I worked up the courage to nudge it with my foot. The bit of brightness on the toe of my shoe stirred something in my memory. I knew it would come up into my conscious mind. Everything always does, eventually. More's the pity.

Anyway, that's what was happening in Theatre Two of Cineplex Raymond. Theatre One was still showing *My Lunch with Robbie*.

I didn't pull away when Robbie put his hand on my wrist. Not then. I hardly remember getting through lunch. Not that either of us ate anything. For some reason, we didn't think to cancel the order. It was three appetizers and dessert, what we always do. So after the calamari, the soup came and was taken away cold, then the salad came and was taken away warm, then the sherbet came and was taken away soup. Our waiter got a little more arch every time he said, 'Was everything all right, gentlemen?'

Jesus Christ. I was sitting there crying (unobtrusively of course, after all I *am* the son of actors) and Robbie was practically holding my hand, and here was this idiot asking us over and over if everything was all right. I was tempted to blow my nose on the tablecloth and say, 'Lovely, thank you. There's your tip.'

I did dry up eventually, long enough to ask Robbie the requisite questions. Yes, he had tested positive. When? Several weeks ago. Why hadn't he told me before this? He didn't want to alarm me.

Alarm. That's when I pulled away. At least, my wrist moved back, just a fraction. Robbie felt the movement and lifted his hand.

'Look,' I said, putting my hand in my lap. 'I didn't mean ...'

'It's all right,' he said gently.

'Will you put your damned hand down?' I didn't mean to snap, but his hand was still poised in the air, palm toward me, fingertips pink and smooth as a boy's.

'Now look, Robbie,' I said, 'you've been diagnosed as HIV positive, right?' He nodded. This was more like it. I've been lecturing Robbie for decades, after all. 'Well, that's not necessarily a death sentence and you know it. You could go on for years before ... And they're doing research all the time. They're very, very close to finding something.'

He let me gabble on, reassuring myself. He must have known what was ringing in my head. Twenty-two years. It's been twenty-two years. They're not backdating that far, are they? Are they? Of course not. Besides, we were virgins when we met. And we've never run in the same pack, for all it's a small world.

He must have known what I was thinking. He always has. And he just let me go on. Didn't call my bluff. That's what went wrong between us as a couple. He always brought out the worst in me, then forgave it. Presumptuous little –

Anyway, the moment came when there was nothing left to say. All we could do was crumple our unused napkins, pay for our uneaten food (Robbie left a tip, I refused) put on our coats and stand on the sidewalk outside, looking at each other.

I did ask, dry-mouthed, if he wanted me to come back to his place with him. He shook his head and smiled. I wish I had left it at that. But oh no. I had to say, 'Is there anything …?' with just enough of a pause to cue him to raise that hand again and stop me.

Damn him. Damn me. But the thing is, if the question had been fully asked, Robbie might just have answered it. And he might have said what he said twenty-two years ago. 'Stay with me until I fall asleep.'

But the moment passed, as moments do. And the light changed. And I went my way, and he went

His.

The Brave Time. There it was. The memory triggered by that strip of light under the closet door.

The Brave Time. My mother whispering, 'This is the Brave Time, darling,' then kissing me briefly and disappearing in a waft of Pancake Number 2 Fair. Then my father saying, 'Time to be brave, old fellow,' and scrunching my hair and waggling my head before disappearing too. His pancake was Number 7 Swarthy, but it smelled the same.

The Brave Time was something they had cooked up to keep me quiet in the wings while they were both on stage. God forbid that I make a fuss and distract the audience.

Jesus. I can't have been more than four when my memory of this kicks in. I was in the wings because my parents were on the road, hotels were sleazy and babysitters cost money. This was, of course, before they became *the* May Mallory and *the* Hugh Andrew.

150

Oh, it probably wasn't as bad as it sounds, or as bad as I remember it. There would have been other actors milling around. And they would have smelled like my parents and fussed over me as actors do over children. And there would have been stagehands and of course a stage manager with two eyes on the script and a third eye on the stage. These were frequently women, but even as men they would have had that worried, motherly air that stage managers always have.

So there was nothing going on that a social worker today could rubber-stamp as neglect or abuse. All that was happening was that a four-year-old boy had cold armpits and bags under his eyes night after night from trying to be his parents' salvation. If I'd had a moustache and a briefcase, I would have looked as middle-aged as I felt.

Because it was a job. Make no mistake. And I did it well. Sometimes there was just a single thickness of velour between me and big, black Audience that must never know I was there. Once I put the tip of my foot into the strip of stage light between the floor and the hem of the teaser. The teaser moved a little, rippled all the way up its height, like a black waterfall. I pulled my foot back, wondering in near panic if I had destroyed illusion, as my mother would say.

You see, I really believed that if I destroyed Illusion, then black, eyeless Audience would swallow my parents whole. And Illusion was such a fragile thing, so easily destroyed. A noise backstage, a flubbed line, and brick wall shivering like the painted canvas it was, and poor Illusion had had it. I pictured her as a thin, anxious-eyed lady forever wringing her hands. Not much protection for my mother and father, but all they had. All I had too.

So I sat still as death in the wings, listening to my parents' stage voices, preserving Illusion with every ounce of my four-year-old self, wishing desperately that the scene would end and my mother and father could step safely back out of the light.

Brave Time indeed. Sucker Time more like it. My God. No wonder I became 'the intellectual's Stephen King' and 'Capote in eclipse'. No wonder the first time I sat down to write, out came oogah-boogah. I was fucking terrified.

Everything backstage is *alive.* It has a kind of heightened reality, a life of its own. It waits, the way a vampire in his coffin waits for sundown. It can't move, but it's aware of you, and it's just waiting to get you.

The jealousy of props. The way the eyesockets of a mask look at you and hate you for being animate. The way a silver-painted wooden hatchet yearns for your neck. There was a coffin in one place I had to sit and wait. And in another, there was a guillotine, complete with neck-notch and basket and blade poised high. I kept my eyes on the knotted rope that held the blade suspended. Were its fibres fraying? Was it slowly, like a snake, working itself out of its knot? Would the blade fall with a clang and kill Illusion once and for all? And if I ran and tried to catch it, would it slice me in half?

The saddest thing is, until I told Robbie about all this (Robbie again!) I didn't realize how much power I had. He had to point it out to me.

'Do you know what you could have done, Raymond?' he said, elbow propped on pillow, cheek resting on hand. We had just been to bed for the first time, and were doing the tell-me-all-about-yourself-I-want-to-know-everything bit. 'To put an end to all that nonsense?'

'What?' I asked, trying to sound indulgent. Robbie had told me beforehand that he was a virgin. I never told him.

'You could have destroyed that wimp Illusion once and for all, and probably have gotten a roar of approval from Audience, just by running out on stage and yelling for your mother and father to come and take you home.'

As I said before, Robbie does have a way of popping things. I had sensed all along that he was not impressed by the fact that I was The Son Of. But he really popped it when he said what he did. I actually felt something go pop inside me, maybe that last little bubble of awe I still had for my parents.

Because I'll give them this much. They were beautiful, my parents. Oh, they were gorgeous. A pair of lovely, talented children who really believed that the lives they were living had something to do with reality. For what it's worth, my head is still full of the love songs they sang to each other on stage:

'Someday I'll find you,
Moonlight behind you ...'
'I'll see you again
Whenever spring breaks through again ...'

Oh dear. Picture a grainy, smudged newspaper photograph. There's my father looking manfully into the camera, my mother looking adoringly up at him, and me not knowing where to look. I was horribly shy of the media then. Hated the spotlight. My, how we change. Anyway, the accompanying article, a puff from a local rag in one of the thousands of burgs my parents dragged me through, would read something like this:

'Family comes first for the increasingly popular team of Mallory and Andrew. Their names may be in lights, but their hearts are with their son, five/ten/fifteen year old Raymond.

'With her unique combination of vivacity and warmth, May Mallory insists, "Raymond is the one we do it all for. And we just don't know what we'd do without him." Her big eyes are moist as she reaches for her son's hand. He twists away, as embarrassed as any five/ten/fifteen year old at a mother's open affection, and perhaps showing some of the shyness unique to actors' children.

'His father, compelling stage presence Hugh Andrew, laughs heartily and concurs. "It's been a different sort of life for Raymond. He's had a lot to get used to. He's changed schools every year or so. Sometimes he's had tutors on the road. But I think it's been character-building in a way. He's old beyond his years, aren't you, son?" He attempts to ruffle the boy's ducking head ...'

I showed Robbie one of my scrapbooks, chock-a-block with this kind of trash. His one comment was, 'Mayhugh. May and Hugh. Did you make your name up or did they?'

'They did. They made their own up, too. My father's name was Carel Idachuck and my mother's was Olive Blount. He gave himself the two first names he couldn't decide between, and she named herself after an actress-cum-whore aunt of hers who boarded the *Titanic* once too often.'

'Mother of God,' Robbie said, still flipping through the scrapbook. I had brought it to bed to show him. 'When did it hit you?'

'What?'

'That your parents couldn't possibly love you. When did you really know it?'

'Oh, for God's sake!' I said. 'I *hate* that kind of self-indulgent crap. It reminds me of everybody's very first short story. The Big Bad Mummy-Daddy. No matter what the story's about, the Big Bad MummyDaddy is at the centre of it.'

'All right,' he said softly. 'I'm sorry.'

But I couldn't let it go. Because of course, Robbie had *really* popped it that time, and I was hurting. I shoved the blankets down and swung my feet out of bed. But then I just sat on the edge. I had meant to get up and walk out of the room, but I didn't. I wish I had. No I don't.

'My parents did what they could,' I said, sitting on the edge of the bed and feeling Robbie's eyes on me. I wished I was wearing something. I could imagine how white and vulnerable my bare back looked to him. 'What's more important,' I went on in my lectern voice, 'they did what they wanted. That probably made them more loving toward me than they would have been if we'd all lived together in a bungalow and she'd made meatloaf and he'd sold shoes.'

It was bullshit, of course. That was the first time Robbie ever saw through me. He was right on both counts. I *should* have run out on stage and hollered at the two of them to stop fucking around trying to be Noel and Gertie, and just be my parents. And there *was* a moment when I realized that they did not love me and never had and never would.

You see, I did my job so well, I preserved my parents in such perfect illusion, I stayed so quietly in the wings that they hardly knew I was there. And what was the payoff? What was my big reward? One moment. One very, very bad moment of standing (where else?) in the wings, watching them onstage.

How old was I? I could have been six or sixteen. Whenever the penny finally drops, precise time and place become irrelevant. But I do remember what I saw and heard. My parents, *the* May Mallory and *the* Hugh Andrew, hand in hand, facing out, singing a Coward medley. Ending with:

'Tho' my world may go awry,
In my heart will ever lie
Just the echo of a sigh,
Goodbye...'

My father's voice was rough. My mother had tears in her eyes. And they were singing to Audience. To Audience. How could I have missed that all those years? Audience, that they had feared and pandered to. Audience that I had protected them from. That was what they loved. Not each other. And certainly not me.

I didn't cry. Not then. No, I continued to be very brave in the wings of my parents' lives. I was braver still when I was twenty and they were both killed in a highway pileup on their way to Stratford for the season. My bravery was even documented:

'... their son, aspiring writer Raymond Mayhugh, is courageously calm in the face of ...'

No, I didn't cry until I was sitting on the edge of the bed and felt Robbie's arms come round me from behind. He crossed his wrists over my chest and rocked me. He put his cheek next to mine and our faces both stung from the wet salt.

I cried again yesterday in the closet. I cried for the belatedness of that embrace. My God. I was already thirty when I felt those arms come round me. Oh, I had long ago figured out that the girl of my dreams was a boy, but he just never materialized until I was giving my opening lecture for Writing 100 in September of 1968 and looked down and saw Robbie.

Yes, I really was thirty in 1968. Talk about missing the boat. There I was with my nonexistent sideburns and my tie, looking out over a forest of hair. This was the first year a writing course was being offered, so all the artsy fartsies in the world were out there, with their liberal prejudices glittering in their eyes. What I could see of their eyes. There were a few diehards, of course, boys who looked depressingly like me and girls in T-straps and sweater sets. But they would be stomped to death in no time by the peace-signers.

And there was Robbie.

Who was to make me what I am today.

A professional bastard, who trades on being a selfish, cynical S O B.

Now, thanks to Robbie, I'm invited on talk shows to be rude. I'm the Sayer of the Unsayable. I give an opinion and the audience screams in pain. One sacred cow after another is plopped down in front of me, trussed and bound:

The Family: 'Family is an accident that happens to you at birth. If you're smart, you crawl free of the wreckage before you're thirty-five.'

Abortion: 'Only in *certain* cases should it be retroactive, and then *only* up to twenty-two years.'

Capital punishment: 'Are you talking about death or taxes?'

My sexual orientation: 'That sounds like something you have to register for. What I am is a faggot. Can you say faggot? I *thought* you could.'

But how, you may ask, was sweet, angelic Robbie responsible for the spewing of professional bile? Well, the Cult of Nastiness was still yet to be when I looked down from my lectern in 1968 and saw him for the first time. I was, again, thirty, conservatively dressed, well-adjusted and well-meaning. I had progressed from being a good child to being a good adult. In the ten years since my parents' death, I had dutifully gotten three degrees in English and was, predictably, teaching same at Royal University.

The department head had gotten wind of the fact that I not only wrote short stories but had actually published a few in tiny literary journals with names like *Prairie Oyster* and *Wheat Germ*. So he dumped the task of setting up a creative writing program on me. And there I was.

It may be evident by now that I don't believe in a universe that is unfolding as it should. I suppose I believe in a universe that is unravelling as it will. But the fact is, I looked down, saw that angel looking up at me, and felt something stirring between my shoulder blades. Yes, something actually seemed to unfold from me. Okay, so it turned out to be bat wings. At the time, what I felt was a sudden possibility, as if someone had granted me an all-encompassing permission.

So I oped my lips and spake and there came forth the first of my now-famous introductory lectures. I informed the hairy jungle that I didn't give a damn if this was the dawning of the Age of Asparagus. If they wanted to change the world, the parking lot was just outside and soapboxes could be scavenged. If they wanted to plumb their spiritual shallows, the Theology Department would review their applications. If they wanted to exorcize their angst, couches and Kleenex were available down in Psychology. But if they wanted to learn to write, they were welcome to stay put.

Then, over the noise of scraping chairs and departing feet, I gave the ones who dared to stay a bitch of an assignment. They were to analyse Thomas Nashe's *A Litany in Time of Plague* from social, historical, religious and literary standpoints, and Nashe himself as a man of his time and place. Minimum 1,500 words, typed, double-spaced, under my office door before next class. Goodbye, and yes, you may applaud.

Well, the essays trickled in. I only had about twelve students left. Robbie's essay arrived neither first nor last. I kept it. Naturally. Not that there was much to it besides the usual undergraduate straining. But one bit did jump out at me:

'Nashe's dates preclude his having had any first-hand experience of the plague. Moreover, the cleverness of the poem's rhyme and the bounciness of its rhythm give the lie to its earnest repetition of "I am sick, I must die. / Lord have mercy on us!"

'Nevertheless, Nashe both damns and saves himself in the fifth verse: "Wit with his wantonness / Tasteth death's bitterness; / Hell's executioner / Hath no ears for to hear / what vain art can reply. / I am sick, I must die. / Lord, have mercy on us!"

'The plague is the common plague of mortality. The cool tap of its finger has wakened Nashe one night when there was no moon to pick out the gilt in his ceiling. He has lain awake staring up into the unrelieved darkness, and has acknowledged the eternal plague that plagues us all.'

Well. Well well. Not just another pretty face. I asked Robbie to drop into my office to discuss his paper. He took the bait. Trouble is, he swallowed the hook.

Or did I?

I came out of the closet eventually. Yesterday, I mean. Lest you think, dear reader, that I am scratching this on the walls in my own blood by the light coming in under the door, no, I'm all comfy at my big black lacquer-finish desk in my elegant aerie. Robbie helped me move in here eight years ago. Robbie's helped me do all kinds of things. He's always been there, seeing me through. He was there when I quit teaching and stepped out into space. He was there when I published my first bestseller, and my second and my third. Robbie defers. He subordinates himself. He's backup, is Robbie, and he's content to be.

I don't get it, and I never will. I'm a taker. I love grabbing things. The last hors d'oeuvre on the plate. The limelight, especially when I don't deserve it. I'm living proof that you *can* profit through gaining the world. As for losing one's soul, well, if such a thing exists, I've probably managed to hang on to that too. Life being as unfair as it is, I was most likely born saved. Or if not, I saved myself by giving at the office. And that, Ladies and Germs, is what the Brave Time was all about.

Odd. I've never thought of it that way. I always assumed that I was the damned one, and Robbie the saved. I think Robbie assumed it too. It's to his credit that even though he'd been trying to jump Jesus' bones for years when I met him, he never tried to convert me. I'm pretty sure he prayed for me. Now and then for no reason I'd break out in a sweat, or a hair would stand up on the back of my neck, and I'd think, yup, the little bugger's at it again.

I never 'got' this part of Robbie. For all his talk about being an accidental Christian, he put a hell of a lot of work into it. Spent hours of his life apologizing for things he'd done or said or thought that just might have hurt the Cosmic Wimp's feelings.

But for all that, he wasn't what I would call a religious type. He lacked that toothy, psychotic cheerfulness they all seem to have. And he was never a prude.

'All right,' I said to him once in bed, 'are you a Christian when you go down on me?'

'Of course.'

'And does Jesus approve? Does he bless you for doing it? Is it some kind of communion?'

'Yes to all questions.' I guess he saw the look on my face, because he moved closer and kissed me and said, 'Raymond, why do you expect everything to be conditional and exclusive?'

'Because everything is. Welcome to the world, Robbie.'

He shook his head. 'Grace is like rain. That's what everybody forgets. Grace is like rain.'

'Oh, come off it, Robbie. If it's all that easy, why do you keep curtsying and scratching your chest and apologizing?'

'Confession isn't apology.'

'Like hell it isn't. You tell some old man in a dress what you've done wrong all week and he makes you write a hundred Hail Marys on the blackboard, right?'

'Oh, Raymond,' he said, closing his eyes and lying back. 'You have such a talent for getting things just wrong enough.'

'Stop evading. Do you tell the priest about me?'

He opened his eyes. 'Of course I do.'

'You tell a Catholic priest that you're fucking a *man*? Out of wedlock, no less?' He nodded. 'Then what happens?'

He smiled. 'My penances do tend to be a bit on the heavy side,' he said, looking at the ceiling.

'Robbie, for Christ's sake. Can't you see how patently absurd that is? How hypocritical?'

'Absurd, yes. Hypocritical, no.' He propped himself up on one elbow and looked at me earnestly. 'It isn't enough for me to be an accidental Christian any more, Raymond. The church is my dark glass. The thing I must see through. I can't look directly at God. I can't go it alone. I need communion and blessing. My confession is a taking stock of all that. It's an acknowledgement of my separation from God. And as for my penances ...' He was silent and looked away.

'Don't stop now,' I said. 'I'm on tenterhooks, as usual.'

Still looking away, he said, 'Well, the priests do get to know you. It's not all that impersonal. They're just people. They have a job to do and rules to follow. They *must* regard my loving you as sin. And they must impose a heavy penance.' He put a hand on my chest and kneaded me like a cat. 'But they hate it, Raymond. I can tell. I can hear it in their voices. It's almost a penance for *them.* It's as if they're confessing to *me.* The church is their dark glass too.'

Dark glass. Oh my God. Dark glass.

'They're my dark glass, Raymond. Through every one of them, I see you. It's your face, always. I pick them up in order to see you.'

That's Robbie. Drunk and for once bitter. A year or so after I pushed him out of my bed, we met by chance in one of the bars. After the requisite awkwardness, we managed to talk. And drink. I got to the point of congratulating him on landing on his feet. Several thousand times, from what I was hearing.

Christ, I was bombed. Everything appeared to be under water. But I remember Robbie giving me this very naked look, and saying what he said about his partners being a dark glass through which to see me. And I didn't make the connection until now.

Damn you, Robbie. I never asked to be your God. All right, your faith did infuriate me. I resented the way it buffered you from life, from pain. The way it neutralized even my acid. But it never occurred to me to destroy it. I didn't even think I could. I just wanted to get away from it. Which meant, so I thought, getting away from you.

You see, I thought your faith was part of you, Robbie. I respected it, the way you never did. I didn't see it as a teddy bear you would hug when the going was good, kick away when the going got rough, and search the attic for now, when the going's as rough as it gets.

I just wanted to be rid of you. I was tired of being your dark other. Tired of having the worst brought out in me and forgiven by you. You had become my saving grace, Robbie. And who, deep down, does not hate his saving grace?

Oh yes, oh yes. I could go on, adroitly rationalizing what I did to the boy. Even now, as I look back and suppress a shudder, my actions make perfect sense to me.

I had to make him hate me. So I waited until we were at a party. Can you believe that? Out in public, I told Robbie that I didn't want to sleep with him any more. I told him I was tired of him, that sex with him was a bore. That I barely had time for him now, what with all the others.

It was lies. The fact is, I hadn't been unfaithful to him. I just let him think I had been. After all, I intended to be. Starting that night, I was going to build a wall of conquests between myself and him.

Oh, Robbie. I can still see you trying to take some of your drink, and your lower lip crumpling against the glass. Why didn't you throw that drink in my face? Why did you just stand there and try not to cry, then say, 'Raymond, please take me home'?

I tried to duck out of it by putting you in a cab, but you begged me to come with you, which I did with very bad grace. I let you know that I intended to get back to the party, and that I didn't have all night.

I saw you into your apartment, where you started to sob, so I said, 'Robbie, why don't you look at me and see the shallow, selfish bastard I am? I don't know what you do see when you look at me, but the fact is, you could spit through me. So why don't you?'

'Because I love you, Raymond. I'll love you till I die.'

'There's nothing here to love, Robbie. Look, take a pill. Go to sleep. Wake up tomorrow furious with me, which is what you should be now, and go out and get laid.'

That hurt you worse than anything else. When you could speak, in a dry little voice (all your spit seemed to have gone for tears), you said, 'Are you really going back to the party?'

'Yes, I'm really going back to the party.'

'Will you stay here with me until I fall asleep?'

'All right.'

But I didn't. I stayed fifteen minutes then left, pretending not to notice you were still awake, trying to ignore the sensation of your eyes on my back.

I am sitting here now, appalled at my twenty-two-years-ago self. Yes, it does happen. I do sometimes appal myself. After the fact. At the time, I'm so busy collecting evidence of my existence, so exhilarated by my bastardliness, that it's like watching a play. I guess, deep down, I still expect everybody to retreat out of the light when their scenes are over and go to messy little rooms and take off their makeup. But afterwards. Oh, afterwards.

Robbie in fact did go out and get laid. And once he started, he became a legend. With that cherubic face and boyish build, he had no problem, no problem at all. Except, of course, that he lost his God. And he never quite found me again.

But time does do funny things. It turns the stone in your shoe into a hole in your foot. And in time the skin grows over the hole and you forget all about the stone, until one day when it pokes out at your elbow.

Robbie and I inevitably rubbed shoulders, on campus and in bars. He got used to carrying his torch and I to being the unattainable love object. We fell into the habit of having lunch. And though we never touched each other again, in a way the whole thing was like a comfortable old-shoe marriage. Everything was cool. Until yesterday.

Now, I'm afraid nothing is ever going to be cool again. Which wouldn't be a problem, except that cool is my element.

I can be cool about my tears in the restaurant. They were a combination of shock, fear and sentiment for old time's sake. As for my hiding out in the closet, well, I was traumatized, wasn't I? Momentarily paralysed by survivor guilt. And writing this is obviously catharsis. Exorcism. You name it.

But there are two things I can't be cool about. One is the fact that I seem to have miscarried my book. Remember my book? Well, here it is. A bit small. Decidedly premature. But all there is. I wonder what I'm going to tell Sam. Hey, Sam, you know that autobiography you've been panting for? Well, it's a short story. With a Big Bad MummyDaddy smack in the middle.

But that's nothing compared to what else I can't be cool about. The fact is, I have been guilty of a monumental failure of the imagination.

All along, I've assumed that Robbie would be there. At the end of my life, I mean. Not me at the end of his. Oh sure, I'd scamper off, get famous doing this or that. But then I'd come home, and there he'd be. In spite of my having pushed him away, there he'd be.

Of course, there he still is. Except that the situation has changed. Just a little. In time, his hair will fall out in clumps. And he will get horribly thin, like a concentration camp inmate. And at the very end, there will be dementia and diapers. I hate paragraphs that end, 'This isn't the way it was supposed to be.' But this isn't the way it was supposed to be.

How was it supposed to be? Why, with Robbie first as my usher, gently guiding me to my seat in the next world, then as my archivist. My curator. The keeper of my shrine. I've always had a dim picture in the back of my mind of quiet, slow-moving people going through my effects. 'These were the poems he admired,' they say, peeking into my file marked Poems. 'These were his thoughts,' they murmur, reading my diaries. And leafing through my scrapbooks, they intone, 'This was his life.'

I have spent my life laying myself out for burial. I have become my own memorial, my own museum.

And somehow Robbie was to see to it. He was to be there. Cherishing. Loving. All those years, I counted on his loving me. I never for a moment counted on my loving him.

But I do. I do love him. The stone in my shoe has come out at my elbow.

That's bad enough. But far worse is knowing how to assuage the pain. That is terrifying. You see, I could assuage it in one of two ways. I could turn Robbie into words, words, words. I could fictionalize, catalogue and file him. Rationalize him down to nothing and go on adoring myself as much as before. That would be one way. I could do it. Sure I could. I've done it all my life.

Or I could put down my pen and entertain a notion that's been nudging the back of my mind all day. It's not so much a notion as a kind of home movie, jerky and silent, the camera angles awkward.

I see myself sitting on the side of a bathtub, sleeves rolled up, towel over my shoulder. There's a thin little man in the tub. I'm sponging his shoulders, dipping the sponge then squeezing it, dipping then squeezing. I wash him all over. His hairless chest, his shrivelled stomach, his scrotum the texture of flower petals, his penis that trusts my hand.

When he's clean I pick him up out of the water. His head falls against my shoulder and his eyes close. I feel the cool circle of his ear at my neck.

I don't know what I'm going to do. Either way, I'm so very scared. Either way, I am sick, I must die. Either way, Lord have mercy.

As an actor, I was taught that if my audience didn't laugh or cry on cue, it was because I had either blown the timing or simply failed to move them. Again, I'm an actor who writes. So I won't presume to tell anybody how to read a story of mine, much less how to enjoy it. (As if enjoyment were somehow their responsibility, and the lack thereof their fault!)

I'm going to approach 'A Litany in Time of Plague' as an actor would a script. The story is essentially dramatic. Writing Raymond's monologue was, for me, virtually indistinguishable from playing him. But before I start, I have to take a moment to be my own director. A director's first task is to come up with one word or short phrase that expresses in a nutshell what the play is about. Not long ago, I saw a high school production of *Hamlet* that was all about *parents* – specifically, *fathers*. The director had wisely tapped into his teenaged actors' ambivalence toward parental authority, with the result that the many scenes between parents and children just crackled, and Laertes' anguished, 'Where is my father?' was one of the most moving stage moments I have ever witnessed.

But we're not doing *Hamlet*, we're doing 'A Litany in Time of Plague', which I would say is, in a word, about *salvation*. (It helps to know the playwright, and to know that virtually everything she writes is about salvation.)

Time now to switch back to being an actor. What does Raymond *want*? The answer to this question will make sense (or nonsense) out of every step I take on stage. One way to find the answer is to examine other works in which Raymond appears. No, this isn't cheating. Any actor cast as Falstaff or Clytemnestra would be foolish not to study those characters in all their literary manifestations.

So, having done my research, I would say that Raymond wants to save Raymond. (The answer to the question of motive must always take the form of an active verb. It's fine for directors to come up with airy-fairy abstract concepts like *salvation*. But I can't *play* salvation. All I can do is try to *save*.)

In 'Author Of', as a blocked writer, Raymond saves himself from literary starvation by cannibalizing Arley. In 'Lifesaver', he saves himself from a living death by escaping into fantasy. In 'A Litany in Time of Plague', there's a struggle going on, one that is still not resolved at the story's end. The struggle is internal, and it involves Raymond trying to save himself from his own salvation. That salvation consists of first acknowledging his love for the AIDs-stricken Robbie, then putting that love into action by taking his old friend into his own home and helping him to die. ('In time, his hair will fall out in clumps. And he will get horribly thin, like a concentration camp inmate. And at the very end, there will be dementia and diapers.') This prospect both obsesses and terrifies Raymond. It means in effect dying and being reborn as a radically different person. Equally terrifying, however, is the knowledge that he doesn't have to do it: 'I could turn Robbie into words, words, words. I could fictionalize, catalogue and file him. Rationalize him down to nothing and go on adoring myself as much as before.'

Okay. I've got a motivation. I've got a conflict, too. As Raymond, I very much want to save myself. But I want to do it *on my own terms.*

It's time to stop thinking in the abstract, however, and actually shove my feet into Raymond's shoes. What does it feel like to be Raymond? I'm going to sample one brief moment in the script, in hopes that it will contain, the way a single hair contains one's entire DNA history, everything that Raymond is, was and shall be:

My problem is that I'm so bloody conscious of everything. I keep track. God, do I keep track. If I go to a movie, I clip the ad from the paper and glue it into a scrapbook, along with my ticket stub. I keep stories and poems from magazines. Playbills. Christmas cards. I'm obsessed with keepsakes. I must make a mark, leave a dropping. I can't let a moment pass without cataloguing it. Even when I'm drunk I make a mental note of precisely how drunk I am, and the next day remember everything in Technicolor 3-D. No 'Lost Weekend' for this boy.

Catching the essential rhythm of a character is as important as pinpointing his prime motivation. The rhythm of Raymond's speech here and throughout is compulsive and driven: subject/verb; subject/verb; *I* do this; *I* do that. It's restless. I can see him pacing. Throwing himself into a chair. Getting up immediately and pacing again. He's a hollow man and he knows it. The knowledge terrifies him. He tries to drown out his conscience with words, words, words. He tries to fill the hole in the middle of his life with proof of his own existence.

His first words are 'my problem.' They beg the response, 'Who cares?' But that is precisely my task. I have to *make* the audience care. And I can only do that indirectly, by loving Raymond as myself. Which means finding the Raymond inside Kathleen.

An actor is trained to give a very subdued, non-dramatic first reading of a script. Histrionics are discouraged, not only because at such an early stage they would be based on nothing, but also because they could distract the actor from any real stirring of empathy with the character.

Upon rereading 'A Litany in Time of Plague' for the first time in years, I found two passages that brought about that feeling of spooky recognition we sometimes experience when reading a book or watching a play. One of them had to do with Raymond's love/hate relationship with the theatre: 'The jealousy of props. The way the eyesockets of a mask look at you and hate you for being animate. The way a silver-painted wooden hatchet yearns for your neck.' When I read that, I was suddenly back in the unfinished basement of my childhood, imagining the damage the wringer washer and table saw were just dying to do to me.

The second passage that was almost too close for comfort is this one: 'I've always had a dim picture in the back of my mind of quiet, slow-moving people going through my effects. "These were the poems he admired," they say, peeking into my file marked Poems. "These were his thoughts," they murmur, reading my diaries. And leafing through my scrapbooks, they intone, "This was his life." I have spent my life laying myself out for burial. I have become my own memorial, my own museum.' Sometimes my characters have a courage that I lack. In that passage Raymond says so nakedly what I could only gloss with humour in *Holy Writ*: '... I court oblivion by keeping multiple copies of all my reviews, good and bad, clipped together in handy press-release-style packets. I never send a letter without making a copy, and store all letters received in carefully labelled files. And yes, Reader, I do keep a diary, lest, God forbid, my future biographers be in the slightest doubt as to how I spent my days.'

A motive. A sense of the character's rhythm. A growing feeling of empathy with that character. These are the things an actor takes along on what is essentially a journey of discovery. To write Raymond was to play him, which in turn was to learn to love him.

As for the audience, they will laugh or cry, or not, at will.

CURTAIN

DAVID BURR

TERRY GRIGGS
Self-Portrait

I SUPPOSE I have to begin by confessing that my childhood was a normal one, although that word hardly captures how much fun it was. And perhaps it wasn't normal at all. My parents owned a fishing/tourist camp that was located on a large stretch of property on the north shore of Manitoulin Island, near Little Current. This land included miles of shoreline, forests, fields, a river, a bay in front of our house, etc., and it was the work of my childhood to get to know every inch of it. I did not spend hours sitting in my room precociously reading literary classics (with one exception, which I'll get to), but rather spent my days exploring, fishing, swimming, boating, tree climbing and basically just running – if there is motion in my prose, I suspect this early energetic take on the world to be a source.

On the other hand, my temperament was not entirely sunny and blithe. There are several photos of a very young me looking vexed and moody, standing off to one side, brow crumpled, trying to puzzle something or someone out. The child I remember being was dreamy, hypersensitive, empathetic, too easily hurt. I was deeply content with solitary play, although not unsociable, either. The family atmosphere was genial, humour a defining characteristic and a filter through which events were usually viewed. My parents had limited formal educations, but were smart and kind. They no doubt had some of the usual adult troubles, but they also had the maturity not to drag these through the hearts and minds of their children. No improving cultural enrichments were offered, no coddling encouragements of innate talents, but then again there were no crippling expectations, nor pressures to perform or excel. If a writer needs a nasty upbringing, a fund of trauma and deprivation to draw from, my parents didn't provide it.

Books were not entirely absent, although I was hardly a bookworm.

Reading was simply one of many activities, and engaged in lightly, as far as I can recall. There was a modest shelf of books in our living room, cast-offs from somebody's book club – they not only looked, but were, unread. I had books in my room with which I sometimes played library, and I loved cycling to the real library in town. It was a one-room stone building, a converted jail, and had a lovely atmosphere – hushed and greenish, like an indoor glade. The librarian only added to the thrill of it by being mildly alarming – the rouge, the tight perm, the glasses (so fifties!), the raspy voice, the crabbiness a kid might incur by speaking above a whisper. As for what I signed out, books like Enid Blyton's *The Castle of Adventure,* I remember more for their sensuous qualities than their contents: their heft and smell, the texture of the paper, their marks and scars. I was most likely a reader-in-waiting, but my world was secure and full – and it didn't happen. Not even when I read that one classic, or two, *Alice in Wonderland* and *Through the Looking-Glass,* which was a truly illuminating experience.

As my brother and I were the Camp's 'children', we were often fussed over by visitors, made to feel special, taken on excursions, given treats and presents. Not a bad situation, believe me, and I highly recommend it for any kid who can get her hands on it. One day I was invited to go to town with a pleasant smiling woman, couldn't tell you who, and was allowed to choose a gift for myself from the Five & Dime. I considered a number of items and finally settled upon a Whitman Classics edition of *Alice* – cheap, no Tenniel illustrations, but very promising-looking. I read it that day and was struck with pleasure. I was enormously proud of myself, simply for having read it, I suppose, but also to have experienced something so funny and rich – there were words in that book that charmed and absolutely thrilled me. When I got to the end, I signed my name to the last page with a flourish – my first author signing, and my full endorsement of what I had discovered within. *You've stupidly written in your new book,* my brother pointed out. This did not, for once, provoke tears, for I was so brimful of potent satisfaction – had the book rendered me momentarily invulnerable? – that I simply picked it up and read it again, and again. But no others, at least not so memorably.

Which is not to say that there weren't other sources of story. You need look no further than the Catholic Church for a packed and bizarre fund of that. As well, anecdote came with the summer breezes, for our camp was always full of people, many of them American (never tight-lipped), and many of whom returned year after year – so you got the ongoing saga. In town there was a whole community of interwoven narratives of which I was aware (to a degree) and a part. Hence my immediate attraction to *Under Milk Wood* when I later encountered it – I had lived the form.

My parents, too, although they probably would have regarded themselves as unexceptional people, had unusual childhoods, and had lived through the Depression and the war, and not at a safe distance, either. They had stories to tell and knew how to tell them. And there was also a considerable fund of untold stories, from the war mostly, of which I was keenly aware. Here was a troubling and mysterious narrative source, unarticulated, yet so close it was almost tangible to me. It was this, I assumed, that gave my parents, my protectors, their periodic nightmares. Such a circumstance could not help but intrigue a certain kind of child.

The Island is a source I draw from, a place I inhabit imaginatively, and by moving back I wondered at the time if I'd be polluting that source with my actual presence. I don't think it has – the formative experience is safely bottled and still available. Who knows, my living on Manitoulin might free me up to write about other things, might land me somewhere else fictionally. Or, it could lull me right to sleep – a need satisfied.

There *is* something about this place, and I'm not the only one who feels it, but because I am drawn to language, that's where I try to work it out, or simply house it. Islanders who have moved away often have no resistance and end up moving back. (*Don't know why* .... I'll hear them say.) Any number of people who have come here for vacation, either keep returning, or become residents. I met a couple recently who used to travel here four times a year from Switzerland, and finally just moved altogether.

You know that line in Yeats's 'Lake Isle of Innisfree': 'And I shall have some peace there, for peace comes / dropping slow'? It's *that* kind of place. You feel far removed from the rest of the world and its urgencies. Sounds Edenic, I realize, and of course the Island does have its share of grim old realities, and yet it has something else, too, something indefinable that seems to act as a tonic for the spirit. Damned if I know what it is.

* * *

School. I went to it, and was schooled indifferently, as is the Canadian way. As far as teachers go, at least in this out-of-the-way place, you got whatever the school board could catch in their net. At times some pretty strange fish.

My first round, grades one to eight, happened in a three-room Catholic school, although I was not taught by nuns. (Thank *God.*) My performance as a student varied a great deal, since, really, I don't think I got the point of the whole exercise. Sometimes I came up for air and scored respectable marks; other times I plunged into the dreaming depths where I concerned myself with other things. In reading, I was not a 'flying squirrel' as was my friend, Mary Kotva – who later became a veterinarian, interestingly enough – but some other more pedestrian rodent. Nor was I like my brother, who was extremely focused and motivated, *the* top student all the way through. But I discovered something in school – that I loved to write. Stranger still, when I did, it was noticed. There were a few teachers along the way who by the quality of their response, a kind of startled excitement, supported the idea (mine) that this was something I could do.

I recall writing a play once, performing it in front of everyone, the whole school, and kids killing themselves laughing. *Too* funny, was that teacher's dismissive assessment.

In high school, grades nine through eleven, in Little Current, I was active and outgoing, joined all the clubs, played all the sports, won athletic awards, was even the prom queen ... and dashed off heaps of poetry, besides. One time a fellow student recommended a book to me, which she said was *quite good.* I took one look at the title and turned up my nose, for I thought it was going to be about hairdos, make-up, and the deployment of feminine wiles – I was not your run-of-the-mill prom queen. Hairdos indeed, the book was *The Feminine Mystique,* that seminal feminist work. (Ha, ha.) Imagine – reading it might have changed my life.

But my life changed anyway. My parents decided it was time to leave the Island (long story), and moved to Southern Ontario, to a small town near London. So. Talk about paradise lost – and regained – for it was then that happiness in earnest deserted me, and reading in earnest began.

Leaving the Island was only difficult in retrospect, really, for I was game enough at the time, eager to check out the big world beyond the channel. The trouble was, I ended up in another rural community, but one that was completely different from the one I was familiar with. At the high school I attended in Strathroy, I found the students to be dull, narrow-minded, far more knowing than I was, but using that knowing-ness to make life smaller, meaner. Cruelty seemed to be a social style. I was of course no longer in the centre of things, and puzzled by the cliques and the rigid hierarchy of high school popularity. It was mostly the tone of the place that got to me – flat and joyless. So I gravitated toward the more interesting people – the oddballs, the outsiders, the readers. These kids discussed books with enough enthusiasm that I wanted to be part of it. Ray Bradbury, C. S. Lewis, Robert Heinlein ('grokking' and 'water brothers' and all that crazy stuff), all engaging enough at the time, and how could a title like *Stranger in a Strange Land* not appeal? I began haunting the school library (first school I'd been in that had one), where I discovered Dylan Thomas, Aldous Huxley, James Joyce. I ordered a pile of books through a school book club, one of which was *Great Expectations* – I was hooked. Seeing that I was so keen, my brother's girlfriend offered me the books from her university English course: Faulkner, Beckett, Gunter Grass. From my English teacher, Evan Pike, I heard about poets like Gwendolyn MacEwen and Leonard Cohen – *Canadian* writers, what next! This same teacher drove me to Toronto to take part in a poetry competition, where I read a poem of my own as well as my rendition of another from an English text. I won a signed copy of Raymond Souster's *Ten Elephants on Yonge Street* for my 'unusual' recitation, but not, alas, for my own poem.

All in all, it might seem that I took refuge in reading, although I think it was more that I found in books the fascinating world I had been expecting to find when I left the Island. The odd thing was how suddenly I was there, smack dab in the house of fiction, lounging about easy as you please. At one point my English teacher asked me (the expert) to assess an anthology of poetry he was thinking about teaching. Anyway, it helped me take revenge on the serious boredom my surroundings were causing me. Once, in math class, I insisted on reading a poem aloud, and did, while my poor harassed teacher hovered in the front of the room with a sick smile on his face. I can still hear one of the other students muttering *shut up* under his breath. Not everyone is susceptible to poetic revelation, I guess. Actually, it took me a while to figure that one out.

Your book, *The Speaking Earth,* I came upon a little later, as I see the publishing date is 1973. With that title and its cover – a close-up photo of field grasses – I would have been immediately drawn to it, since it brings together something I find irresistible – a natural and a verbal intricacy.

I started university in 1972, a couple of years after leaving high school, after travelling in Europe and Mexico, and just generally goofing off. At twenty-one, in my last childhood act of trailing after my older brother, I enrolled at Western in London, Ontario – his Alma Mater – which I only discovered later to be a conservative and rich kids' university. He studied economics and law – I didn't. The sentiment in the air at the time: arts degrees are useless, study something that will lead to employment. So, taking the bull by the horns, I decided to major in anthropology – plenty of employment in that field surely, whatever the hell it was. I had also tried a journalism course in my first year, thinking I might do that, but part of the program was taught by a man named Brian Keyes, if I remember correctly, whose whole nutbar course was devoted to 'subliminal seduction in advertising' – all those phallic images in cigarette ads that made people rush out in droves and buy particular brands, was the gist of it. He gave my assignment a low grade, and made some negative comments, to the effect that I didn't know how to write and would likely never learn. I don't think I believed him, but it was shaming nonetheless, and so off I went to tackle the cattle culture of the Masai, and *The Raw and the Cooked,* and mother-brother-sister-son relationships. Filiation is a racehorse, I wrote on one of my exams ... yes, well, I didn't last too long in that particular discipline, either.

After dropping anthropology, I hightailed it to the English department and signed up for the honours program, which is what I had longed to do in the first place. My plans were vague – I can always teach, or go into law, I explained to those who never do get the point of a liberal education, although I had no intention of doing the latter, and the thought of teaching always makes my heart sink. I did know that I wanted to immerse myself in poetry and literature and be in the presence of those who felt the same. The cut-throat politics of English departments are well known and lately they seem to be packed with careerists, books being merely objects they climb on to get to the top.

But at the time, I felt I had found my place, or at least a place where I could comfortably indulge a passion. This was pre-theory, before literary study became a 'science', and no one had yet declared authors irrelevant. I had some terrific classes, and naturally tended to gravitate toward the teachers who were also writers – Stan Dragland, Don McKay, Les Arnold, and later, Larry Garber and James Reaney. In my first year, I had figured out how to write an essay (surprising my teacher, Tom Tausky, by actually taking his improving comments to heart), and thereafter began to play with the form. I had creative energy to burn, and this is where I did it – I wanted to see how flexible the essay was, how it could be blown open, or tightened, or invigorated. I wrote a number of collage essays, which included visual materials, used odd packaging – once a tiny essay in a discarded balloon bag – even wrote one in heroic couplets. Amazingly, people were quite open to this, and where not, I still tried to infuse the essays with a different or unexpected approach. Western did not offer creative writing courses at the time. If they had, I probably would have taken them, although the idea of 'writing workshops' and all that makes me want to clear the area – fast.

As far as university life goes, I didn't get very involved, and stayed pretty much on the periphery of things. I socialized some (more with teachers than students), read and studied, and worked part-time to pay my way. I felt busy enough, and writing, outside of some poetry here and there, I deferred to a later date. I did plan on getting to it, though.

The writers who engaged me most at the time, outside of the 'myriad-minded' Shakespeare, were the modernists – Woolf, Forster, Lawrence, and among the poets, Wallace Stevens, T. S. Eliot, Theodore Roethke. And, closer to home, Don McKay and Michael Ondaatje. (Michael, a friend of Stan's, often came to London in his pre-fame days, and gave marvellous readings, which were of course followed by some fine parties.) When I went on to graduate school – the motivating factor being money; I received a scholarship – the one thing that irked me particularly was the attitude of many grad students to the writers they were studying – a kind of chummy, gossipy equality, as though we were all pals hanging out together. Some essential respect for the work was being eroded, and maybe I was beginning to see the whole endeavour as a bit parasitical. At any rate, after a year of it I realized that I'd had my fill of schooling – I had developed a definite immunity to the classroom. After

I graduated, I was as unemployable as ever, and since I regarded 'career' and 'vocation' as entirely separate matters, I thought I should at least get on with the latter and more important of the two.

To backtrack a moment, I did during my undergraduate time take a year off, and it was then that I started to switch from poetry to prose. The first story I wrote was about St. Teresa of Avila, my patron saint, which, I suppose, is as good a place to start this transcendent business as any. (The Catholic Church required the infants in their flock to be christened with saint's names, and my parents seemingly complied ... I've only recently discovered that I was actually named after a favourite movie star of my mother's – Teresa Wright.)

My MA thesis dragged on a bit – I finished in 1979 – and shortly after that I began to write, with no intention of letting up, even though it was pretty stop-and-go. The first thing I discovered was how difficult it was to sit still. Skittish, dodgy, too easily deflected into reading, I was nonetheless determined to get something down, and did eventually. I wrote three or four stories and started sending these out to the literary magazines, having picked up the idea that this was part of the process.

Early on, I had gotten into the practice of showing my efforts to Stan Dragland, whom I had met in my second year, almost the moment I stepped into the English department. I took his course in Canadian literature, and, like many others, was immediately drawn to his unpretentious manner, his humour and his creative intelligence. Sensitive to what you were about, he also gave sharp editorial advice, good news or bad still encouraging of the work at hand. Curiously, I ended up in that same CanLit course twenty-five years later, no longer the student, but, thanks to Stan, the one whose book was being studied. Anyway, Stan became my unofficial editor, and for a while there, along with another writer-friend, Jean McKay, we passed stories around looking for some trusted, but objective, feedback.

There were writers-in-residence when I was an undergraduate – Margaret Avison, Margaret Laurence, Alice Munro – but I would never have even considered approaching them. Too shy, for one thing, and I wasn't too clear on what exactly their function was. (I remember sitting a few seats behind Alice Munro on a downtown bus, thrilled, and watching her with acute interest as she stared out the window, taking it all in.) After I began writing my stories, a friend who was in charge of the writer-in-residence program urged me to make an appointment with the current one – Matt Cohen. I did, and we had the most hilariously uncomfortable encounter, as I could scarcely speak, and, no doubt infected by my reticence, he didn't do much better. I had given him two stories, one entirely forgettable – he tried to make helpful remarks without being crushing – and of the other, he said only that it should be published, and in *Canadian Forum,* and here was the address. The interview was spare, but the advice was excellent, with almost a touch of magic in it, or so I thought. I did send it, and it was accepted – my first acceptance. Keep writing, Sam Solecki, the editor then, had jotted on a note, and those two words of encouragement I floated like a little banner in my head for years. That story was 'Harrier', which appeared about a year later in 1982 – with none other than Alice Munro on the cover. Not long after this, I was approached by Don McKay, then an editor of Brick Books, about republishing it, and that's how *Harrier* as a chapbook came to be.

Generally, I was fortunate in placing the stories that I sent out, which is a good thing as I tended to lose interest in getting them published after one or two tries. I had no sense of writing for an audience, although a mini one began to grow, I suppose, usually in the wake of readings, which I did from fairly early on. For sure, I have never suffered from lack of encouragement, from friends, especially Stan, from other writers along the way, from readers (I love readers – the things they'll put up with), and most of all from *you.* I will always treasure that first letter you sent me out of the blue about 'India', another early story that appeared in the *Malahat Review.*

Of the stories in *Quickening* first published in magazines: 'India' (*Malahat Review,* 1983), 'Patronage' (*Room of One's Own,* 1985), 'A Bird Story' (*Malahat Review,* 1987), 'Casting Off' (*The New Quarterly,* 1988), 'Man with the Axe', 'A Laughing Woman', 'Visitation' (*The New Quarterly,* 1989), 'Quickening' (*Malahat Review,* 1989), 'Oral History' (*Malahat Review,* 1989), 'Cutting the Devil's Throat' (Malahat Review, 1990).

And, finally, a word on how I turned from 'someone who wrote' into 'a writer.' Actually, I'm not so sure that transformation occurred, as I do prefer the process to the identity. I would much rather inscribe 'someone who writes', or tries to, on my tax form – it would explain my income, anyway. This is not some form of awshucks modesty, but because I value writing and my involvement in it so much, and it comes so close to what I am, or wish to be, that it's really a secret – a hidden identity. I feel terribly exposed when someone calls me a writer in public. If I were a better liar I would claim to be almost anything else. (Paul Theroux tells inquisitive strangers that he's 'in publishing'.) You see, I could have used that elusive profession, after all. Hey, maybe I *am* an anthropologist, tackling the cattle culture of Manitoulin ...

How was *Quickening* received? In two instalments basically, pre- and post–GG nomination. Both times received well for the most part, enthusiastically as they say. Because the Canada Council changed the timing of their awards announcement then (1990–91), my book had been out for almost a year before it somehow ended up on the short list. So I had the initial reviews, shorties usually, in *Books in Canada* and *Quill & Quire* and a few other places, and then a year later reviews in the *Globe*, the *Toronto Star*, the *Vancouver Sun*.

The approval conferred by that nomination does bring with it all kinds of attention that would not normally arrive at one's door: family (taken utterly by surprise), neighbours, a whole range of unknown others, from within and without the writing community. The GG for fiction has since been eclipsed by the Giller, beside which it looks like a dowdy and earnest older sister (although lately it has spruced up a bit), and there are so many awards flying around it must be harder now not to be at least sideswiped by one. More distinction to the writer who can claim on the book blurb – *Nominated for Dickall!*

You ask what kind of impact the book had and I really couldn't say. Not much, I expect, but the experience was a positive one for me. I felt that I had a foot in the door and that I might just get on with this writing business. Art, rather – business being another matter entirely. If some people were willing to let down their critical guard and find in it, say, a pleasure in sentences put together a certain way, or a sense of life shaded slightly differently, or a hitherto unvoiced feeling put into words, then that was of great worth to me. If I could please myself, minimally anyway, and find in language what I was looking for, at least come close to it, then that was really something. *Quickening* gave me hope, and my next book, *The Lusty Man*, took it away. But that's life – the writing life in particular.

What prompted me to write *The Lusty Man?* The prompting has all but vanished, but as I recall, I had a feeling at the time that stories weren't working out, that I had become over-preoccupied with form at the expense of readerly content. What I now realize is that I have this creative requirement – a restlessness – to move house. I see a form I haven't tried and, hermit-crab-wise, can't resist taking up residence. After *The Lusty Man* I wrote a children's novel, and I've been thinking about an essay collection, maybe a mystery, and perhaps a dyspeptic travel book, a *Toujours Providence Bay* from someone who can't quite manage the fab year in Provence or Tuscany – ahh, the charms of Northern Ontario, the cuisine, the colourful characters speaking in their local yokelese! (A tourist said recently of Manitoulin to a local store owner, 'I find it amusing that people actually live here.') By the time I'm finished, I expect I'll be writing dictionaries and how-to books.

The genesis of *The Lusty Man* certainly involved the Lusty Man icon itself. It's a Janus-faced Iron Age stone figure that can be found in Northern Ireland (and was once located on Lustymore Island, hence the playful name). Photographs of the figure often show up in books about Ireland, so I didn't think it was all that obscure a reference. At any rate, a range of characters and ideas gathered around that image for me and grew into the novel. Some of the stories in *Quickening* have a density that could have been expanded into a longer form – I can look into them and see a fair distance. In writing *The Lusty Man* I decided to use more of what I could see, and in a way the novel is made up of stories that open up into one another.

A contradiction I work with is that I am not a wordy person – not in conversation or on the page. And yet the old head brims. Which is not to say I'm brilliant, only hive-headed. (My dream life is so absurdly packed that I wake up most mornings needing a holiday.) What I am saying, I guess, is that a lot of my imaginative equity ends up in these peculiar tight-lipped verbal purses. I should be writing poetry. Or, I should loosen up.

I will madly persist, however, even though novel-writing doesn't suit my temperament much. The process is too long, too dogged. It's like inviting someone interesting to dinner, and they end up staying for two or three years. I get these ideas all the time for novels, for stories, but don't so readily run to answer the door any more. *That idea doesn't look like Mormons,* I'm thinking as I peer warily through the window curtain, *but it might be.*

But stories, yes, I do want to try my hand at writing a few again. Possibly it's the form I'm best suited to, as I love language – charged, heightened – and style and narrative. (You know, I do find it annoying when critics say I pay no attention to the story in stories, simply because it is not done in the usual way, or they can't be bothered to read with a degree of attention.) As Elizabeth Bowen has said, 'The short story avoids routine, it is the most fluid and experimental of forms.' At a time when even literary novels are becoming more formulaic, the story may be the best and most artistically open place to play.

Which brings me back to *The Lusty Man*. 'Pissy', is how you describe its reception, and I have to agree. The reviews were largely terrific, although I know reviews don't count for much. Whenever I read from it anywhere, the response was overwhelming, and, I can only assume, genuine. The book seemed to be poised on the verge of something, but what that something turned out to be was disappearance. Well, it *was* a first novel, coming from a small literary press – so what did I expect? Also, as you suggest, it is not naturalistic, which is still a literary no-no in English Canada, nor is there much tolerance for the inventively structured, even lightly so, unless of course you receive recognition outside of the country; then you're on your way. As you say, too, it is comic *and* mythic, and certainly the former quality seemed to mark it instantly as being a trivial and not a serious work (one of the less ecstatic reviews compared it to a TV sitcom). Something else – hard to credit I know – is the titillating effect that the cover seemed to have. (Underwater swimmer, female, nude, beautifully photographed.) Believe me, I fielded far more questions about it than I did about the novel itself. Between that and the title – 'Is your husband the lusty man, heh heh?' – I began to feel as if I had released the book at a prep school filled with sniggering twelve-year-old boys. One bookstore clerk told me that customers would turn the book around on the shelf, if facing out, so that the cover wouldn't show. Then, what the venturesome reader got was not eroticism, but sexual irreverence and farce, which women seemed to love, and men, generally, *did not.* Curious. All in all, though, *The Lusty Man* did not cause much of a stir, and that may have been quite simply because it's a shitty novel. But interesting shit, I thought.

MOMMA HAD A BABY
Terry Griggs

AND HER HEAD POPPED OFF. My cousin Nile had spread himself out on the lawn, lethal as any chemical, and was decapitating dandelions with his thumbnail. Flicked sunheads spun haywire this way and that, ditsy blondes. *Momma had a baby* (pause) *and her head popped off* (flick). Another (flick) and another (flick). If the dandelions had been further along, he'd be blowing them bare, infesting everyone's lawns with his wishes, banks of yellow gold erupting days later, the flower of his desire for biceps, for cool cash, maybe a call from the Leafs' manager. ('Look, Keon's injured. We *need* you!') As far as nature was concerned, Nile was better than dogs' hindquarters, pant legs, and wind put together. Restless in fields, unwashed, he went about her pollinating business like a pimp. I felt for Nile the same degree of relatedness one might feel for a nightcrawler – a cousinage that had more to do with inhabiting the same stretch of earth than sharing anything as intimate as genetic material. But, twelve years old, with an undescended testicle, Nile was the love interest, take it or leave it.

Inside was estrogen city, all women, mostly related, the air fibrous with connection. And even the few who weren't blood knew each other inside out, friends and neighbours who were practically sewn together, chain-stitched, with their knowledge and informed speculation about one another. Only one person stood on the edge of this dense familiarity like someone having an out-of-body experience, and that was a woman who'd recently moved here from some smug Southern Ontario town, and appeared to have her jaw rusted shut. She was remembering, was all. A younger sister who had succumbed to scarlet fever at the age of fifteen had arrived unbidden in her head and now after all these years rode there like a conquering whip-snapping queen in a chariot. Naturally, this gave her a somewhat self-absorbed expression.

Anyway, they were all packed into Auntie Viv's living room for a last-minute, hold-your-breath baby shower. Very last minute, time stretched tight as a drum over Mother's huge belly. She was two weeks late and Auntie Viv thought this little party might break the monotony, if not the water. Mother hoped not, her water that is, for she was beached on Viv's newly upholstered sofa, formerly a spirit-lowering beige and brown tweed, now red and slick as an internal organ, enough colour and texture to make you giddy. Viv had put up bilious fleshy drapes to match, and Mother figured this show-off reason was the real one for the shower, not her.

A fountain of dandelion heads spraying up outside past the window caught Mother's attention. *The Birth of Venus,* she thought, even though she had only ever seen a commercial version of that famous painting, a picture in a magazine advertising shampoo. Still, wouldn't it be lovely, a fresh-water baby rising out of the lake on a clamshell, dandelion heads flocking the feathery-soft air? So beautiful, so easy. Mother was terrified of dying in childbirth, and understood her fear to be a restraining band, wide as a strop, holding her baby back. She entertained a morbid notion that already she had marked the baby, that it would be reticent and fearful all its life, and she prayed it would find a source of courage somewhere deep inside itself. If she lived, she resolved to call her baby Hero, boy or girl. If she died, Morie would call it Stu if it was a boy, and Sue if it was a girl. That being the extent of it, Mother vowed to hold out at least until the naming formalities were concluded.

For her part, Auntie Viv was more than curious to see this baby, on account of Mother simultaneously losing her virginity and committing adultery scarcely hours into her marriage. She probably set some sort of record for the town, though it's not the kind of accomplishment you'd want to print up. Might be printed on the baby's face, mind you: Cousin Tony's visage appearing clear and crisp as a photograph, reproductive values more conclusive than the Shroud of Turin. This notion tickled Auntie Viv, for she considered her sister-in-law to be simpy and shallow as a pool. Piously nice. Let Mother pretend otherwise but marriage had corrupted her, the cracks were beginning to show. Auntie Viv smiled her fox smile and wrenched her push-up bra back into place. Damn thing was chomping on her ribs *just like* something invented by a man.

When you think Viv had only cooked up this shower idea the day before, Mother was getting a pretty good haul. Not that she needed more sleepers in neuter green or yellow – no one willing to commit her firm opinions as to the baby's sex in material terms – or teeny tiny vests (already outgrown) that made the whole assembly chant *Awwwww* when she held them up for ritual gift inspection and approval. And, since this was her fifth shower to date, she had enough fuzzy blankets and quilts at home to bury the kid alive. Most of those present had contributed plenty to the prospective infant, dearly hoping that at this rate they weren't going to have to fork out for its education, too.

My grandmother, Albertha Pinkham, veteran of all five, knew enough to bring her gift in instalments. So far, the oddly shaped packages wrapped in brown paper and stuck with adhesive contained wooden slats, spindles, rockers and a seat. She promised to knock the rocking chair together and paint it once she had the squalling evidence in her large sliver-flecked hands. Albertha had ironed her linen dress for the first shower, gesture enough she felt, and now it was so wrinkled it might have been in pain. Gruesome. A sartorial senescence mimicking her own decline. She bowed her head and dropped a brief prayer into the creases along the lines of *No stupid games, okay? And do You think we could get on with the show here?* By show, she did not mean more teething rings and baby wipes, but contractions, a crescendo of them, sudden and strong, a muscular fanfare announcing the arrival of.... Glancing over at her child, stranded on Viv's hideous sofa, a giant's collapsed kidney, she recognized that aura of fear, Mother's stricken look, like that of an animal about to be clubbed. Albertha tacked a stern postscript onto her prayer: *Remember, I go first.* Don't mess up. How far afield had those rumours about her daughter's infidelity actually drifted? Divine punishment? Well, really, grandbabies weren't so thick on the ground around here that anyone, divine or otherwise, should gripe if one came swaddled in a story or two. What was life without embroidery, anyway? Coarse cotton, that's all. Plain as unsullied paper, too plain for words.

Momma had a baby...

'What is that noise I keep hearing?'

'Nile, that lunk. Out on the grass.'

and her head popped off.

Death, you know, crashing the party, mute as a shadow falling through the window. The uninvited guest. Which isn't exactly true, for my other grandmother, Gramma Young, had been issuing special invitations for years, beaming signals into the black depths of space, courting that one polygamous alien, violent lover, terminal seducer. Thus far she was unrequited, and a regular menace on the subject.

'My *last* shower,' she sighed, sailing this hoary news across the room. As her foreboding announcement was the very one she had made at the other four showers, no one was buying it. Any sympathies aroused had already been slashed to the bone.

'Mine too. We're *all* hoping that.'

'Pine. A rough pine box, nothin' fancy for me.'

'Chin up, Gramma. This is supposed to be a happy occasion. Think, real soon there'll be a new baby to cuddle.'

'I'll never see it.'

'C'mon, none of that talk now.'

'New life comes into the world, old life's booted out.'

'Amen, and praise the Lord!' said Auntie Viv, who'd been sneaking swigs from one of the flower vases she kept topped up with gin. The longevity of Viv's birthday roses always amazed Uncle Clyde, a phenomenon he could only attribute to some secret source of power generated by Viv herself.

'Tastes like soap.' Gramma Young was chewing with athletic effort one of Batty Pock's shortbread squares.

Instantly, a message written in apologetic smiles, a kind of facial shorthand, was flashed to Batty that said, *Never mind her, the old coot.*

Batty shifted uncomfortably in her chair. Whatever did happen to that soap powder, the box sitting on the counter when she was searching for the extra flour?

'Mother,' warned Aunt Faith, seizing any opportunity to pay Gramma back, coin for coin, for every admonishing word she'd received as a child. Faith was the snappy sister, my least favourite aunt. She had resentment the way some people have religion – visibly – she wore it like a prow. If feeling slighted, overworked, neglected, she would take her husband Earl apart molecule by molecule, then reassemble him, a lesser man. She was Nile's mother, and he her son, and they fit together like a mathematical problem you could work on most of your life and never figure out.

Drop dead, Gramma was about to retort – she absolutely refused to let Faith have the last word – when, unaccountably, it *was* and she *did.* Drop dead. But the drop was so slight, gentle as ash drifting down, it was as if a quieting finger had been placed lovingly on her heart to untrouble its agitated and relentless motion. Indeed, Gramma had cried wolf for so long that her death was as tame and friendly as a panting, tail-thumping companion lolling at her feet. *I rest my case,* her body finally said, and in such an understated, such a gracious and accomplished manner, that no one, not even she, noticed her passing, She sat very, very still, and said nothing further.

Minnie Evans screamed, a startled little product, but it was only at Nile, who had smushed his face up against the window. Give him six years and he might almost resemble James Dean, but at the moment, features flatly pressed into the glass, he could have easily passed for a package of plastic-wrapped chicken thighs from the Red & White.

An intuitive awareness of something amiss perhaps sparked the inevitable birthing stories. Ancient Mariners all, women trotted out their individual traumas, sparing Mother nothing in the way of still births, haemorrhages, Caesarean sections, and marathon labours. Babies' shrill kitten cries repeatedly stabbed the air, and gallons of lost, fictional, and phantom blood sloshed through the room.

My girl cousin, Amy, who had made a bow-hat out of an upturned tinfoil plate and the discarded gift bows, rose as if on a wave of this unsettling talk and placed it on Gramma Young's head. This festive and improvisational bit of haberdashery slipped, caught on a stiff curl, and came to rest at a rakish and merry angle.

'She'd dead,' said the woman from the south who had not yet uttered a single word. At least she spent her embarrassed verbal fund well. It was to the point.

'Pardon?' someone asked.

'What?'

'Oh God, look at Gramma Young.'

'My arse,' said Auntie Viv, 'stick a pin in her.'

'Oh my God.'

'She's only asleep.'

'Faking it.'

'No. No I don't think so.'

'Give her a little push, Minnie.'

'Not *me*.'

'Heavens,' said Albertha, reaching out to give Eve Young a wakening nudge, this *other* grandmother to whom she had rarely ever spoken, certainly nothing beyond courtesies. If you could call a grunt a courtesy. Truth was she didn't have time for whiners, and now she realized, touch telling no lie, that Eve didn't have time at all, it had withdrawn itself from her, its animating caress, its ticking breath.

They all shivered and stared at one another.

'I'll call Glanville, why don't I?' This was Marion Goodwin, the undertaker's wife. Marion usually managed to appal and fascinate in about equal measure. What was it like being married to the Gland Man was a question that swam up from a depth and circled visibly close to the surface. Imagine his unearthly cold hands reaching for you in bed at night (sheets reeking of formaldehyde), hands fat and grub-white that only hours before had been palpating the internal organs of corpses, drawing blood out of bodies with the same ease and indifference with which they might drain Freshie out of coolers at a picnic.

Marion wrote poetry, verse boxes that never seemed to contain humans, but heavily featured dewdrops, sunsets and an array of symbols inert as stone markers. These she published in the local paper. *More embalmed mots,* the editor would groan when he saw her approaching down the walk, clutching yet another torso-thick bundle of paper in her arms, that unnerving pink smile of hers indelibly printed on her face.

'Viv,' ordered Albertha, 'call the ambulance.'

'Hey,' said Viv, as she sashayed out of the room, 'I've just thought of a great name for a female comedy group.' She stuck her head back in to deliver the punchline. 'Titters.'

An outbreak of giggles erupted and was quickly suppressed.

'Viv's in shock,' said someone, kindly.

By this time Nile had taken off, pelting away like a hunted man. Soon he'd be tearing through fields, running and running, long grass singing past.

'It's coming,' said Mother.

'So's Christmas,' snapped Minnie Evans. A novice to the potency of sarcasm, she promptly fell apart weeping buckets.

'What is, dear? The ambulance?'

'Already? Alec won't set out on a run till he's had a coffee and a smoke.'

'The baby,' Mother whispered. This a mumbled, prayer-faint revelation that was indeed underlined by Alec's keening flashing progress down the street.

'What baby?' demanded Aunt Faith.

Then a single dawning *Oh!* of recollection was all it took for everyone to fly into action. Mother was rescued from Viv's sofa by a dozen pair of hands, bundled into a shawl warm as a nest, and delivered with midwifely solicitations and endearments to the ambulance revving its engine at the door.

One thing you have to say for it, the trip to the hospital was cost-efficient. Not only did Mother, thrown suddenly into racking convulsive labour, have to share the ambulance with Gramma Young, cooling rapidly and inviting no intimacies, but Alec stopped at the Perdue's place halfway there to pick up pie-padded Horace and wedge him in as well. Horace had swallowed his pencil stub while working on a crossword. '*Women,*' he confided to the male-grey upholstery into which his face was pressed. You had to wonder if that was the word he choked on filling in the puzzle, or whether he considered his emergency eclipsed by the usual female problems. Women, there was no escaping them.

And to prove it, I added my weight to the world. Nine pounds fifteen ounces of pure solid self. Mere minutes after they wheeled Mother into the delivery room, some intern had me by the heels. Well. My first bat's-eye view of the situation was not consoling. The room swung muzzy, as though rubbed in grease. Mother lay bloody and limp, a brutalized body cast aside. Pain seared up my backside (never trust a doctor), and I let go a river of sound, my tongue a flailing, undisciplined instrument. But I must have known even then, grabbing at the air (I had Albertha's hands!), that the power would eventually be mine to carve that river into the precise and commanding language I needed. For the present, raw underspeech. I said: *Mother, don't leave me.* I said: *Nile, get your balls in order, boy, your Hero's come to town.*

As for 'Momma Had a Baby', I wouldn't want to dictate how anyone should read it, but if it were me, I'd tackle it head on, as it were. There is no gentle setting of the scene or quiet preamble to the story, no writerly spider-to-the-fly invitation. It begins with the title, disallowing any hesitation or pussy-footing around, and by the 'And' of the first sentence you should be in. It's sort of like stepping on loose gravel and off you go, propelled with a certain velocity through the narrative.

I was pleased when Kim Jernigan of the *New Quarterly* immediately recognized the child's game/saying that it's based on, for I didn't want the reference to be obscure, but hadn't ever heard it myself until my son, then five years old and keeping me apprised of kid culture, demonstrated. The sinister innocence of it, concluding with the unexpected *coup* of the dandelion head flipping up into the air, I found both chilling and funny. And true – mothers *do* lose their heads, and sometimes their lives.

If the story has 'felicitations and pleasures' to offer, I like to think that has something to do with what it catches in its weave. 'Momma' is comic, which should be a pleasure in itself, but it's not a trivializing comedy, nor a contemptuous one, for it concerns itself with what is largely unresolvable in human affairs: the mysteries and brutalities of death, and birth; the male-female divide; the tension between individual desire and community demand. It is about what is borne in the social undercurrent – and sometimes literally born out of it – what petty resentments and suspicions, what stark loves and fears. It is about what people want and want to escape at the same time. These matters are spoken of less baldly in the language of the story, in what I hope is in a more subtle and resonant way, for subtlety and resonance are definitely pleasures.

I like the narrator's prenatal wryness, her worldliness – even though she isn't in the world yet – her storytelling prowess and assertiveness, and how at the end it is language alone, her call and need, that may save her mother. She is certainly not the child her mother is expecting, as is usually the case, and ditto the reader – certainly not the narrator. Hero (the myth of Hero and Leander not incidental here) was actually conceived at the end of another story, 'The Discovery of Honey,' and she got to narrate that one too – a fertile and omniscient ovum.

I have to confess a liking for Aunt Viv. She also appears in the 'Honey' story, 'playing her nose like a Hawaiian guitar,' and she has her own story called '*Joie de* Viv' kicking around in my files, in rough draft appropriately enough.

Inside/outside is a structural element of the story, which at the end gives an extra boost to the feeling of release. I like to think the reader gets a birthing as well. It's a small courtesy to the claustrophobes among us, and I personally prefer open-endedness and freedom. No way I want to get locked into anything, not even a fiction.

What can I say about the dialogue? Generally, I use as little as possible (no playwright here), and, as in 'Momma', it's functional. In a few strokes it delineates character, moves things along in an economical way, takes the reader to the surface for a quick gulp of air, before being plunged back into the text once again.

As it is a story about birth, *and* death, *and* sex, the language and imagery is largely visceral. You could take just about any line and find that this is so. In the first paragraph, say, you have, 'head ... decapitating ... thumbnail ... sunheads ... ditsy blondes ... If the dandelions had been further along, he'd be blowing them bare ... the flower of his desire for biceps ... hindquarters ... pimp ... genetic material ... undescended testicle.' And then there is also a recurring spiritual or other-worldly reference that intersects the physical throughout: 'an out-of-body experience', 'Viv's newly upholstered sofa, formerly a spirit-lowering beige and brown tweed, now red and slick as an internal organ', 'a fresh-water baby rising out of the lake on a clamshell', 'Cousin Tony's visage appearing clear and crisp as a photograph, reproductive values more conclusive than the shroud of Turin', 'She bowed her head and dropped a brief prayer into the creases', 'Gramma Young, had been issuing special invitations for years, beaming signals into the black depths of space....'

This is the weave I mentioned, language interconnected and making patterns. The neat thing about it is that you're not much aware of it on a first reading, but if the story has an impact at all it is because of this deeper reading that occurs perhaps unconsciously as one is chasing down the story. As a child I spent a great deal of time studying the lake, what was happening on the surface (waves, light), and on the bottom when visible (rocks, crayfish, undulating weeds), and in between (currents, minnows, bass). This was how I learned to read, and how I want to write.

1999

ELISE LEVINE
Range

MY SHARPEST SENSE of writing is that it bears a central relationship to wordlessness – the blank spaces, the white margins at the edges of our daily lives. Translating from these infinite white fields into sound and sense – trying to lay bare a gesture, a feeling, a deeper structure or congruence that contains the stingingly, psychologically accurate, and to render these in a way a reader can apprehend – is what I think I'm attempting when I sit in my room and write. A language, a map, of our human edges: how I think of fiction.

About that room: it drives me up the wall.

For me, writing involves confinement, drudgery, boredom. Frustration. In trying to get the story to work, there's so much back and forth, endless revising, locked up alone at my desk. What's exciting is when lift happens – when I feel the story coming clear and taking over, strutting. Hey gorgeous! When I feel I'm realizing my original impulse for wanting to write the stubbornly secretive thing in the first place.

When a story first occurs to me, it usually comes in the form of the opening and closing lines. Before these lines announce themselves, I might have a sense of an image, or emotional cluster, a person or situation dense with emotional cross-currents. But when I get those lines, I know that if I pay enough time and attention, I can locate the story and pull it through to the other side – the other side being the page turned by the reader.

I start with handwritten notes I store in file folders. Lines, parts of scenes. Sketches of ideas, characters. Notes on how various aspects will connect, what will happen. Structure. A sense of tone, what formal devices to use.

I have notes by the bushel almost. Ideas are easy – developing them, being able to commit to the time required to do that, is what's so hard. For me to actually begin working on a particular piece, I have to experience a feeling of urgency, that there is some critical imperative to bring the story – compressed, a dark star – out. In other words, writing is a process of excavating what is embedded, an extended drive to fill in the centres of the truth of a character. I think of a mouth spotlit, opening and closing in a blacked-out theatre. I flirt with notions of some strange operatic experience, part Monteverdi, Messiaen, Ligeti, PJ Harvey – equal parts aria and recitative, with performers well versed in the uses of extended techniques. Ahistorical, forever playing away on a lost stage, in a pocket out of time. My job is to press my forehead against the stage door and peek through a peephole, and to try to describe, as faithfully as I can, what I see and hear.

Once I actually begin to work on a piece, which I do on my computer, I rewrite extensively, chronically. I'm committed, I don't allow myself to give up. I shuttle backwards, forwards, at once minutely – comma by comma, paragraph by paragraph – and overall, sweepingly, trying to keep the structure tight, trying to get at this shy, fabulous, proud creature. I find myself falling short at every turn, lamenting the gap between what I want to do and what I'm able to do. (Although sometimes I surprise myself in pleasant ways.) I keep lists of words, phrases. I might write down overheard scraps of conversation. Mostly I feel I'm lazy, brazenly haphazard, guilty of not committing enough.

As the piece begins to emerge as a whole, I try to shape (the material feels plastic, three-dimensional). I try to listen as hard as I can for the way the piece should sound (the material is musical, involving timbre and pitch, pulse and rhythm and hypermetre, it unfolds over time, is, like music, abstract). I try to look as hard as I can (fast flat lines or textured and painterly), to imagine. Content dictates form, form equals content: I keep going, and if I'm lucky, I at times find myself awed in the presence of this beautiful, mysterious tautology.

So writing, for me, occurs in the course of a sustained act of imagining, one that involves a mixture of mystery and pragmatism, of things that fall from the sky and those that come only through the stubborn dailiness of solitary, hard work.

What I'm trying to imagine is how and who we are in the world: this is the fictive baseline on which any story is threaded. The imagination is a high-functioning instrument, essentially, critically moral in nature, playing at a discipline radical in its attempts to envision the other: you, me, thou. Longing's rebus. I see it as expansive, expressive, wide-ranging, fundamentally in opposition to that which limits and flattens, empties, destroys, hates. Silences.

If trying to write well requires a vigilant angling toward subtlety, clarity and precision in the act of finding an expressive language to depict human nature, it also requires a willingness to bump up against the strengths and limitations of narrative and language, of making fiction. This means risking being labelled 'unconventional', 'poetic', 'experimental' – these underhandedly pejorative terms that smack of a conservative, underimagining, reactive view of literary fiction very much in contrast to commonly held views of other contemporary arts.

My earliest memory of being me, of selfhood, is from before I could read or write – before I was allowed to cross the road by myself – when I stood one afternoon on the sidewalk in front of my house gripping a notebook and pencil, spying on a house on the other side of the street, scrawling over the paper as if seized.

This is an intensely physical memory that grips me still.

For all the gruesome, gruelling day-in and day-outness that is for me the hallmark of writing, there is, however, this physicality to it which remains breathtakingly pleasurable. From confinement to liberation, exhilaration. It reminds me of the time, once, when I drove across Wyoming shortly after I'd finished a draft of something, when I felt as if my skin were smoking, then lifting, tumbling across the sky. Going, gone, as I got closer to home.

Yippee-i-o.

ALWAYS THE SNOW
Elise Levine

HIS MOTHER CALLS first thing one morning, crying because some princess has died – by the way, early predictions are saying a wealth of snow. Remind her, when is he coming to visit, should she get lift tickets? She's having the roof of her *porte cochère* repaired, can he hear the racket?

He is in a city his mother has never visited. It's fall: ripe warm weather, Midwestern lake-effect flurries still months away. His wife is beside him in bed, a tender crumble, half asleep – she mewed softly against him when the phone rang, turned over when he picked up, himself barely awake yet. Outside on the sidewalks the golden leaves are crisp as toast. Through the open window he can hear children crunching them on the way to school, their pipsqueak voices bouncing like red rubber balls through the yeasty air.

And it's sad, his mother is gasping. Isn't it all so very, terribly sad? Hasn't she been weepy since sunrise? Her bed precipitate, as if she'd woken already knowing the worst: some Diana or other, beautiful and brave, chic in mint-green Chanel, this tangled spirit of a girl dead in the crushed back seat of a limousine, in a tunnel in Paris. It's as if she'd hardly needed to haul herself to a half-sitting position with the oversized pillows and Euro shams plumped behind her, herself primed, hand on the TV remote, the news fireballing off satellites and contrailing at her in high definition. Hardly needed the excuse.

Mom, he says, trying to get a word in edgewise – she is almost unstoppable, he thinks, like a force of nature.

If he comes for Christmas, she wheezes energetically, they can take a sleigh ride up to the yurt.

He ponders the word *denature*. He'll have to look it up. Though it pains him – a pronounced, almost hallucinatory light, migraine-strength, annunciatory – to admit he doesn't know something. He understands: this is not a good character trait to have. His wife – whom he adores – tells him this all the time.

Still, he thinks of that pain, that winging regret, with guilty pleasure: it is, he thinks, what makes him *him* – his mind well-stocked, a heady fortress.

He checks the clock radio on the nightstand beside the bed. Overslept!

Fully awake now, phone jammed between shoulder and ear, his spine sags. He fingers his narrow chest, the warty microphiliac nipples, tips turned inward as if attuned to interior states, self-reflective, a bit dreamy, the sparse hairs he imagines must feel like those of an old man's – like grass that never quite took.

Later, his wife said the night before.

He'd just asked her, again. Rather clumsily, too – point blank, naked.

Don't you want to start a family?

Even to his own ears he'd sounded defensive. He was struck, then, by the thought of how an aggrieved man is like an untended plot of dry ground, the very air he breathes ungenerous as drought. How love withers on the fucking vine.

Again, she refused to answer. Then she jabbed at her pillow, and that was that.

For hours, he listened to her breathe among rooms he'd never enter – never grasp their rare proportions, glimpse the damask and silk, the heirloom portraits, a dizzying perfume dilating each hidden chamber – where he might grow hopelessly lost to himself, lost in her, where at the farthestmost inner reaches a little prince sits by a roaring fire, playing a game of his own devising, a game called the future.

Now, sitting on the edge of the bed this fine fall morning – while behind his back, cozened by sheets and coverlets, sateen and chenille, his wife lies, still asleep, or pretending to be – he grasps how your future can live on without you, in a place you might never reach.

Instantly, he feels stung to the core. *Debride*, he thinks. Another word he'll have to look up.

When did his wife first begin to avoid him?

At Whole Foods one evening the previous month, for no reason he could fathom, she'd stalked irritably in front of him – her head making

little jerking motions as if ticking items she'd found fault with off a list –
as he dutifully wheeled their cart past freezers of green tea soy ice cream
and microwaveable palaak paneer, the store lights even and bland as a
sugar-free glaze, a meringue of long-term conjugal content. Strangely, it
teased from his memory the time shortly before they were married,
when he screwed her at White Sands, New Mexico, right in the open –
three years past, give or take – and he'd come too fast for her pleasure,
pulled out clasping the ring of the condom and looked up, gasping and
sweaty, disoriented, into a scorching blizzard, a microsuede sensur-
round. And felt himself alone, witlessly unhappy.

From somewhere outside now, children's voices ride the air. He feels
awash, all his hopes and dreams down the drain. It's the little things that
slay him.

Authentic Mongolian, his mother is saying breathily. Isn't that
totally fabulous?

Mom, he says again, trying not to shrill – suddenly he's remembering
the time he broke the eggs.

Tragically, he was thirteen years old, bound to his mother for the
summer in a dull resort town – scuffing his heels through the parking lot
of Silver Creek Comestibles, that home away from home in the mountains, toting the grocery bags in which their provisions had been cra-
dled, you bet the clerks and baggers knew how bitterly his mother
complained if her eggs, her quart of juniper berries and her out-of-
season, flash-frozen venison steaks weren't handled with care. Devastat-
ing: unlike his older brother who was spending his vacation rafting on
the Colorado River, *this* young sir was shackled though it was killing
him, he would expire he knew before he reached twenty, already suicidal
impulses racked his gangly frame, he would quit prep school and join
the ROTC and be disinherited, he would that very fall drive his new Can-
nondale bike over the hills and never come back.

The gist was, his mother's pedicure was at two and she was miles
ahead of him, he could never keep up – he stopped for people getting in
and out of their cars, even in parking lots he let traffic have the right of
way when traffic had the right of way.

Which she never did – she would never let traffic, let other's people's
business, their right of way, get in the way of her pedicures, her appoint-
ments. Wasn't she on the board of everything in town, didn't she and her

husband donate to everything, not a substantial amount, but enough to feel entitled to their money's inflated worth? Or so he guessed even back then.

Wasn't she a woman with red hair touched up more and more frequently as she aged to maintain the original colour? Who was still pretty if not overweight by her circle's standards, who wore good shoes matched to good handbags, valued bone china for its durability over porcelain – entertained a host of other discriminating notions concerning etiquette and art and child-rearing practices she owed to her mother-in-law, that rich controlling bitch, from whom however she had learned a thing or two, including how to set a formal table and play her cards right? Who explicitly encouraged her youngest son to do the same?

Who that afternoon in the lot was telling him to *be careful*, at the same time indicating he should *hurry up*, in that insinuatingly high-pitched voice of hers, entitled, *narcissistic*, he remembers, as if he could ever forget.

Apparently he dragged his feet to spite her, to cast judgement, apparently he'd dragged at her his whole life, held her back. Even after years of EST as a child, accompanied by his older brother – be part of the solution! and not the problem – while she and his father sat in the main hall with the adults.

He ceased his slow progress through the parking lot altogether, tightened his grip on the handles of the grocery bags. Prickle of sagebrush in his nose and throat. Lush profusion of richly waxed Beemers, early editions of SUVs – endlessly shiny whites and blues, bright discs and oblongs boggling the light. He was praying: his first religious moment.

Praying for a car to swing out of its parking space and ding her into eternity – her trumpeting throat melting, turning to dust, cities crumbling and ruinous salt deserts arising like the Utah flats he cast his eyes upon from the window of the RV his family rented when he was eleven, his brother having only seconds before forced him to eat fraternal snot during an unsupervised moment, their parents having stepped out of the vehicle to snap some scenic shots.

As he prayed, he yanked viciously at the handles of the bags in his hand, swinging them – pissy little savage! he thinks back. She had always made him less than himself.

And so the moment passed. History: the brilliant yolky mess. A dozen suns beyond repair. For the rest of his life he's never heard the end.

Now, all these years later, phone still to his ear, he holds his hands in front of him, fingers splayed, and adds in what else.

He broke his collarbone once, falling off his bike, jetting it beyond care down Dorchester Drive.

He broke a toe, stubbed against a rock during a school trip to Yosemite, where he and his best friend were lost for three frantic pain-addled hours, until they found their way back to the main trail, upon which they feigned sheer stoner indifference.

He had an extra bone growing in his left shoulder, which was surgically removed when he was nine. Years twelve through eighteen he was pimpled, his jokes were pure cornball, he secretly favoured Schiele over Klee – works pored over on countless lonely museum visits. And Hawaii, don't even mention Hawaii, the unfortunate collision with the tiki torch, the split brow and stitches when he was seven.

Worse, to this day he has always been smarter than his daddy dude, who made a killing in industrial real estate.

He curls his fingers toward him, examines the cuticles, the nails ridged, thickening ever so gradually over the years. *He has always been part of the problem.*

He holds the phone away from his ear. Gives his head a shake, mentally brushes himself off. Because it is fall, time passes – time passes, and God is he grateful. Outside the window the children's voices toss and turn like apples, spiralling objects, englobed as if engorged by the warm autumnal air. His wife is pretending to be asleep – fine, let her pretend, he'll grant her the privacy of her feelings.

At the very least, he'll avoid another fight.

He sighs. Some sourness in his stomach, a touch of indigestion – something he ate. Something that didn't go down well, a nascent insight rising in him – testes to trachea – a little elevator of intuition. Oddly, he thinks of asking his mother about it.

But he's not sure how to phrase it, he has to admit. Which he hates – the having to admit that he only knows what he knows. Some flatness he suspects inside himself. A force, pressing. Old newspapers bundled tightly together – what was ever in them?

A throttled sob chokes him. Must. Keep. Airway. Open.

(That so-called wife of his. It's not like she'd ever lift a finger to save him.)

Was he really – had he hopelessly been – is he – too much to bear?

Some question he suspects only his mother can answer.

Who has no idea what her flighty son is talking about, Mom this, Mom that, when all she wants is a little nice communication. Is that so much to ask?

She exhausts herself easily. Grows, in a heartbeat, tired, and moves on.

Take crashes. She doesn't kid herself, she knows what's coming: hot rain, menopause, flash floods of memory like dirty buttermilk – the car spinning out of control. She'd survived – stepped almost instantly back into her life as a hale twelve-year-old in knee socks and pigtails, smoke and charred debris haloing her, ambulance sirens lulling her – while her seven-year-old brother hadn't. Her feebly transplanted New Orleans mama talking a mean streak forever after – *why wasn't it you?*

Despite bearing her mother's blame for having survived when her brother had not, *selfish child* – she excelled in school, won a scholarship, in the parlance of the day hooked a husband from a good family, from the earliest ages trained her two sons to open car doors for her, to wear blazers and ties with their shorts when visiting their paternal grand-mother (those gold-buttoned, blue-blazered little men opening, closing doors for their mother fattened on pan-seared foie gras – give her credit, she knows, for one glorious year there was fen-phen by the bushel, then a flurry of MRIs and ultrasounds to check her ticker). She cultivated champagne tastes, in any blind tasting of various caviars she to this day unfailingly picks the Beluga.

In other words – in other ways – she kept her mouth shut. Took what she could get. Hermès scarves. Shoes, glorious shoes – what she doesn't know about shoes! And window treatments and soaking tubs. EST ses-sions learning to be part of the solution, to detest problems of any kind, years of shirty bullshit from her mother-in-law, dead, finally fucking dead, the past June. Undertaking a mid-life conversion to Christianity (United Church) so each Sunday she could beg baby Jesus to forgive her and miraculously, week after week without fail, he would.

Taking up residence, finally, in this vacation home in the luxe mountains, a community free of Hispanics and beggars and democrats, *toujours les montagnes, toujours les neiges.* Pure and cold, like her heart: she pictures a vast storehouse of jewel-bright snow, perpetually poised in pre-melt. All that arterial plaque dammed inside her, and nothing can get in. Safe: nothing can touch her. At long last she is safe.

Besides, there's news of her wine futures, and more. There must always be more.

She is lying in bed in a foreign city not so different from her own as to afford her the certitudes of exile, reflecting while her husband clasps the phone to his ear, his mother on the line – those two never stop, do they? Buying herself time to think. Items one through infinity.

A woman rapidly depleting her collagen-elasticity surplus – and with insufficient funds for certain surgical interventions or extended sojourns at swank spas – she has nonetheless married a man ten years younger than herself.

Increasingly at dinner parties, she finds herself seated across the table from sons of famous fathers, young men – younger than her – who believe their pens are penises, or is it the other way around? She can never quite remember. She watches the wring of their exposed throats in the V of their shirts as they talk, gesture, laugh, and she imagines sinking her teeth into them, there, a whisper above the collarbone, there at the fine jawline.

Meanwhile the women, their shoulders bare, navels flashing beneath sleek cropped tops when they stand to cut lewd jokes and clear the table, their interesting, accomplished haircuts bobbing, shining in the low light – well, she thinks, such pretty moments can't last forever. Despite the daily grind at the gym: hip-hop step, advanced ashtanga yoga.

She would give it some thought, she'd said, finally, late last night.

Fine, he said. Sleep on it.

Now it is morning. She should get up, make her way out of the room, start her day. En garde. Carpe diem. Next year in Jerusalem. Her husband will be expecting her answer.

But some paralysis prevents her from taking action. It's as if her limbs, torso, are full of some fine particulate matter, a fine-mesh screen or filter is inside her, something slowly calcifying, cementing. The effect's been worsening the past few months. Ever since her husband began asking what she's thinking. What she wants. Fuck you, she thinks, each time he confronts her, fuck you.

Like the night before, after dinner, when the white dishes made moons on the black granite counter. She'd stared at them, until he left the room, hands clenched.

What is it like to wish a person dead?

She pretends not to know all about that, being not generally a dishonest person. Though on occasion for the hell of it she lies like a vixen, a mink, the biting red foxes that slip across the hay-mown fields of sleep sometimes.

She was married once before. A long story, long ago, another place, you name it. When her best friend since first grade died – *Jane, Jane, tall as a crane*, though she was improbably petite, a girl-child even as a woman, except she wasn't that either, she was tough as nails, climbed mountains in Switzerland, dived in underwater caves and not big ones either, they were too easy! instead she opted to push her way in zero-visibility sumps, shove her heavy tanks of breathing gases in front of her, squeeze herself in and out of the tightest restrictions – when Jane died in one of these caves, on a dive, Jane's best friend's husband had been there with her, had been implicated, though he'd grieved piteously, as well he should have: Jane, according to the findings of the inquest, had been in her first trimester. With Jane dead, he confessed to the affair.

So Jane's best friend (this is how she sometimes thinks of herself – some primacy, some pinnacle of intimacy in that first relationship, unrepeatable) is here now, divorced, remarried. About those old days – long gone, good riddance – she has mostly never breathed a word, words nested inside words inside her, one adventure story after another, and sometimes she just gets tired.

(A cool honeycombing drive inside her, in which she is herself embedded, all queenly and remote. It is like watching TV, only better. Much better, thanks.)

She shifts, with tremendous effort moves to the far side of the mattress and sits where her second husband can't reach her, can't put out a friendly paw and rub her back, mouth *I love you* or *God I hate my mother*, again.

Really – she should arise, get up, go. She's done it before.

But: there is the exhaustion.

There is the light outside. Fierce, stabbed through with those cricket voices, killing little things that only serve to remind her, sharp motes drifting through the open window into the room where she sits – how many years ago, now? – if she could brush the memory off she would, perched like a nervous canary at this small table at an outdoor café, Paris, New York, whatever superturboed, blinding empire of lucre or famine she finds herself in, triple-divorced and once-widowed, practised at all the tedious *envois* pleated about her like a lovely skirt, rendering her unable to move, emptiness avalanching around her as she remembers this moment – poised on the edge of the bed. The double-dare of her body, twisting.

I wrote 'Always the Snow' probably over the course of two years, working on numerous drafts, putting it aside, coming back to it, trying to get the tone right, tightening the material considerably, locating the most important threads and links – what I think of as the pulse points – opening certain themes up, adding in a little air to breathe.

In the end, I opted for a simple tripartite structure, set in a very focused present-tense situation – three characters' points of view, one morning, the duration of a short phone call – and then within each section set up and exploded that framework, moving in and out of the characters' memories, and including, at the close, a parenthetical shift into the future.

I wanted to evoke the hopes, fears, sorrows – the nature and texture – of these characters' lives. To do this, I relied heavily on the use of compression to show them propelling through their highly charged emotions and thoughts. This is the action of the narrative, the central dynamic that moves the piece along from start to finish. Why shouldn't our rich, commanding interior lives drive a story?

ANNABEL LYON
Interview

MY DAD TAUGHT ME to write when I was small. He had been a journalist and newspaper editor for many years and taught me some particularly ruthless lessons about style that I've had trouble giving up. The main one, which I've accepted as dogma, was to cut out all extraneous words. If you've said something in six words and you can say it in four, you're obliged – by logic, by aesthetics, by Occam's razor, by principles of elegance and an acquired radar for pretentious bullshit – to say it in four.

So: I grew up in Coquitlam, a suburb of Vancouver. It rained.

My dad bought a lot of newspapers and magazines. On any given weekend we'd have the *Vancouver Sun*, the *Globe and Mail*, the *Financial Post*, the *New York Times*, the *Economist*, and the *New Yorker*. He also had a lot of books – most of Orwell and Waugh, one or two Hemingway, one or two Russian, a lot of history, classics, books about East Africa, where he had lived – and by the time I was in double digits I was allowed the run of them. At first (particularly after I read William Golding's *Lord of the Flies* at ten and spooked the hell out of myself) he would gently suggest books, but I usually ignored him. I guess I was a little bit precocious but I liked children's books too – Madeleine L'Engle, Ursula K. LeGuin, Tolkien. I loved *Harriet the Spy*. I couldn't get through *Anne of Green Gables*. My mother had books too, but they were more eclectic: German books, art books, the *Epic of Gilgamesh*, a Koran. She taught me to read before kindergarten and took me to the library pretty much whenever I wanted. She would read whatever I was reading and talk about it with me. My brother and sister and I weren't allowed a lot of TV. I was lucky to grow up in a house where reading was encouraged and writing was considered a serious occupation for an adult.

The piano arrived when I was five, my mother's idea. My sister and I got lessons. I stuck at it like a weasel until I was nineteen, which is strange because I really had little aptitude for it. Imagine wanting to be a basketball player and not having a basketball player's body: that was me and the piano. I teach it now and I see some kids' hands just fit the instrument. Mine didn't. I had a natural ear and practised enough to get through my exams, though not enough to make up for my physical limitations. Looking back, I wish I had either practised harder or chucked it and had more fun as a teenager. For a while I dreamed about a concert career, they way kids dream about the NBA. It took me a relatively long time to grow up and realize this wasn't going to happen.

Lessons from piano that apply to writing: be patient, because for the first several years most of what you produce will be unbearable and mastery of your medium will take decades. Work on your technique. Be disciplined. Practise. Listen to the sounds you're making. Listen to the rhythms. Seek and value criticism. Sit up straight.

School was easier, who knows why. A tidy mind is as much a fluke as an athletic body. I was the bright kid in class, the pain in the ass with all the answers. I liked pleasing adults. It took me a long time to figure out that there was pleasure to be had in displeasing them too; unfortunately I was well out of my teens by then. You would have wanted me for your kid, probably, for a while there – thirteen, fourteen, fifteen – at least on paper: great grades, dressed like my brother, never smoked, never drank, never did drugs, never asked for money, never crashed the car, never trashed the house, never stayed out late, no scary boyfriends, no tattoos, no problem. Tofu child. I'd like to meet that creepy little kid now and say, Hey, wake up. What's the matter with you?

I remember reading Machiavelli in grade ten, Thomas More earlier than that, and a lot of Evelyn Waugh earlier still. I thought *Black Mischief,* where they eat the girl, was hilarious. Hemingway, Aldous Huxley for some reason, Oscar Wilde. I remember being very morose for most of high school. Isn't that normal? I really have forgotten most of those years, so essentially boring and irrelevant to later life. French and German class were useful, but otherwise – vectors and volleyball rules and how to play the flute. I mean, come on.

After high school (we were living in Calgary just then, for a couple of years), I took some time off school to work and finish my piano exams. Work was Northland MacDonald's, in the far northwest of the city, across the street from my old high school. Usually they put me on drive-thru because I was less shy about pushing pies and fries over the speaker than face to face. On my breaks I sat in the staff room in the basement eating cheese sandwiches from home – oh, they hated me – reading *Dubliners* and *One Day in the Life of Ivan Denisovich*. The one good job I remember was getting sent out to clean takeout bags and other identifying crap off the Northland Drive median, to help maintain a good corporate image. You had your mountains, you had your traffic, you had your garbage bag and your pointy stick and your whooshing prairie air.

The week we moved back to Vancouver, January 1989, it hit minus forty. I remember that. I remember reading *The Tin Drum* in the hotel room and the airport, waiting for the plane to thaw. I remember when we got to sweet Vancouver, they were in a cold snap too, minus nine, and there was a dragon in the hotel lobby because it was coming up to Chinese New Year.

I started university a year later – Simon Fraser University, in Burnaby, British Columbia – at nineteen, after I decided not to pursue a music degree at the University of British Columbia (read: I balked at the prospect of auditioning). Philosophy major with English and French literature minors. I liked philosophy because it was hard. If that sounds arrogant, then you've discovered I had added arrogance to moroseness at that time. I also had a black T-shirt which I think I wore rather too often. My first published story, a few years later, was called 'Black'. I was, am, young. I suppose I ought to be embarrassed about this sort of thing, but, really, who cares? It's all too generic to take very seriously.

I was ticking along, teaching piano by then, getting a bang out of Seamus Heaney and Hermann Hesse and my ethics seminars, when the English department offered a creative writing class and I thought, that's different, that's for me, I can do that, hello! Over here! What possessed me? I sat down and wrote a couple of stories for a portfolio, the first stories I'd written in a decade, and was accepted, and discovered in that class that there were such things as creative writing departments at universities and small literary magazines that published stories by little types like me. This was all news. Then everything sped up for a term or two and suddenly it was time to think about graduate school. It was assumed I'd want to go directly to a doctoral program; it was assumed

I'd want to go to a good school in the States. To derail this terrifying train (or at least to postpone it a little) I applied to do a master's in creative writing at UBC and was accepted. Well, it's just two years, I thought. I can always do the doctorate after.

I had submitted the kind of portfolio I've since learned they don't really want: they asked, if I recall, for thirty pages of writing in two genres, so I provided one hundred pages in four: story, novel, children's and poetry. (That was then, in a nutshell.) I took courses in short story, novel, screenplay and poetry, with short story as the planet and the others as the moons. Short story was co-taught in my first year by Leona Gom and Linda Svendsen, and Linda became my thesis adviser in second year. I learned important stuff from each class I took – about structure in screenplay, about compression in poetry – but short story was where I wanted to apply what I'd learned.

Can I say a word here about creative writing programs? Why do some people insist writing can't be taught? (If the same people believe their own writing benefits from being edited then they are hypocrites who should close their mouths. And if they don't believe their own writing benefits from being edited then they are insufferable egotists who should close their mouths. And if they don't, themselves, write, then they don't know what they're talking about and should close their mouths. QED). Linda, for instance, taught me I relied too much on lists (of adjectives, or characters, of colours, of *words*), that I should think in terms of conflict and change, that I should force my characters to make decisions and to act. I also learned a lot from the workshop context (another source of contempt for CrWr detractors), watching my peers wrestle the same problems from an analytical distance I couldn't always achieve with my own work.

We also loaned each other books, and talked about books, and slapped ourselves on the forehead and rolled our eyes when we realized the person we were talking to hadn't read some book we were devoted to. I started reading much more than I'd had time for during my undergrad, and discovered authors who had a sound I loved and wanted to imitate – Joy Williams, Mary Robison, Denis Johnson, Amy Hempel, Frederick Barthelme. So deep was I sunk in philosophy, I hadn't heard of Richard Ford before entering the program. Reading and writing are two sides of a coin, and my own prose would sound very different now if I hadn't encountered those authors then, at that crucial point when I was trying to write serious fiction for the first time. I think it's important to note these writers are all American only if you happen to be extremely insecure about your own national identity (which I'm not).

At UBC I also worked on PRISM *international*, the creative writing department's literary magazine, as fiction editor. (I think nobody else wanted the job). Reading hundreds of submissions and having to analyse each one, to articulate what made it work or what it lacked, made me more ruthless with my own stories, and (though I didn't realize it at the time) wary of submitting to magazines myself. I knew my stories weren't ready, and I knew the rough ride they'd get from some witch like me sitting in the office at the other end.

After I graduated from UBC (pink trim on the grad gown for us flaky MFA types, you better believe it), Linda Svendsen called one day to say she'd sent four of my stories to John Metcalf at the Porcupine's Quill and he wanted to see more. She then sent me his letter (which I obviously wasn't supposed to see), saying who was this Lyon and could one work with her or was she difficult? That was in the spring of 1996. I worked on *Oxygen* for another four years. It came out in May 2000. Amazingly (for a [1] first book of [2] short stories from a [3] small press) it was widely reviewed, and well reviewed, and the criticisms – lack of structure, brevity, opaque character motivations, cuteness in the prose – were criticisms I had already levelled at myself, and was trying to address in my new stories. So I was happy.

WATCH ME
Annabel Lyon

MARIE'S BROTHER CALLED to tell her the junkies were gone.

'Since when?' she asked.

'Two days,' Steven said. 'But mum has their babies.'

'Oh, surprise.'

'I know, Marie, but two days. She says she's running out of activities.'

'Someone should report those people.'

'Someone did. Mum reported them to me and now I'm reporting them to you.'

'You know what I mean.'

'I know I'm going this afternoon and you're coming. Pick you up in an hour.'

'Oh, Steven.' She cut him off with the tip of her finger and poked her mother's number.

'Beth?' Laura, her mother, answered. Beth was the woman junkie.

'No.'

'Oh, Marie,' said her mother. 'Now, I wish you had been here for lunch. I made this pesto salad such that the curtains smell of garlic.'

'How are things?'

'Well,' Laura said. 'I'm surprised you can't smell it down the phone, it's that strong.'

'I can't smell it,' Marie said.

* * *

Steven stood in the doorway of Marie's apartment, wiping his glasses on his sweater. He held them up to the light and squinted and wiped them some more. 'Well, that's it,' he said. He put his glasses back on and looked at her intently for a moment, like he was testing them.

'No.' Marie sat in a wicker armchair, hugging a red cushion.

213

'Where's your pretty coat?' He meant her new anorak of vanilla corduroy.

'Mum dislikes that coat. Just go on your own.'

'Stop sulking,' he said, getting it from the closet and throwing it on her lap. 'She phones me because you act like such a goddamn groupie. You know I can't do this without you.'

Marie pushed her arms through the sleeves and reached into the pockets. 'I don't see what you're so afraid of,' she said, pulling on black leather gloves and making slow fists to work her fingers in.

* * *

Laura lived out in Langley, farm country a good two hours' drive from Vancouver. As they left the city behind the land opened up and flattened out. Marie sensed large animals, furtive cows and horses, fading in and out of the waning day.

'She just wants to talk,' she said.

'I know what she wants,' Steven said.

Laura was in her front yard, playing with the twins from next door. They had jagged translucent teeth and hot sweet eyes, like fudge oozing. They wore plastic boots, quilted space-suit overalls and miniature turtlenecks. Laura wore jeans, black rubber boots and their dead father's shirt. Her grey hair was stuffed up attractively under a baseball cap.

'You're just in time,' she said. 'We're going to shellac some gourds.'

The twins belonged to a couple of gentle junkies, Beth and Morty, for whom basic excursions – to the gas station or the supermarket – were perplexing epics. Often Laura found herself putting Natalie and Dylan to bed and getting them up again in the morning because their parents had run out of postage stamps.

'They're taking advantage of you,' Marie said.

'They're nice kids,' Laura said.

Steven had a soft spot for little Dylan. He taught him dog tricks. 'Come on, Dylan! Come here, boy!' he called from the end of the yard. Dylan loved Steven with the stupid love of small children. He romped over, grinning. Steven slapped his thighs, corralled Dylan with his forearms, then held a fist high in the air. 'Up, boy!' Dylan jumped, trying to reach the fist. 'Higher!' Steven ordered. 'Atta boy.'

Natalie studied Marie blankly before turning to cuddle with Laura.

Apparently Marie lacked every appealing quality she knew to look for in her own species.

'Did you phone hospitals?' Marie asked, hugging her coat.

Inside, Laura laid some newspaper on the kitchen table and used a teaspoon to prise the lid from a tin of clear varnish. 'Here we go,' she said. Natalie and Dylan sat on the big kitchen chairs, smiling and breathing and kicking their legs. Laura dipped a pastry brush into the shellac and started to gloss a fat yellow gourd. She wore her wedding ring on her thumb.

'Beth and Morty went picking at Singh's,' she said in the slow, balanced voice of someone working carefully with both hands. Singh's was a strawberry farm.

'In that truck?' Marie said. 'That's an old truck. Anyway, it's October.'

Laura looked up at her and back at the gourd. 'We're going to do this,' she said. 'Then we're going down for the night. Let's just hold our fire until then. Steven?'

'Mum?' Steven said.

'I need you to look at the washing machine. It's thumping again.'

'Somebody needs to,' he said.

'Your father used to grease it with a little Vaseline, if you wouldn't mind.'

Steven went downstairs and Marie sat next to Natalie.

'We have certain responsibilities here,' Marie said.

'Don't start me,' Laura said.

'You're taking the easy way out,' Marie continued. 'This babysitting, for instance.'

'These ones, easy? Ha!'

'Ha!' Dylan said.

'Make the call, mum. You'll feel better.'

'Ha,' Dylan said, studying her.

'Hi,' she said. Natalie giggled.

'All right, you two.' Laura seized a twin under each arm and swept them, kicking and howling, upstairs. Marie picked up a science magazine with her father's name on the mailing label and began to read an article on robotics.

'I should cancel that,' Laura said, coming back into the kitchen a few minutes later. She opened the fridge and started pulling foods out and setting them on the counter. 'I never bothered.'

'Don't you dare.' Marie didn't look up.

'Pumpkin,' Laura said.

'Remember when he gave me that microscope? Remember how he was the only one who ever called me Molly? Can I have his slide projector?'

'I gave it to charity.'

'Jesus,' Marie said. She started to cry.

'Stop that, chicken,' Laura said. 'You have his armchair, his cushions, his good gloves, his antique typewriter and his bifocals.'

'I told you always to check with me first.'

'I have every right to dispose of my husband's things. Now reach me the cilantro.'

Marie didn't move.

'What did I raise?' Laura asked the ceiling.

Marie got the little wad of green leaves from a drawer in the fridge and dangled it under the cold tap while Laura skinned chicken thighs. 'Daddy hated cilantro,' she said.

'This is Aztec soup. Daddy loved this.' Laura slammed a knife down on the counter. 'Please go watch TV,' she said.

* * *

After supper they sat at the kitchen table and spoke like family.

'Your father never liked those children.'

'Daddy died before they were born. What's the matter with you?'

'He disliked them in the womb. Beth was sticking out all over at the time of the accident.'

'He did not. He did no such thing.'

'This does not sound like him at all.'

'There are lots of things you children don't necessarily know,' Laura said. 'For instance, to conserve water he refused to flush more than once a day.'

'You're making this up,' Marie said.

'It was worst in the morning, the smell but also the colour. Toilets full of yellow. I scrubbed and scrubbed.'

Steven said, 'Did you try the hospitals?'

'Marie's going to do it,' Laura said. 'She wants to.'

They sat her down with a realtor's pad and a pencil. Laura got the black rotary phone from the kitchen counter and plopped it in her lap. She and Steven smiled expectantly.

'You're only doing this because I'm studying law,' Marie said.

'That's right,' Steven said. 'We believe you can cope.'

Marie phoned and asked if anyone like Beth or Morty had been admitted. She listened and nodded a lot. She drew an abrupt line on the pad, making them jump and crane forward. 'Thank you,' she said, hanging up.

Laura said, 'Would anybody like some tea?'

'Well,' Marie said.

'I would,' Steven said, getting up to help her.

'Well, they're not hospital gone. They're just gone.'

'Banana tea,' Steven said, taking a box from the cupboard and shaking it next to his ear. 'What is banana tea?'

'What it says. You see, Marie, we told you.'

'They also said we should phone the police and report them missing.'

'Now, that's thinking.' The kettle screamed and Laura wetted the pot.

'No, it's not,' Marie said. 'The police will want particulars. They'll send social workers for the babies. Bloodhounds and social workers and forensic pathologists wanting DNA samples.'

'What?' Steven said.

'Blood, wool, cuticles, hair –'

'I can look after them,' Laura said.

'Not indefinitely. And I'm not sure if failure to report missing persons doesn't make this kidnapping,' Marie said. 'I'm not one hundred percent on that. But I think it might be.'

They looked at her, Laura with the kettle, Steven with the tea. 'Marie,' Laura said, 'one day you will have a good job with a pension and dental, and for that I am glad. But in other ways, law school has not made you a better person.'

'I am trying to think ahead,' Marie said.

Laura looked at Steven.

'We'll stay tonight,' he said. 'Tomorrow we'll take a drive into town and check it out. We'll ask some questions.'

'I suppose you'll want to camp in your father's room.'

'Trying to plan,' Marie said.

'Come on, citizen,' Steven said. 'Let's scout some sleeping bags.'

'I'm going to lie down now,' Laura said. 'I'll leave the phone on the hook, but you people have tired me out.'

* * *

Their father's study felt like a sealed room in a shipwreck, fathoms below real air, with its low ceiling, its buttery yellow tone and its fireplace full of books. During the day, the only possible sunlight came from a single window near the ceiling, a rectangular frame stuffed full of colourful glass bricks the size of ice-cubes.

Marie got a heavy glass tumbler from a desk drawer and a bottle of Scotch from the mantel. Next to the bottle was an ornamental pepper plant, dripping waxy red peppers – inch-long, kinked like fingers – in a flare of matt gold foil. The plant was new and made her hungry. She poured a thick finger of Scotch and rinsed it around the glass, then set the glass down. She took the plant and placed it on the floor in the hall, just outside the door, peppers trembling. She took a shoebox down from the bookcase.

Steven came in with an armful of bedding. 'Help me with this?' he said. She set the shoebox next to the stereo. They laid out red sleeping bags and white blankets and pillows in two rough bed shapes, taking up most of the carpeted floor.

Marie got a deck of cards from another drawer.

'Steven,' Laura called.

'Coming,' he called back, looking at Marie.

'You're okay,' she said.

'I know.'

'She just wants to talk.'

'I know. I know she does.' He went upstairs.

Marie took a cassette from the shoebox and hinged it open. On it her father had printed 'Evangeline Ray, June 1967'. She tipped the tape into the stereo and clicked a finger panel. A woman began to sing jazz about her man. She sang deep and clear and behind her voice people were coughing and scraping chairs. When she finished there was a splash of applause.

Marie sat on one of the made-up beds. She tilted her drink back and forth, watching the play of glass-light in the loose white wool. She adopted a yoga position, pressing the glass between the palms of her feet, and leaned forward to deal a hand of solitaire. When the tape ended she put in another one. 'Hello,' her father said. 'We can't take your call right now, but please leave a message after the tone.' She was still listening to the tape unwind its silence when Steven came back.

'Feel like a hand?' Marie asked.

'I feel like taking a trip,' he said. 'Do you feel like that?'

He pulled down a magazine file stuffed with maps and BCAA guidebooks. He spilled the pile across the sleeping bag between them and took the glass from between her feet.

Marie picked up one of the books and flipped through it, half reading about campgrounds and restaurants and inns in southern Alberta, half watching as Steven unfolded a map. He looked surprised as it got bigger and bigger. He looked up at her as though she might be thinking the map was his fault.

'So?' he said.

'Head-Smashed-In-Buffalo-Jump,' she read. 'The Badlands. Hoodoos.'

'Hoodoo you think you are?'

'Sip,' she said. He gave her the glass. Upstairs the phone rang.

'She's thinking about planting runner beans next spring,' Steven said. 'She's going to give everybody earthquake survival packs this year for Christmas. She's worried the Civic won't make it through AirCare.'

'The Civic is okay,' Marie said. 'She barely drives it.'

'That's not the point.'

'Steven,' Laura called.

'That's the point.'

'Stay,' Marie said. 'I'll go.'

Laura was sitting up in bed, quilt pulled to her chin. 'Oh, Marie,' she said. 'Could you please get me a glass of water? It's just that my hip. I didn't want to get out of bed.'

Marie went into the bathroom and rinsed Laura's tooth mug. 'You did too much today,' she called over the water.

'Those children are little energy packets. Where's Steven?'

Marie came out and handed her mug of water. She squinted at Marie's chest. 'Bunny, I wish you wouldn't wear your father's clothes. Are you cold? I'll lend you a sweater.'

Marie didn't answer. Laura turned her head to the window. Her lips tightened and her eyes changed. Marie peeled the sweater off and stuffed it under the covers. 'Here,' she said quickly.

'I have some nice clothes,' Laura said. 'Perhaps when I'm dead you'll want to wear them. That was Beth on the phone.'

'Where are they?'

Laura threw back the quilt. The chunky brown sweater lay against her knee. She shook it out and pulled it over her head, over top of her white nightgown. 'Home.'

Marie looked at the window and saw light in the house next door, sudden yellow rooms scooped from the darkness.

'You children get so angry,' Laura said. 'Steven won't let me touch him, and you act like your father's pencils are shards of the true cross.'

'We miss him.'

'I don't know what you miss. You don't act like children.'

'We aren't.'

Laura rose slowly and pulled her jeans on. 'I've made a decision,' she said, sitting back heavily on the bed.

Marie got Laura's runners from the closet and knelt before her, loosening them. She fitted them onto her feet.

'One more night. Just until morning. They're asleep now, anyway.'

Marie didn't answer.

* * *

'Do you think she's shooting up over there?'

An hour had passed. Steven and Marie sat on the sleeping bags playing war, a card game that involved throwing the deck at one's opponent at strategic moments. Steven had the jack of clubs propped in the bridge of his glasses, while Marie rose periodically to refill their drink. Lena Horne was torching on the stereo, loud.

'She's arguing with them,' Marie said. 'She wants to keep Natalie and Dylan.'

'She needs a pet.'

'She needs two.'

Steven threw a handful of cards at Marie. They fluttered down around her head. 'I see your two pets and I raise you a husband.'

Marie picked the queen of hearts out of the Scotch and licked it off. She held it up to show Steven. 'Ha,' he said.

'Where do we get one?'

Steven cleared his throat and tucked his chin into his chest. 'Examine this rationally,' he said in a deep, bored, familiar voice.

Marie giggled. 'Method, children,' she drawled.

'Remember that Scotch is the drink of the educated man.'

'And, due to the shape of his thorax, Zoot Sims was the greatest saxophone player of all time. This is scientifically provable. The zenith of Western music was Billie Holiday's mouth.'

Steven laughed, then brushed the jack of clubs from his forehead. Laura stood in the doorway, holding the pepper plant.

'It wasn't so much he didn't like them,' she said. 'But he was so afraid they'd be born addicted.'

'Everything o k over there?' Marie asked.

Laura held up the pepper plant and twisted it side to side. 'It's like a little Christmas tree, isn't it? What are you playing?'

'Cards,' Steven said.

'I offered to keep them for another night, but they said I'd done enough.'

Marie turned off the stereo. She made a show of standing up – pulling her jeans straight, brushing off imaginary sleeping-bag lint. She was drunk. 'Excuse me, I have to make a call,' she said.

The kitchen phone was whacked black plastic, cracked and venerable. She knew that phone. Its receiver offered tiny tunnels to hospitals and light.

'Who are you calling?' Steven had followed her upstairs.

She stared at the back of her hand, the one that wasn't gripping the receiver where it lay in its cradle. 'Police,' she said, frowning.

Steven sat down opposite her. He reached over, pinched the jack out of the back of the phone, and held it up like an explanation. Marie relaxed but said, 'Gimme.'

'They came back, Molly. They're right next door.'

'Don't call me that.'

'Molly, Molly, Molly.' He squinted at the plastic jack, then waved it in front of her face like a tiny cobra head. 'You are feeling very, very sleepy.'

'No, I'm not.'

Steven let his hand fall to the table. 'Me either.'

'Where's mum?'

'Down there, fixing our beds.'

'What's wrong with our beds?'

'They're *fine*,' Steven said.'She's just making them even *better*. Are you sure this is a 911 thing?'

'No.'

'We should call somebody, though.'

'Definitely.'

'Even though they came back.'

'It doesn't matter that they came back,' Marie said. 'What matters is they went away.'

Steven took his glasses off.

'Drugs are bad,' Marie said. 'This is how bad drugs are.' She looked up at the kitchen clock, at its five-minute slices of pie. 'You'll still love me, right?'

The fridge fan rattled off, leaving a ticking quiet. Steven reached over to plug the jack back into the phone. 'We all love each other,' he said. 'That's how these things start.'

This story was unusual for me because it went through about ten drafts, and changed substantially with each draft. Usually I'll write a painfully slow first draft, give up, and that's the story. The first draft of 'Watch Me' (written during my tough, terse, suffering, Richard Ford phase) was about a sister and brother who pick up a hitchhiker, drop her off, go to a bar, and watch some mentally handicapped people shoot pool. Draft by draft the extraneous characters and locations dropped out until I was left with the siblings and their mom. (The story had started with the description of the junkies' children, who were actually children I'd watched at a bus stop one day, with a mom who was obviously trying extremely hard to keep her shit together.)

The ending gave me a lot of trouble. It was *Waiting for Godot* for the longest time, with everybody sitting around saying, We must do something!, or listening to the phone ringing, and nobody making a move.

This was very foolish. John sent it back a couple of times saying he didn't understand what was happening on the last page. So (one of the few times I consciously thought about theme or anything resembling theme) I asked myself what Marie was afraid of, and realized it was something pretty basic, and decided to have her just say it straight out, without coyness or symbols or fictional fanciness. 'You'll still love me, right?' Marie asks Steven, and then the story ran clear.

Bibliography

Borsky, Mary.
Influence of the Moon. Erin, Ont.: the Porcupine's Quill, 1995.
Benny Bensky and the Perogy Palace. Toronto: Tundra Books, 2001.
Benny Bensky and the Giant Pumpkin Heist. Toronto: Tundra Books, 2002.

Griggs, Terry.
Harrier. Ilderton, Ont.: Brick Books, 1982.
Quickening. Erin, Ont.: the Porcupine's Quill, 1990.
Tag. Ottawa: Magnum Bookstore, 1991.
The Lusty Man. Erin, Ont.: the Porcupine's Quill, 1995.
Cat's Eye Corner. Vancouver: Raincoast Books, 2000.
Rogues' Wedding. Toronto: Random House Canada, 2002.

Heighton, Steven.
Stalin's Carnival. Kingston: Quarry Press, 1989.
Foreign Ghosts. Ottawa: Oberon Press, 1989.
Flight Paths of the Emperor. Erin, Ont.: the Porcupine's Quill, 1992.
For Gods and Fathers. Ottawa: Magnum Bookstore, 1992.
Théâtre de revenants. Translated by Christine Klein-Lataud. Quebec: L'instant même, 1994.
The Ecstasy of Skeptics: Poems. Toronto: House of Anansi Press, 1994.
On earth as it is. Erin, Ont.: the Porcupine's Quill, 1995.
The Admen Move on Lhasa: Writing and Culture in a Virtual World. Concord, Ont.: House of Anansi Press, 1997.
La Rose de l'Érèbe. Translated by Christine Klein-Lataud. Quebec: L'instant même, 1998.
The Shadow Boxer. Toronto: Alfred A. Knopf, 2000.

Flight Paths of the Emperor. Toronto: Vintage Canada, 2001.
On earth as it is. Toronto: Vintage Canada, 2001.

Levine, Elise.
Driving Men Mad. Erin, Ont.: the Porcupine's Quill, 1995.
Requests and Dedications. Toronto: McClelland and Stewart, 2003.
Driving Men Mad. Toronto: Emblem Editions, 2003.

Lyon, Annabel.
Oxygen. Erin, Ont.: the Porcupine's Quill, 2000.
Oxygen. Toronto: Emblem Editions, 2003.

Miller, K.D.
A Litany in Time of Plague. Erin, Ont.: the Porcupine's Quill, 1994.
Give Me Your Answer. Erin, Ont.: the Porcupine's Quill, 1999.
Holy Writ: A Writer Reflects on Creation and Inspiration. Erin, Ont.:
    the Porcupine's Quill, 2001.

Moore, Lisa.
Degrees of Nakedness. Stratford, Ont.: Mercury Press, 1995.
Open. Toronto: House of Anansi Press, 2002.

Winter, Michael.
Ask Me No Questions. With Linda Phillips and Peter Ringrose.
    Englewood Cliffs, N.J.: Prentice-Hall, 1990.
On a Morning Age Remembers. St. John's: Jarrow Press, 1991.
Creaking in their Skins. Kingston: Quarry Press, 1994.
One Last Good Look. Erin, Ont.: the Porcupine's Quill, 1999.
One Last Good Look. Toronto: House of Anansi Press, 2000.
This All Happened: A Fictional Memoir. Toronto: House of Anansi Press,
    2000.

Acknowledgements

'The Ukrainian Shirt'. Copyright © 2003 by Mary Borsky. Previously published in *The New Quarterly*.

'Momma Had a Baby'. Copyright © 2003 by Terry Griggs. Previously published in *The New Quarterly* and the 1997 *Journey Prize Anthology*.

'Five Paintings of the New Japan', extracted from *Flight Paths of the Emperor* by Steven Heighton. Copyright © 1992 by Steven Heighton. Reprinted by permission of Vintage Canada.

'Always the Snow', extracted from *Driving Men Mad* by Elise Levine. Copyright © 1995 by Elise Levine. Reprinted by permission of Emblem Editions.

'Watch Me', extracted from *Oxygen* by Annabel Lyon. Copyright © 2000 by Annabel Lyon. Reprinted by permission of Emblem Editions.

'A Litany in Time of Plague, extracted from *A Litany in Time of Plague* by K. D. Miller. Copyright © 1994 by K. D. Miller. Reprinted by permission of the author. Lyrics quoted from 'Someday I'll Find You' and 'I'll See You Again' by Noël Coward, used by permission of William Heinemann Ltd.

'Craving', extracted from *Open* by Lisa Moore. Copyright © 2002 by Lisa Moore. Reprinted by permission of House of Anansi Press.

ACKNOWLEDGEMENTS

'Archibald the Arctic', extracted from *One Last Good Look* by Michael Winter. Copyright © 1999 by Michael Winter. Reprinted by permission of House of Anansi Press.

John Metcalf is the Senior Editor at the Porcupine's Quill. His most recent books are *An Aesthetic Underground: A Literary Memoir* and the novella *Forde Abroad*.

Claire Wilkshire teaches English at Memorial University in St. John's. She was a founding member of the fiction collective *The Burning Rock* and her stories are represented along with Lisa Moore's, Michael Winter's and Ramona Dearing's in the Burning Rock anthologies *Hearts Larry Broke* and *Extremities*.